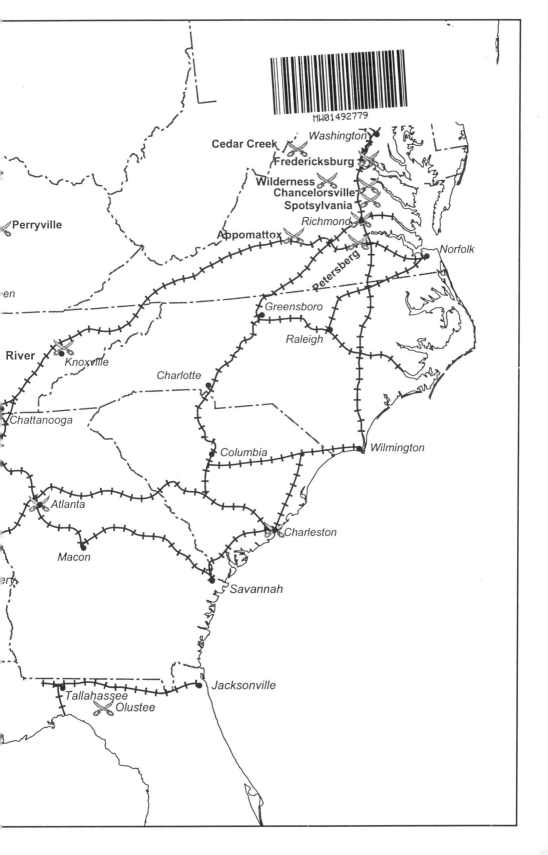

THE STILWELL LETTERS

To Hunter Taylor, a good Virginian

Signed at the Brown House in

McDonough on 11/28/02

RAMoseley

THE STILWELL LETTERS

A Georgian in Longstreet's Corps, Army of Northern Virginia

Edited by

Ronald H. Moseley

Foreword by

Herman Hattaway

Mercer University Press

MMII

The Stilwell Letters

ISBN 0-86554-807-2
MUP/H610

© 2002 Mercer University Press
6316 Peake Road
Macon, Georgia 31210-3960
All rights reserved

First Edition.

∞The paper used in this publication meets the
minimum requirements of American National
Standard for Information Sciences—Permanence of
Paper for Printed Library Materials, ANSI Z39.48-
1992.

Library of Congress Cataloging-in-Publication Data

CIP data are available from the Library of Congress

CONTENTS

Abbreviations and Short Titles

ANV	Army of Northern Virginia
GDAH	Georgia Department of Archives and History
KIA	Killed in action
MEC	Methodist Episcopal Church
OR	Official Records
POW	Prisoner of War
UDC	United Daughters of the Confederacy
WPA	Works Progress Administration

Civil War Day by Day–	E. B. Long with Barbara Long, *The Civil War Day by Day: An Almanac* (New York: Da Capo Press, 1971).
Civil War Dictionary–	Mark M. Boatner III, *The Civil War Dictionary* (New York: Vintage Books, 1988).
Generals in Gray–	Ezra J. Warner, *Generals in Gray: Lives of the Confederate Commanders* (Baton Rouge/London: Louisiana State University Press, 1995).
OR–	*Official Records of the American Civil War*, 128 vols. The version I used was a CD-ROM (Guild Press of Indiana, 1996).
Sears, Chancellorsville–	Stephen W. Sears, *Chancellorsville* (Boston/New York: Houghton Mifflin, 1996).
Sears, Richmond–	Stephen W. Sears, *To the Gates of Richmond: The Peninsula Campaign* (New York: Tichnor & Fields, 1992).

FOREWORD

By

Herman Hattaway

William R. Stilwell while serving in the Confederate Army wrote many letters to his beloved wife, Molly, and a few missives to other folk, which have been saved and are presented herein, helpfully glossed by the editor. "Keep these letters," Stilwell wrote Molly in late 1863, "they may be pearls in time to come." How right he was! What follows on these pages is a real treat. Of course Stilwell felt he never received enough mail. But he did get some from time to time, as well as clothing and other goodies from home. He suffered numerous physical hardships but seems ultimately to have thrived while enduring harsh conditions.

Sometimes Stilwell's writings bordered on being poetic. On 22 July 1862, he noted that:

> when the moon is up in the heavens and gentle wind from the mountains sends forth its still rustlings among the aspen tree under which I stand while the thousands of rattles of the drums are all still and the frogs that sing in the swamp all around are sending forth their beautiful melody while I go from post to post with a little black box in my hand containing the moments of my soul with a little lock of golden braid.

Stilwell was a complex, sensitive and articulate man; he was also a thorough "red neck" in both meanings of that term. First, that is a fair-skinned individual who sunburned easily. He wanted a hat instead of a cap—the latter being a "Kepi" with so short a brim as to offer the wearer no shade. In early 1864, he wrote Molly "the sun has burned me till you would hardly know me." Secondly, like the "stereotypical red neck" he cared unreservedly about the Southern cause, and espoused no tinge of guilt for any alleged wrongness that might have tainted the slave-holding society.

And Stilwell espoused a sharp perception of the Yankee's "other-ness." He wrote to Molly, "we are not going to stop as long as there is an army on Virginia soil and we may invade their country." And when in September 1862 the rebel army did thrust into Maryland, he felt that "we were in a foreign nation." And as they had waded across the Potomac, "the many big brass bands on the banks and played Dixie but when they go on the other side such a yell was never heard which rent the air and echoed down the long extending banks of the river, and here the band struck up the tune of Maryland...."

He seems constantly to have suspected that the war would not last much longer. But no matter what, he was staunch and firm in his commitment: "I don't believe the war can last at farthest twelve months longer (this in July 1862) but time alone will decide that. I am for my God, my family, and my country and I don't think any harm will befall me though I have to suffer and bear hardships and may have to die in Virginia." What an interesting revelation; that no harm would befall him even if he died in combat. Quite simply, in addition to his unstinting faith in God, Stilwell loved his "country." Whether he perceived that as primarily being the state of Georgia, or the would-be Confederate nation—he had an unquestioning affection and loyalty to it. And he was unquestioning in the depth of his faith that God would watch over and sustain it.

He did not always get what he wished he could have to eat, but on occasion there were feasts. He could revel over having had a sumptuous meal; and described one;...." Some man came from home and brought some of our mess some Irish potatoes and we drew peas and boiled it all together with a great big piece of meat as long as a stick and as wide as a piece of tobacco. It did not more than get done till we pitched into it and sure it was the best dinner I ever ate." He was with the force that captured Harper's Ferry, and "We had fine times off of a Yankee sutler's syrup and butter. I would not object to another bite of the same kind. You better believe I sopped both sides of my bread. For several days I have eat beef until I can almost low like a cow though we get the finest kind of beef but don't shorten bread much...." His tastes were typically Southern: preferring pork to beef! He much missed grits and, he noted, "Oh, how I would like to be at home to get some good cornbread and milk." But Stilwell often did secure good things, for he was quite a wheeler-dealer. He made money plying his trade as a leather-crafter. He bought and sold numerous goods, ranging from apples to boots and shoes and to watches, always turning tidy profits. Quite simply, he thrived. "I can eat more than ten men ought to eat and am glad to say that I get plenty to eat. I am as sassy as a big house nigga. Got money and tobacco a plenty for the present."

It is worthwhile for modern readers to think of Stilwell as man of his time and culture. He had a personal regard for certain Negro servants, and sometimes wrote warm greetings or instructions to them in his letters. To speak of a "sassy...big house nigga" was *not* a slur within the context of place and moment. No person feels even a tiny twinge of guilt when he has no perception whatever that his attitudes might be somewhat questionable or immoral.

There were, to be sure, moments when Stilwell's confidence in the rightness of the Southern cause floundered just a bit. In a down mood, he noted that "I wouldn't care if the Confederacy was broken into a thousand fragments anyhow for they treat the army like so many dogs. It is like Pa says, If God blesses us as a nation it can't be hard to get a blessing, for of all the nations on earth, I think in the course of another year we will be the most corrupted, Yankeedom not excepted." But this was a stark variation from Stilwell's more usual feelings.

Victory in battle assuredly elevated his moods. After the great triumph at Fredericksburg, he wrote Molly:

> I am prepared to give you a look at me as I now write. If you could only look sitting in the door of a comfortable tent surrounded by a nice bush arbor, comfortable fire and dressed out in a fine suit of jeans and fine boots with a fine watch in my pocket and fob and chain hanging down, and sitting on a cushion chair with a gold pen to write with, plenty of rations, a pocket full of money, a heavy beard and mustache on my upper lip, plenty of good books to read, now who wouldn't be in the war?

Through the long and hard and calamitous conflict, Stilwell's religious faith sustained him. "Only live right," he wrote Molly, "and God will make it all work out for our good. I am trying to keep my garments unspotted from the world. I want to live so that when I fall either [on] the battlefield or not, all will be well." Stilwell's faith was typical of Southerners—and Americans too—in the mid-nineteenth century. Death occurred so often at younger ages than has become common today, and that induced people to be nearly constantly and keenly aware of its inevitability.

But Stilwell, like all the good Rebels, had faith—not only in the goodness of God, but in the rightness of their cause. He wrote in August 1863: "Oh, Molly, how dark, this indeed is a dark day for the Confederacy, hundreds of our men are deserting and those that remain are discouraged and disheartened and people at home are whipped and want us to give up. To give up is but subjugation, to fight on is but dissolution, to submit is awful, to fight on is death. Oh, what shall we do? To submit, God forbid. To fight on, God deliver. Oh, Molly, when I think of the thousand of mangled forms of human beings crippled [and] torn in pieces, the thousands of widows and fatherless children all over our land, the weeping and moaning and anguish throughout the land, I am compelled to cry out, Oh, God, how long will thou afflict us, how long shall the horrors of war desolate our once happy country."

Stilwell did not waver; on 1 May 1864, he wrote "Oh, that God may bless us and give us peace that we may...worship around our family altar." Later that fateful May he wrote "We have whipped them at every point thus far and I think will in [the] future..." And, again a few lays later: "We feel perfectly confident of success, we have whipped them every time we have fought for the last month and with the blessing of God we can do it again...Our cause is just and must prevail. My prayer is that God will defend the right, his will be done, not mine."

The scenes of war were grim indeed. In mid-June 1864 Stilwell described Malvern Hill:

Here lies the remains of departed heroes with nothing to cover their bones from the heavens above. Many a loving and affectionate husband, father, or brother's bones lies exposed and trodden under foot, here too lies the skeletons of our enemies, thousands upon thousands, all over the fields and woods side by side enemy lie...man in his animal estate is worse than the best of the field but I shall not attempt to describe the scenes of a battlefield after two years has passed since the conflict, and where so many bodies lie moldering in its mother dirt. To you it would be an awful sight, but to me it is not. I have seen so much, ah, too much.

And the civil populace near the battle area were sometime similarly inured; On 15 October 1864. Stilwell wrote, "this whole valley is one barren waste, all the barns, mills and public houses have been burned up by Yankees, crops destroyed, dwellings sacked and plundered.... The other day after the battle, I seen and talked with two ladies while walking about the garden when the Yankee dead was lying all around them. Think of ladies walking over dead men, laughing as though nothing had happened.... Could you do it, Molly?"

Stilwell later entered into the Christian ministry: not extremely well educated, nevertheless he was quite thoughtful and reflective. In keeping with his calling, he seemed to have loved people generally, was gregarious, and always found it easy to make friends. He was also ambitious for his own status and circumstantial well being, and during the war displayed a talent for securing and keeping desirable assignments. He displayed an obvious unstinting dedication, made the best of circumstances, and manifested a considerable degree of bravery and courage; paying in the end for what perhaps eventually bordered on foolhardiness, by sustaining a wound that cost him one of his feet.

Like the rest of the society that crumbled around him, Stilwell had some hard times of mental, spiritual, and cultural readjustments ahead of him. With many difficulties, he persevered, living to the age of 68. He made very slow progress in pursuit of his ministerial credentials, but at last was ordained in the Methodist Episcopal Church (South) and thereafter served in a number of pulpits. His letters written during the great Civil War herein are now available to students, scholars, and enthusiasts who will find them both readable and informative.

Herman M. Hattaway, professor of history and religious studies, is in his thirty-third year at the University of Missouri-Kansas City. A native of Houma, Louisiana, he received a Ph.D. in 1969 at LSU under the tutelage of T. Harry Williams. He is the author, co-author, editor, or co-editor of eleven books. He has also published articles, chapters in books, and reviews numbering in the hundreds. He probably is most known for his co-authorship of two books; *How the North Won: A Military History of the Civil War* (Urbana: University of Illinois Press, 1983) with Archer Jones and *Why the South Lost the Civil War* (Athens: University of Georgia Press, 1986; abridged as *Elements of Confederate Defeat*, 1998) with Archer Jones, Richer E. Beringer and Wiliam Still, Jr. These two books broke considerable ground on "big picture" topics—strategic and socio/political factors that determined the eventual outcome of the War.

In addition to his professorship, Dr. Hattaway is an ordained priest in the Anglican Church in America and is pastor of St. John's Church in Kansas City.

PREFACE

William Ross Stilwell was wed to Mary Fletcher Speer on 8 September 1859 in McDonough, Henry County, Georgia. William was 20 and Mary (Molly) was 18. One month later, on 8 October 1859 they left for northwestern Louisiana where Molly's siblings were settling. Their first son, John Thomas (Tommy) was born on 4 June 1860, barely nine months after the wedding. While in Louisiana, William worked at his trade of harness maker, first in the town of Homer and then in Vernon. Sometime in 1861, with war clouds gathering, William and his family returned to Georgia so that Molly and Tommy would have the protection of Stilwell's extended family. In Georgia, William procrastinated on entering the army, not volunteering until 3 May 1862 to join Company F of the 53rd Regiment Georgia Volunteer Infantry.

Molly was the daughter of Margaret Beavers Everitt and James Madison Speer. The family gradually moved westward occupying various sites in Georgia and Alabama until Margaret died in Chambers County, Alabama in 1847. James immediately remarried a local widow so that his family of five children had proper care. But James died in 1852 and the family was dispersed; the four younger children being assigned to guardians who happened to be McDonough residents. The two oldest of the four were wards of Richard M. Everitt, Margaret's brother; and the two youngest, including Molly, were wards of Thomas Speer, James's brother.

Thomas Speer had moved to McDonough about 1853 with wife Nancy and seven children and promptly established himself as a prominent citizen. By 1860, he had a comfortable house west of town and a farm worked by 19 slaves.[1]

Richard M. Everitt was a McDonough harness and saddle maker. Evidently, his trade was prosperous; in 1860 he had two apprentices.

William Ross Stilwell was the son of Squire Stilwell and Ann Foster Stilwell. Squire was an early settler of Henry County following the lead of his brother, John who became a highly prominent member of the community, both as a farmer and a merchant. Squire did not prosper, as did John and their parents, Elijah and Margaret, who had migrated to Henry County. Squire owned a 67-acre farm about 4 miles south of McDonough that he worked by himself; he had no slaves.

William's mother, Ann Foster was raised in Butts County, adjacent to Henry County on the south where the Fosters were early settlers. Ann's father was deceased but her brother, William operated the family farm in far southwest Butts near the site of Fellowship Presbyterian Church. He owned 23 slaves in 1860. Ann's mother, Margaret, and a sister, Penelope, also lived on the farm. William Ross spent considerable time on this farm in his youth so he knew many of the neighbors, some of whom would be organized into Company I of the 53rd Regiment.

Thus, Squire Stilwell was the poor relation of the family structure. It is likely that he was alcoholic and this would have much to do in forming William Ross's traits and character.

By the time William and Molly returned to Georgia, Squire and Ann had moved from the 67-acre farm near McDonough to be near William Foster's farm in Butts County, probably so that Squire could be the overseer on the farm, the previous young overseer having gone into the army. This would be Molly's home during the first part of the war.

Henry County, lying just south of Atlanta, was situated on the northern border of the cotton belt; it was heavily agricultural with a

---

[1] The Markham House still stands as of December 2001 but is in imminent danger of being torn down.

high slave population, but not so high as areas further south. Up until about 1850, McDonough, the county seat, dominated the farm trade of the area. However, in the late 1840s it was bypassed by the Macon and Western railroad, a link in the Atlanta—Savannah line; thereafter McDonough declined sharply, with much of the trade and legal professions moving to Griffin, a newer town that became a major stop on the railroad. From 1850, McDonough and Henry County would become a quiet backwater area.

But in the 1980s Henry began to liven as the growth of Metropolitan Atlanta reached it. In the decade of the 1990s, Henry was fourth among fast growing counties in the United States. The population more than doubled. It is no longer possible to find any resemblance to the look and feel of Civil War times in modern day Henry County.

Butts County, lying south of Henry farther into the cotton belt and even more intensely agricultural than Henry, never had any pretensions of being a trade or professional center. Griffin took that role. Butts has been influenced to a lesser extent than Henry by the growth of Atlanta. Its 1990 population grew by 27 percent to the year 2000. Most of this growth was concentrated in the northern end of the county. The more isolated southern part, including the area around Fellowship Presbyterian Church is still quiet much like it was in the war period, but there are no remaining cotton fields.

Company F of the 53rd Regiment was the seventh and last volunteer infantry company to be raised in Henry County. That it was the last is significant. The regiment was formed during the first few days of May 1862. Conscription had taken effect on 1 May and all men between eighteen and thirty-five who would bear the honor and benefits of being "volunteers" would have to be in the army or in process on that date. Thus the conscription law drove the formation of Company F and the men of Company F, for a multitude of reasons, delayed volunteering until the last possible moment. If they had not volunteered, they would likely have been dishonored by conscription. This differentiated them from earlier units that had rushed to volunteer as patriots not pushed by the prospect of conscription and this applied to all companies of the 53rd.

Company F was a very large company. On 21 May 1862, 117 enlisted men signed the bounty roll and received their $50 volunteer bonus. Counting the four officers, the company began with a total of 121 men. Few companies started with as many as 100 men; Company I began with approximately ninety-five men.

The 53rd Georgia, on reaching Virginia, was immediately assigned to the brigade commanded by Paul Jones Semmes, a wealthy Columbus, Georgia banker. He was killed at Gettysburg and Goode Bryan became brigade commander until poor health forced his resignation in September 1864. Thereafter, James Philip Simms of Covington, Georgia commanded the brigade until the end of the war.

Shortly after entering Virginia, the brigade was assigned to the division commanded by Lafayette McLaws of Georgia and remained under him until he was relieved of command during the East Tennessee campaign. Joseph Kershaw of South Carolina was then appointed commander and held this position until the end of the war.

James Longstreet was the responsible corps commander throughout the war. Despite his becoming very controversial in postwar times, there is little doubt that Lee always considered him his number one general—"his old war horse." The partisans of General Stonewall Jackson will dispute this vigorously, but they overlook the fact that Lee deliberately gave Longstreet the higher date of rank. His reputation, of course, was based on the superior performance of his units, of which the 53rd Georgia was a part.

After a rocky start, the men of Companies F and I and the remainder of the 53rd Georgia performed very creditably at Antietam, Chancellorsville, Gettysburg, the Wilderness, and Cedar Creek, their performance certainly being on a par with the older units of Longstreet's Corps. Stilwell's reason for procrastinating about volunteering was because of his slight physique, thus hampering his ability to keep up on marches, particularly when he had a heavy load on his back. So as soon as enrolled, he began to maneuver for a special assignment that would relieve him of the burdens of the ordinary infantryman. His efforts were successful as he consecutively held positions of brigade headquarters guard, assistant to the brigade quartermaster, and finally brigade courier. But he maintained daily contact with Companies F and I. During the two-and-a-half years that he served in Longstreet's Corps of the Army of Northern Virginia, Stilwell wrote Molly about once a week. These letters are the treasure available to the reader in the following pages.

BACKGROUND AND
ACKNOWLEDGMENTS

There are 127 letters in the Stilwell collection, many quite lengthy, resulting in one of the larger collections of period Civil War letters written by an active soldier. William Ross Stilwell, a private in Company F of the 53rd Regiment Georgia Volunteer Infantry, wrote practically all of the letters. Most were addressed to his wife, Molly, and contained, among numerous topics, instructions on the training of their children. In one, Stilwell asked that the letters be saved for the sake of posterity and to assist in the religious training of the children.

The family honored his request and in the 1930s the collection was submitted to the United Daughters of the Confederacy (UDC) to be judged in a contest on interesting sets of letters from Confederate soldiers. The collection won an award. In 1940, son "Tommy" of the letters, then the postmaster at Montezuma, Georgia, contributed the letters to the Georgia Department of Archives and History where the full citation is Stilwell, William Ross (1839-1907). Civil War Letters, ac 40-102. In the same year, as W. P. A. Project #5993, the letters were typed, the typescripts were bound by the UDC and placed on a shelf with other *Letters from Confederate Soldiers* which are in a public area of the Archives and freely available to historians and the public. Being easily accessible, the letters have been oft quoted in various Civil War books and publications. Bell Wiley, in his landmark history *Johnny Reb,* (reissued by Louisiana State Press in 1978, 1994 printing) quotes from the letters no less than a dozen times.

I was attracted to the letters through a search of all documents and materials related to the 53rd Georgia as I had a grandfather, John Shirley Elliott, who served as first corporal in Stilwell's company. John also had a younger brother, Bailor S. Elliott, who was second lieutenant of the company. I found the letters invaluable in understanding the wartime experiences of these ancestors. I also realized that they would be valuable to anyone interested in the Civil War and they deserved a wider distribution so I have undertaken the task of publishing the collection.

The typescripts needed much work. In a time of poor spellers, Stilwell was particularly atrocious, and not unusual, the letters were practically devoid of punctuation. Many editors would present similar letters in the vernacular, warts and all. But I decided that the reader would soon tire of attempting to translate the vernacular into recognizable English, particularly in view of the length of the Stilwell collection. Thus, I have corrected the spelling, including correction of proper nouns when sure of the object, and lightly added punctuation. In doing so, *I did not delete or change a single word written by Stilwell* but I have added words as needed for clarity. All added words are enclosed in brackets, [ ]. Checking the typescript version against the originals, I found that the 1940s typist made many errors in attempting to read the handwritten documents. Stilwell's handwriting was not bad but he was writing on all kinds of paper, some of which had faded badly over the years. By understanding the context of the letters, I was able to improve and clarify the typescripts. Stilwell could paint a vivid picture with words. He was not an exceptional writer but probably a great orator. His religious background probably accounts for this. Thus, the reader should approach the words as oral messages, possibly reading some passages aloud.

Producing a clean manuscript of the letters was the easy part. The annotation of the letters has taken over five years. This task has taken so much time because I needed to educate myself on the background, causes, Southern attitudes, culture, and support for the war. My professional life was as a financial executive with an aerospace giant, living for twenty-two years in Southern California separated by 2200 miles from my roots in Georgia. When I had accumulated enough savings to finance my retirement, I returned to Georgia and began my study of antebellum southern history and the Civil War. I intended to apply this learning to my family history; later I applied it to annotating the Stilwell letters.

Many individuals and organizations assisted me in this quest. I became a docent at the Tully Smith House at the Atlanta History Center. The House, built around 1846, was once the center of an 812-acre farm established by a Smith family soon after the central Georgia area was opened to settlement by the Creek Indian land cession of 1821. The treaty area was a slice that ran down the middle of the state from the Chattahoochee River through Macon and included Henry and Butts Counties. My job at the house required that I become familiar with the culture and practices of the early pioneers and continue with their descendants who became the slave owners of the late antebellum period. This helped me to understand my family roots but then became invaluable in understanding William Ross Stilwell. I am obligated to the volunteers and staff of the Tully Smith House for providing the opportunity, and particularly helpful was the house administrator, Chris Brooks.

During the period I have been associated with the Atlanta History Center, they mounted a major permanent exhibit on the Civil War, *Turning Point.* I served as a tour guide for this exhibit, for which Gordon Jones, the initial responsible curator, and later Myers Brown trained me. The exhibit was much influenced by author James McPherson whose views of the war are contained in his book *Battle Cry of Freedom.* He has lectured at the History Center and I am greatly influenced by his account of the causes and pursuit of the war by the South.

Book and museum learning are necessary in understanding the background of the war. But no amount of book study can supply knowledge of the land over which the individuals and units you are studying fought. I have followed Stilwell and his unit on most of the battlefields they trod: out of the West Woods at Antietam, advancing toward the Cornfield and farmer Miller's house; holding the line of Marye's Heights at Fredericksburg; and at the brick church named Salem located between Fredericksburg and Chancellorsville. The church is now a shrine but immediately across the road to the north where the 53rd Georgia made its stand the area is now covered by asphalt—the parking lot for a shopping mall. At Gettysburg, it was the Rose Farm, its woods, the ravine and the Wheat Field; the indescribable thick brush of the Wilderness; and the trenches of Cold Harbor and Petersburg. And finally, I visited the crossing on Cedar Creek where the dawn attack was initiated by Stilwell's brigade. This site today is still very isolated, having only a one-lane bridge to accommodate the occasional local vehicle. The quietness is appropriate because the actual attack was done in much secrecy and thus proceeded very quietly. And this was Stilwell's last battle.

Some of these sites I did on my own, but mostly I was part of group, usually organized and sponsored by the Blue and Gray Education Society, Len Riedel, executive director. Our tour guide would often be Ed Bearss, the superstar of battlefield tours. But there were many other guides and lecturers; Richard McMurray, Brian Steel Wills, Parker Hills, Jim Ogden, Steven Woodworth, and Herman Hattaway are a few of the names that come to mind.

The comments and footnotes on events in the war are derived from this background but I do not attempt to provide a general background of the war's progress. I leave this to Stilwell and his compatriots who were surprisingly aware of what was happening, even on the far-away western front. But for the benefit of the casual reader, in the footnotes, I attempt to deny, affirm, or correct Stilwell's reports and recognize that rumors we know to be false today might have been very real to the participants. When I comment on acts or general events or historic persons not directly associated with Stilwell, I give the source, mostly from standard references.

Most of the effort in annotating the letters went into the identification of the local people mentioned by Stilwell in passing news of them on to Molly. This research gives the editor an opportunity to probe into the class and slavery connection of members of the units and other local personages. Public data tells us much about the makeup of the particular units and communities. The research on local non-historic personages is very different from events and people recognized as historic and I treat them very differently by not listing the source of data on local individuals. The number of sources for this purpose is very limited so that a general description of the search methodology will suffice to enable others wishing to confirm the facts quoted.

Most individuals mentioned were soldiers so their service records are of prime importance. The most convenient access to the records of members of most Georgia infantry units is *Roster of the Confederate Soldiers of Georgia.* Despite the title, the units covered are limited to infantry units in Confederate service and several sources of information such as hospital and prison records were not available to the compilers. The more useful source is the Compiled Service Records of Confederate Soldiers that is on microfilm, the most convenient set to me being at the Georgia Department of Archives and History. The microfilm records are much more complete as to units covered and data items included and are less prone to error than Henderson.

William Ross Stilwell was a member of Company F, 53rd Regiment Georgia Volunteer Infantry that was organized and re-cruited in Henry County Georgia, thus practically all the members were Henry County inhabitants. However, Molly was living with Stilwell mother's family for much of the war in Butts County, just to the south of Henry. Stilwell, in his youth, had spent much time here and had a wide range of acquaintances in this neighborhood. The 53rd Regiment also had a company (I) organized and recruited from Butts, and Stilwell often mentioned these individuals.

Ninety percent of the quoted civilian data on individuals men-tioned by Stilwell is derived from US Census data, primarily from the censuses of 1860 and 1870. The primary organization of the data was by county; data on each individual organized by house-hold unit was entered on ledger sheets and later bound, there being one book for an average-sized county, and the pages numbered sequentially. This allows for indexing with names being referenced to page numbers. Each page is available as a microfilm image and there are several published index books available for each state.

The 1860 Census of Free Inhabitants contains columns for name, sex, age, color, occupation, value of real estate, value of personal property, and place of birth. Other miscellaneous data includes identifying those that can't read or write. There was a separate slave census, each slave identified by age and sex and listed under the owner's name. There are no indexes for the Slave Census. The 1870 census was very similar to the 1860 free census except that all inhabitants were now free. In addition to counting the inhabitants, there was an agricultural census of each farm that includes an incredible amount of detail. There is no index to the agricultural census.

The microfilm census records that I utilized were the collections at the Georgia Department of Archives and History, the Atlanta History Center, and the Georgia Room of the Cobb County, Georgia, Public Library. I am much obligated to the staffs of these institutions for their assistance.

There are county histories that assist in providing data on selective individuals but are mostly beneficial on understanding the history and background community information of Henry and Butts Counties. Most valuable was *Henry County Georgia, Mother of Counties,* by Vessie Thrasher Rainer. Also valuable was *First Families of Henry County Georgia.* There is also a *History of Butts County Georgia 1825-1976,* which was of some help.

There are two manuscript publications filed in the family history section at the Georgia Department of Archives and History. One is written by Eva Fulton Stilwell, the daughter-in-law of our William Ross and his second wife, Callie Jane Kennedy and covers the Stilwell family and their predecessors, the Houston, Foster, and Duffey lines. For Molly's lines, the Speers and Everitts, there is a document written and placed in the files by Mrs. James H. Elliott, Jr. Both of these documents are helpful in defining family lineage.

The later history of the Fosters is not covered by any documentation. As Molly was residing with William Foster and suddenly departed, we wonder what circumstances caused this event.

For this information, we must examine the tombstones in the Fellowship Presbyterian Church Cemetery located in far southwest Butts County. The little modern church building is nondescript, but the setting and the cemetery are magnificent—the church is set in a grove of towering oaks, bounded by a huge magnolia tree and the cemetery is enclosed by a dry stone wall, very rare in this area. Considering the age of the cemetery, the names on the tombstones, and their Presbyterian religious persuasion, the soil of the cemetery is probably as rich in Scots-Irish genes as any place on earth. My thanks go to Brenda King of the Butts Genealogy Society who directed me to this lovely place.

I also appreciate the assistance of my wife, June, who helped me with the grammar and syntax; to Mack Moseley who orally offered a rich background of Henry County history; to Joseph Moore, also a Henry County expert who read and commented on the text of this book and gave me a couple of valuable leads on the persons mentioned. Last, but not least, I appreciate the encouragement of Harry Stillwell, grandson of "Tommy" of the letters.

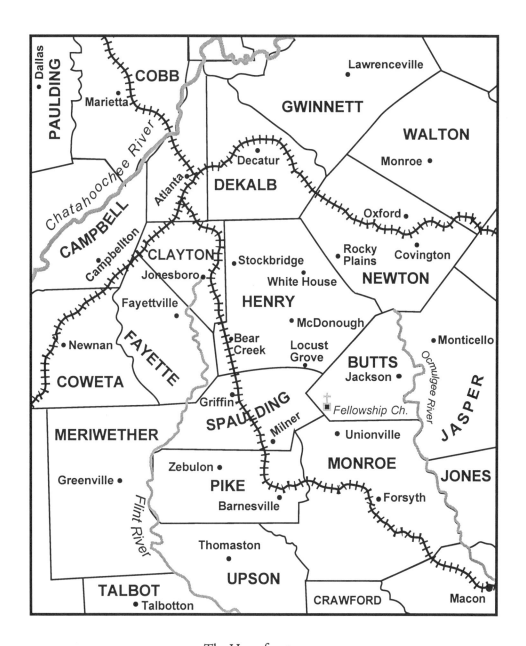

The Homefront.

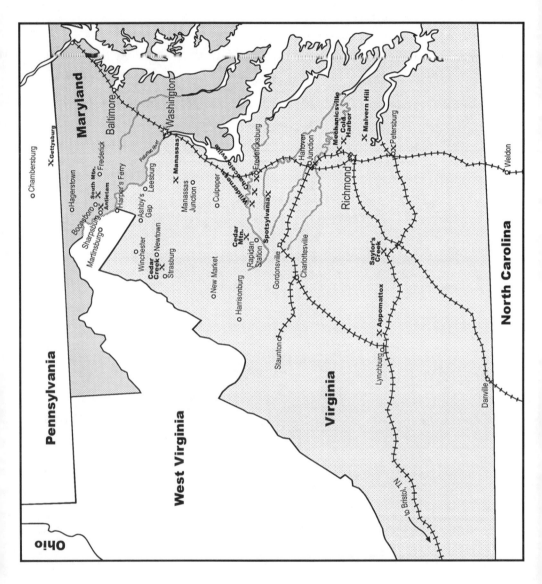

The Virginia Front.

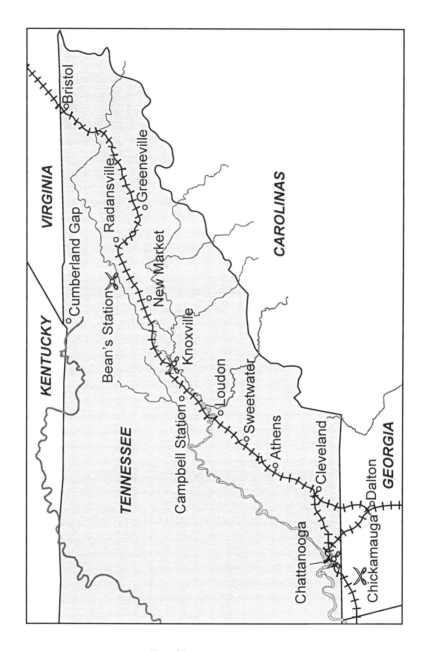

East Tennessee.

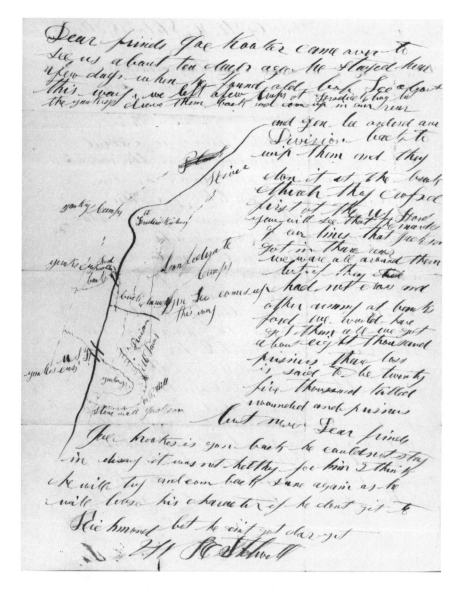

See p. 155 for the letter written here. Stilwell included this map on the letter.

1

THE SEVEN DAYS

The Confederacy is in dire danger. General George B. McClellan with his huge Union Army is within seven miles of the capital city of Richmond. Every available southern soldier is being rushed to the front in the northern outskirts of Richmond to join General Robert E. Lee's Army of Northern Virginia. This is General Lee's baptism by fire as commander of a large army. On 25 June Lee began the movement intended to destroy McClellan or at the least to force him away from Richmond. So began what will be known as the Seven Days Battle.

June 26, 1862—Near Petersburg, Virginia.

Dear Molly:

I feel thankful to Almighty God that I am permitted to write you for the cars have just run off the tracks breaking every box on the train wounding eight or ten men, how it was that nearly all of them were not killed? I got my arm hurt a little but not but very little. We have to stay here until the engine goes 21 miles and returns. We would have got to Richmond tonight if the cars had not run off. We have fared tolerable well. I have not time to give any details of our trip but will perhaps in my next.

My health is very good. The health of the regiment is very good. All of the boys that you know escaped unhurt. Everything is so excited that I can't write. Molly, I am as well satisfied as I could be under the circumstances. I will have to close as the train will be here in a few minutes. I close for the present. Kiss my boy. I remain your affectionate husband until death.

W. R. Stilwell

Remember me

———

The 53rd Regiment reached Richmond in the middle of the Seven Days Battle, which will reach its climax at Malvern Hill on July 1, the day this letter was written.

Richmond, Virginia, July 1, 1862

Dear Molly:

I am permitted to write to you again. We arrived here Thursday at twelve o'clock and were armed with guns taken from the Yankees the day before. They had been fighting two days when we got here and have been ever since. We marched twenty miles the next day after we got here, carried thirty pounds and were ordered in to line of battle the next day. The march made me sick and I was not able to go. Our regiment is in pursuit of the Yankee now. We have driven them back at every point and taken all their cannons. I have not been to the battlefield but the boys that have say that there are at least ten thousand sacks of salt and coffee and sugar. It is not worth while for me to write much about the battle for you will hear more about it than I will before you get this. It is my opinion that this battle will close the war. It is thought that we will capture the whole army. Stonewall Jackson is in their rear and we are in front, they have burnt all their commissary stores, blown up the ammunition. We have taken at least five thousand prisoners. I learn that the Yankees are still retreating this morning. I hope I will be able to join my regiment tomorrow.

I have not seen William Darnell yet and don't know when I will.[1] I don't know whether he is killed or not. I won't get to see

---

[1] William Darnell was a brother-in-law to WRS; Darnell was married to Jane Penelope Stilwell, WRS' older sister. They had two small daughters in 1860. At that time,

him until the battle is over anyhow. I have seen some of the most awful sights since I have been here that ever any man was permitted to look at, men lying in great piles, dead and dying, some with no legs, no arms, nose or eyes shot off or out. The wounded are cared for the best they can be. We left our tents in Richmond but have our flies.[2] We had to leave everything but what we could carry on our backs. We get plenty to eat such as it is, hard crackers and crackers hard.

We had a very tiresome trip. We left Griffin Monday twelve noon, arrived in Atlanta four pm, left at six, got to Augusta nine am Tuesday. We came through Williamsburg [Wilmington (?)], Goldsboro and then on through South Carolina. I wrote to you the other side of Petersburg, Va. where the cars broke down. I suppose you got it. The second box of the train from the engine broke down and fell down on the track and all the cars behind stove up against it. Some of the boxes of the car was in the two others, some on the end, pieces of planks and cast iron flying, men jumping off the train but nobody killed, how was it God only knows.

Molly, I have just heard that they won't let any letters go off from Richmond until this battle is over but I will send this one in and see. I don't know when I can write. I just have to pick my chance. I could not write this plain like I wanted to. I have to write it on my knee. I am as well satisfied as I could be under the circumstances. I want you to write soon. Direct your letters to Richmond as I told you. Give my respects to all, kiss my baby, oh lordy.

I must come to a close for the present. I hope not for ever. Write soon. I remain your affectionate husband until death.

W. R. Stilwell

I will write again the first opportunity.

Darnell was probably William Foster's overseer. Darnell was a private in Company H, 27th Infantry Regiment, Henry County "Zachry Rangers" and, as far as I know, survived the war. He and his family cannot be located in the 1870 Georgia census.

[2] A sheet made of tent-like material that can give some shelter.

———

The regiment first saw service in a reserve role on 29 June at Savage's Station and was involved in a comedy of errors wherein they came under friendly fire from another regiment, panicked and ran a short distance before stopping to reorganize. On July 1, in the battle of Malvern Hill, their line of battle fractured into many pieces with many of the men getting lost in the surrounding swamps. Malvern Hill was a disaster for the Confederates, demonstrating again the futility of charging well-positioned artillery but the cautious McClellan continued his retreat to the protection of the Union gunboats.

Fifteen miles below Richmond, Virginia, July 4, 1862
Dear Molly:
Thanks be to God I have been spared to write to you once more. I left camp on Tuesday in pursuit of the enemy towards Yorktown and have driven them 15 miles to James River on their gunboats. Where they will go now I don't know nor I don't know where we will go from here.

Molly, it would be folly for me to attempt to describe the hardships and dangers that I have come through since I came here. I have been where bullets fly thick and fast and bombshells burst all round and in all the horrors of battle. We have not been the advance guard on the battle but in just as much danger.[3] God save me from ever seeing the awful sights that I have seen for the last week. As for hardships, we have no tents, half rations of meat and crackers or bakers bread, and no pan to fry our meat in. We just cut off and throw it in the fire and broil it. That is the way we live. My knapsack is at camps near Richmond and I don't know whether I will ever see it again or not. I have lost both of my blankets, went off when I was gone and of course I could not help it but I sleep on Yankee blankets, drink their coffee and sugar. We have had one of

---

[3] WRS is exaggerating. The unit had no direct contact with the enemy but was subjected to artillery fire. Also remember that WRS was sick and not with the unit for most of this time.

4

the greatest battles ever fought on this continent and have drove the grand army of the north from every position they have taken. We have lost a great many men but that must needs have been. We have taken over ten thousand prisoners. I hope that this will stop the war but it may not. Molly, I thought of you and Tommy when we were in the battle, when I was looking every minute for the balls or bomb to kill me. I don't know when I may be killed; it may be in a few days and it may never be, but I expect to try to die like a brave man fighting for the right of his country, and try to die the death of the righteous that my last end may be like His. It is not near as wicked here as I expected to find it. There was only one or two men killed in our regiment A good many struck in our company with bombs but none very bad, only Bud Whitard.[4] He was wounded in the hand. There have been a great many of my old friends killed. Perry Sowell was killed.[5] Every man in Peeble's Company that went off the fourth of March is sick, killed, wounded and missing except six.[6] They have been cut to pieces almost. I saw James Speer but I

---

[4] Probably H. V. Whitaker, a fifty-two-year-old illiterate house carpenter, widowed with two teen-age children. He was discharged from service on 5 August 1862, probably because of the hand wound. He was present in the regiment as a substitute for Uriah Alexander who was a farmer and owner of four slaves. Alexander, married and the father of six children, was the thirty-two-year old youngest son of a Henry County pioneer. Alexander does not appear in the 1870 census of Henry County. Whitaker married Mary McCoy in April 1865 but they can't be located in the 1870 census.

[5] Perry Sowell was a member of a large Henry County family that supplied several soldiers to the cause. A private in Company A, 44th Infantry, he was killed on 26 June 1862 at Ellerson's Mill on Beaver Dam Creek. He was believed to be about 33 years old and there is no record of his having been married but the whole family, living near Bear Creek (now Hampton) in Henry County was missed in the 1860 census. One of the editor's grandfathers was the assistant marshal responsible for the 1860 census of Henry County.

[6] Captain William H. Peebles was organizer and commander of Company A, 44th Georgia Infantry, "Weems Guards." The 44th would lose 335 of its 514 men in the Battle of Ellison's Mill on Beaver Dam Creek on 26 June 1862. Again on 1 July, they suffered severely at Malvern Hill, with 65 of 142 men either dead or wounded. *Official Records of the American Civil War*, 128 vols., 11/2:656. Before the war Peebles was a young doctor, educated at Augusta Georgia, Philadelphia and New York, practicing in Bear Creek (Hampton) in Henry County. In 1861, he married Eliza Ann Weems of the family for which Company A was named. He survived the war and resumed his practice in Bear

can't get to see Darnell yet, can't find his regiment but learn he is not killed. I reckon it is so.[7]

I have a bad chance to write. This is a piece of paper that I have borrowed and have to write on my knee but it is the best I can do. You must write often to me for I can't get to buy anything here with money and I had just as soon spend it on writing as anything and will therefore write often when I can, but I don't know when I sit down to write but what the old drum will commence the long roll and then you hear "Fall in, fall in!" and then such jerking to get on your tricks was never heard and here we go through mud and water knee and thigh deep. I don't any more mind wading through a mud hole here than I would a little stream at home. If you did, it would do no good. We are treated very bad but we take it all like good soldiers. My health is very good. I can eat fat meat covered in fire coals and ashes. Sleep sound all night on the wet ground, get up next morning all right.

Molly, I could write a half dozen pages but have not paper. Write soon and let me know what my baby has to say about the friends and all the news. Tell all of them to write. Give my love to all. No more at present but ever remain your affectionate husband until death.

W. R. Stilwell
Yours forever
Farewell, W. R. Stilwell

––––––

WRS visits his former neighbors in the units from the two towns where he and Molly had lived in Louisiana; Homer of Claiborne Parish and Vernon of Jackson Parish. They were part of the 2nd Louisiana Volunteer Infantry and had been fighting in Virginia since

Creek where he raised two sons. According to the 1870 census he and WRS were likely next-door neighbors.

[7]James Speer, son of Thomas Speer, was third sergeant of Company G, 19th Regiment, "Henry Guards." In 1860, he was a 28-year-old unmarried community schoolteacher.

mid–1861. This was a zouave outfit that became part of what was known as "Lee's Tigers." The zouaves modeled themselves on the Algerian infantry of the French colonial army and were famous for their gaudy uniforms.

Fifteen miles below Richmond, Virginia, July 6, 1862
Dear Molly:

I wrote to you the other day but having another opportunity of writing I thought I would write again. We are still here and don't know when we will leave. We may stay here two weeks or we may leave in fifty minutes. A soldier don't know anything but to obey orders. My health is still good and also the health of the company and regiment. I feel thankful that our regiment came out so well, two or three killed and ten or twelve wounded. I was on the battlefield yesterday and God deliver me from ever seeing another battlefield. Some think that this fight will end the war and that we will have no more fighting to do. All that I can say is God grant it. One thing I know, we routed and whipped the Yankees. They have gone to their gunboats and some say that they are leaving as fast as they can. I hope they may never come back here again. This is twice they have tried to get to Richmond and they went so far as to have on their flags "Richmond or Hell by Saturday Night." Some of the boys say that they got to both places. I don't know. I know some of them went to Richmond, the other place I don't know.

I have had a chance to visit some of my friends since the battle. I have been with William Darnell for the last two days. Saw him last night, he looked as well as I ever saw him. He was detailed to drive a wagon and was not in the fight. Jug was wounded but not bad.[8] William tells me that the government owes him about one hundred and forty dollars. I also saw the Second Louisiana Regiment Homer Guards and Vernon Guards. There are not many

---

[8] "Jug" has not been identified other than as a member of the 27th Regiment who lived near William Darnell's home.

of them left.[9] I saw Dock Witch, Elie Ragland, West Reams, all of whom are in good health. I saw Manrow too; Jones Lloyd is at the sick camp. Nat Knight is dead, Monrow Kent and Jerry Leack were killed.

Molly, you can write to Sister [Martha Ragland]. I learn that we still hold Vicksburg and your letter will go. It is not worthwhile for me to say that I live hard for I don't wish to grumble for if I can just live through and get home to enjoy your and baby's company I shall feel thankful to God and that is my daily prayer. I think of you when I lie down and when I rise up, when I go out and when I come in, when bullets fly and cannon roar. I am trying to keep in good spirits but can't help feeling bad for I am gone from them that I love but God knows the heart of all men and I feel if we will look to him that all will be well at last. I want to hear from Mother and Grandma very bad. I hope I will get a letter from you soon. Today is Sunday and as pretty a day as I ever saw. I think that you will write to me today.

We had a powerful rain here on Wednesday after the great battle on Tuesday. The fighting commenced on Wednesday and lasted just a week. I write on Yankee paper and I have two splendid Yankee blankets. It is impossible to describe their loss. They burnt up great houses of stores. From the best information that I can gain we had about three hundred thousand men here.[10] I have no idea of their forces. I have no idea that they will keep all of their men here now. Where the next fight will be I can't tell. I think that both armies are tired and want to close the war. It is said that McClellan's men is completely demoralized. I hope it is so and it looks to me like they ought to be, being whipped as they are. Richmond is the largest city that I ever saw, being twenty-five

---

[9] The 2nd Louisiana lost three color bearers and then the regimental commander in charging Malvern Hill. The second-in-command took up the flag, then he too was killed. These Louisianians lost 182 dead or wounded, more than any other unit save one. They finally halted and withdrew without reaching their objective. Sears, *To the Gates of Richmond: The Peninsula Campaign* (New York: Tichnor & Fields, 1992).

[10] Actually 92,400, the largest army Lee would command during the entire war. Sears, *To the Gates of Richmond*, 332.

miles round and five through. The capitol is placed on a very high hill right in the middle of the city. I went up in it and went out on top where I could see all over the whole city. It is a beautiful sight. While I write there are some of the sights of camp life to be seen, some men writing, some cooking their little meat over the fire, singing, smoking, cleaning guns, and in fact all the work that several thousand men would be doing placed as we are, all thinking of one day getting home. We know that all can't get home but all think it is not me, it is someone else.

Molly, I am about done this letter, I was obliged to write with pencil. I don't know whether you can read it or not but hope that you can. I have done the best that I could this time. This is the fourth letter I have written since I left home and will continue to write when I can. Give my love to all and tell all to write. Kiss my boy and may God spare you and him and me too.

Yours until death,

W. R. Stilwell

––––––

Richmond has been saved by Lee's aggressive tactics and McClellan's timidity. By now, with two weeks service on the battle line, WRS is playing the part of the seasoned soldier indifferent to the spartan living conditions and dangers of battle, yet he wonders if devotion to his family will make him less of a soldier. Some sickness is beginning to occur in his unit; one soldier has died of fever.

Three miles east of Richmond, Virginia, July 10, 1862
Dear Molly:
You will perceive that we have moved since I wrote your last. On the evening of [the] eighth we were ordered to sleep by our arms and on the morning of the ninth at three o'clock the old drum commenced the long roll and we knew that something was to pay and then you could hear all over the swamp. "Fall in, fall in!" Off we put, not knowing where but to our great satisfaction we were marched back to our old camps. Men fell tired down on every side

and Captain Brown was surprised to see me roll up in the camp the third man in our company, though I was very tired.[11]

I almost hate to write back to you how we live for we take it like good boys. I have lived on half cracker a day and on parched corn and was glad to get it, and waded through mud and water. Slept on the ground without any thing but still I live and am blest with good health. I have got my knapsack and all of my things except my blankets and bedtick but I don't need them. There is some sickness in our company and one death. Jerry Goss died at the hospital in Richmond with the fever.[12]

Molly, you would have been surprised to have seen me and Bob McDonald washing out shirts and drawers the other day.[13] We did not have any clothes but what we had on for eight or ten days and we went about half mile from camp, pulled off stark naked and went to washing like good fellows, dried and then put on again. We are very good hands at the business.

How long we will stay here I know not. We will live better here than we have been living. There are a great many rumors here about our going back to Georgia and about peace but we don't believe anything we hear. You know a great deal more about the war and the movements of troops than I do. We don't know anything but to do what we are told. Everything here is so high that I don't pretend to buy but very little. Meal is worth four dollars per bushel and everything is very high. Molly, I shall have to stop in a few minutes for dress parade, but may write more in the morning.

---

[11] Sheridan Ragland Brown, captain and commander of Company F since June 11, replaced Thomas Sloan who was appointed Lieutenant Colonel. He was a 29-year-old farmer with a 21-year-old wife and two small children and owned seven slaves. He was wounded at Gettysburg and resigned with a disability on 23 September 1864. After the war he would have a family of four children in 1870 and by the 1880s he would be one of the largest cotton farmers in Henry County.

[12] Jerry Goss was a private in Company F of the 53rd who died on 8 July. He was a 33-year-old Henry County tenant farmer with a 22-year-old wife and no children. He had married Susan Gardner in 1859 and she remarried in December 1866.

[13] R. A. McDonald was a Griffin dentist married to Uncle John Stilwell's oldest daughter. He was 29 years old with one small child in 1860. In 1870, he was still practicing dentistry in Griffin and he and his wife had three children.

Morning, and it is still raining. Molly, I learn than there have no letters gone from Richmond since the fight commenced. I expect you are very uneasy about me. I have written you four or five letters since I got here. I have a chance to send this to Griffin by hand. Molly, when you get the letters that I have written to you it will give you some of the news of the fight. I was in the great fight on Tuesday but was not hurt.[14] Two or three of our regiment were killed and ten or fifteen wounded. I had bomb shells to strike very close to me and throw dirt and rocks all over me but, Molly, may God save me from ever seeing another such a fight. It is awful to think about.

I will write more. I thought I would have got a letter from you before now but have not. You must not neglect to write as I want to hear from you very bad. While I write it is raining very hard but I am dry. I have seen some of the boys that have just come from home and was glad to hear that you had good rains and hope that there will be good crops made. I hope that I will get home some day to enjoy what little [crops] we will make but when, I know not. I feel that I am a long ways from home but I enjoy myself as well as I can. You know how I feel better than I can tell you with my pen, but Molly, my duty to my country demands my service and I must obey. I trust that the worst of the fighting is over. The North admits that we whip them very bad. Just give us the breastworks that they had and there are not men enough in the north to whip us. I never saw nor heard of such in my life but our boys charged them wherever they came to them and they would run every time, sure.

I am wet and can not write much. If my letters do not go by mail I will send them by hand whenever I can. I will try to send some by Mr. Dave Evans when he comes. Your letters will come to me if you will back [address] them as I told you.[15]

---

[14] WRS is referring to the Battle of Malvern Hill but he had written a letter on the day of the battle stating that he was sick and not with his unit. However every southerner basks in the glory of sending McClellan back to his boats and saving Richmond and every soldier claimed a part of the victory.

[15] David Evans was a well-to-do Butts County farmer who lived in the vicinity of Molly's temporary quarters with the Fosters. He owned 10 slaves in 1860. He had several

Molly, I rested very well last night having my blankets to lie on and a fly to sleep under for the first time in over a week. I don't mind lying on grubs and rocks. I think if it was not for my family that I would make a good soldier but when I think of you and Tommy and that is all the time most, it makes me feel bad but let us trust in God and all will be well in the end. Oh, that this unholy war would come to a close, but we must wait the time of Him that made all things.

Molly, I will have to close my letter for the man by whom I send is going to start. I think that the mail will be open in a few days. Molly, I want Tommy's ambrotype if you can get it. Send it by some one that is coming here.[16] It would do me good to look at it when the golden sun was setting in the west and when the silver moon was sending its beautiful rays through the tall pines of Virginia. While the poor boys are sleeping in their little white houses, have I often sat with my face towards the land of Dixie and the tears would run down my cheeks while I thought of thee and my little baby. But I must close for this time. May God bless thee, my dear, and my baby and may he permit us to meet once more on earth and if not, in heaven, is the prayer of your own loving and affectionate husband until death.

W.R. Stilwell
Write soon and often

———

Stilwell is still awed by the victory over McClellan. The Confederates were amazed at the amount of booty abandoned or destroyed by the Union Army during their withdrawal. Their plentiful supplies are indicative of McClellan's careful preparation. WRS's letter

---

sons in the Confederate Army including two in Company I of the 53rd. It was customary for such men to make trips to and fro from army areas bringing mail, clothing, and food to local soldiers. In this role, these men provided considerable assistance to the troops and to the cause.

[16] An ambrotype was an early type of photograph made by imaging a negative on glass backed by a dark surface.

writing was interrupted by a summons to the headquarters of his brigade commander, Paul Jones Semmes of Columbus, Georgia. Contrary to general historical reporting, he was not the brother of Admiral Raphael Semmes of Confederate Navy fame. Their grandfathers had been brothers thus making them second cousins.

Three Miles below Richmond, Virginia, July 14, 1862
Dear Molly:
I have another opportunity of writing and sending it by hand. Mr. Dave Evans will leave for home tomorrow. I am in good health this morning though I feel very drowsy having just come off picket last night, having been on twenty-four hours. I had to stand two hours and off four. We stood at the Yankees' camp and I went over part of their camp. It is a sight worth looking at. Such a war as I never thought I would look at. You could find anything almost that you wanted to. I have no doubt but they lost and destroyed ten millions of dollars worth of property in those runs, they say retreats, but it looks more to me like a routed and whipped army. Old McClellan made a speech to his grand army in which he said "Men, you may think that things look dark but all is right." But, alas, his men saw the darkness theirselves and they know that it is dark. I don't know where they are. The last I heard of them they were trying to get on their gunboats and General Stuart was driving them in. I hope they will never try to come to Richmond anymore.[17] It is thought that peace will be made in a short time. God grant it, for war is a terrible thing to all the world. I would be willing to quit it. You may talk about men seeing the monkey and the elephant but if they haven't seen both since we came here I don't know anything about them, though for my part I have taken it very well and feel thankful that I have come out so well.[18] I can assure you that the battlefield is not a delightful place to be at.

---

[17] General J. E. B. (Jeb) Stuart, Lee's talented cavalry commander.
[18] "Seeing the monkey and elephant" were slang expressions meaning to experience combat for the first time.

Molly, I have just been detailed to go to General Semmes headquarters and will have to go in a few minutes.[19] I intended to write you a long letter but won't have time. I don't know what the general wants with me. He sent down for a steady reliable man and they detailed me. I must close. Give my respects to all my friends Tell Uncle William [Foster] that Mr. Evans can tell him more about the scenes here than I can write and to go and see him. He saw me at the Yankee's camp. I will write again soon. Write often to your ever loving and affectionate husband. Kiss my baby and tell him Pa wants to see him. Yours until death.

W.R. Stilwell

————

Stilwell recounts the advantages of his new position as a brigade headquarters guard. Nonetheless, he will also be in daily contact with his old unit. WRS adds a private note for Molly that is a love letter. He has a poetic way with words, which is strange considering his poor education.

General Semmes' Headquarters, July 15, 1862
Dear Molly:
I wrote a few lines yesterday and gave it to Bob McDonald to give to Mr. Evans as I had to leave the regiment and I don't know whether he got it or not. So I thought I would write again this morning and send it by him as I have found out what I have to do here. The general sent to our regiment for a sober, steady and reliable man to come to his quarters. So I was detailed. He wanted

---

[19] Paul Jones Semmes was a wealthy farmer and banker in Columbus, Georgia. He was 47 years old, married with four children still at home in 1860, including twin boys, age 7. Long interested in the militia, he served as captain of the Columbus Guards from 1846 to 1861. At the outbreak of the war, Semmes was elected colonel of the 2nd Georgia Infantry and took his regiment to Virginia. Promoted to brigadier general on 11 March 1862, he participated in Magruder's defense of Yorktown and Williamsburg, and also served in Magruder's division at the battle of Seven Pines. During the Seven Days, he was a brigade commander in McLaw's division of Longstreet's corps. Ezra J. Warner, *Generals in Gray* (Baton Rouge/London: Louisiana University Press, 1995) 272.

me and eleven more from the different regiments in his brigade to guard his quarters. I am very glad that I was chosen for I fare a great deal better here than at the regiment. I have to stand about four hours in the day. I get plenty to eat and no drilling to do and will not have to be in battle as long as I stay here. I will stay as long as we remain in this brigade and that may be a long time. I hope it will be until the war closes. Me getting here should console you very much as I am a great deal better satisfied than before. I don't have to be exposed to the weather. I get to sleep in a house and the place my regiment will stay is a short distance from me so that can see them any day that I want to. General Semmes is from Columbus, Georgia, and is a very nice gentleman.

I have not received any letter from you yet. I don't know what is the matter though suppose that you have written to me before now. I want you to write at least once a week and I will write as often, and perhaps more, as I will have a good chance to write as long as I stay here. I must bring my letter to a close as Mr. Stevens[20] is going to leave shortly. I will write a few lines private on an extra page. Give my respects to all the friends. Let me know what my boy has to say about Pa.

Yours as ever,

W.R. Stilwell

[Private addendum]

Molly, night before last while I was on guard and the moon was throwing its golden light down through the tall trees around me and the gentle breeze was blowing its whistling sound through the leaves of autumn and I was walking from post to post the brass band of the Second Georgia Regiment marched up in front of General Semmes tent to serenade him as he was their colonel when the war commenced and I was thinking of my family in the distant land, they commenced playing and harps would sound their shrill notes and the sound would ring and echo down the long range of valleys.

.[20]Mr. Stevens has not been identified

The tears would run down my face while I would turn it up to look at the moon and pray God to preserve my little family.

Molly, did you let the day pass by that we were married on without thinking of me or did you remember it? Oh, what a change has come over this wide extended land in three years. Do you remember the evening we walked down in the garden at the Hatch place and how happy we were? But those days have passed and gone and I dwell in a far distant land from you but God's ways are past finding out and what seems to us a curse is often a blessing and we should say "Thy will be done." I thank God that I am still permitted to read the bible and can worship God as I desire and here I am glad to say by being where I am I can get off to myself where I can read and sing and enjoy myself very well. It is not so in the regiment. You have to always be in a crowd where you are surrounded with all kinds of persons but here at headquarters I can keep company with no one but those I choose to keep company with.

Molly, I wrote to you in the letter I sent by Mr. Evans about my clothes. All that you will want to know is that you can be governed by circumstances. If you know that we have come back to Richmond at any time you can send them if you have a good chance. Mr. Evans talked like he would come back before long and if he does that would be a good chance for me to get them. But I suppose you will do what is for the best.

I will begin to close my letter. You direct your letters to Richmond no matter where I go until I write to you different. They will be sent to me anywhere in the Confederate States. Molly, you don't know how bad I want to see you and Tommy. I can't hardly recollect how he looks. I don't expect he would know me. I shaved off part of my beard the other day for the first time since I left home. I don't want my beard dabbling in my grub, let others do as they please. I don't think I will cut off the beard on my chin this winter.

I have not seen Darnell yet nor heard anything from him since I wrote. Molly, remember me when the sun sets in the west and pray that we may soon meet again. Oh, what a meeting it would be. I believe it will be and that before a great while though I may be mistaken. But let us trust in God and it will come to pass in the morning. Kiss my baby. I kissed your letter. I will kiss this one. May the love of God and the communion of his Holy Spirit be with you all, now, henceforth and forever more is my prayer. Give my love to all the friends. Yours until death.

W. R. Stilwell

Probably every Confederate soldier accused his home relations of being lax in writing to him. They did not realize that as soldiers they had considerable idle time while those at home were very busy trying to keep their households in food and shelter without the benefits of the absentee's usual contributions. It is now the height of the summer season and the food is good and plentiful. Stilwell demonstrates what can be done if a soldier is willing to forage. The question of Colonel Doyal's "sickness" and the quality of his second-in-command, Lt. Colonel Sloan, is a background subject about which WRS is very reticent.

Headquarters, General Semmes, 4 miles east of Richmond, Virginia. July 22, 1862

My Dear Molly:

Through kind providence I am permitted to write to you again though I have poor encouragement to do so for I have been gone from home one month tomorrow and have written more than a dozen letters and have looked with longing eyes for an answer but without success, though I don't lay it to your charge for I feel confident that you have written before now. I shall still look with eager eyes until I get one.

I saw Sandy Parker the other day who informed me that Mother was very bad the last he heard from her which increased my desire very much to get a letter.[21] I thought that you would have sent

---

[21] Alexander Parker was a private in Company I of the 53rd. In 1860, he was a thirty-year-old small farmer living in the Indian Springs area of Butts County. He and his

a letter by him. You should never let an opportunity of that kind pass for I am sure to get letters that way. I don't suppose you knew he was coming.

Thanks be to kind providence this leaves me in good health and enjoying myself as well as could be expected. I suppose you will have got my letters which I sent by Mr. Evans before you get this and I need not say anything more about my home at the general's quarters, suffice it to say if I can get to stay here until the war closes I shall feel glad. My labor is very light. I have to stand two hours in the day and two in the night, which you know is a very light thing. I had rather stand in the night than in the day. When it rains they let me go in the house and when the moon is up in the heavens and the gentle wind from the mountains sends forth its still rustlings among the aspen tree under which I stand while the thousands of rattles of the drums are all still and the frogs that sing in the swamp all around are sending forth their beautiful melody while I go from post to post with a little black box in my hand containing the moments of my soul with a little lock of golden braid. It is often pressed to my lips and in the other hand is placed my little bible which the world could not buy. Then comes up the sad thought, "Home, home sweet home, when shall I get there?" While thus engaged I am suddenly aroused by the sergeant of the guard who says, "Your time is out." Thus the hours fly like minutes. It is the most beautiful place to meditate that I ever seen. Many times I while thus walking my line I think how sweetly you and Tommy are sleeping beneath the care of some guardian angel and again know that Molly is thinking of me. I have often times dreamed of being at home but when I would wake up I would find it a mistake. I think I shall get home but when, I don't know. I shall leave that to the future and do the best I can for the present. You do the same and trust in God for the rest.

I have a great deal of playtime. I can go anywhere when I am not on guard. The other day my messmate and I, for I have but one,

---

twenty-six-year-old wife Martha, had three children. He was killed on 28 June 1864 near Petersburg VA.

went huckleberry hunting. We had the good luck to get a good many. We had some sugar that we drew and we concluded we would have some pies. So we set to work and made some five or six and they were splendid too, just such as are sold to the boys for fifty cents, but that isn't all, we ate as many as we wanted to and put the rest in the cupboard for we cook in a kitchen and some unnamed pup stole them so ever since that when we make anything good, and we do that most everyday, we either eat it up or hide it. The best dinner that I ever ate in my life was after we came back from following the Yankees. I had nothing to eat hardly for ten days, only crackers and parched corn and had to press the corn as the wagon passed and when we got back some man came from home and brought some of our mess some Irish potatoes and we drew some peas and we boiled it all together with a great big piece of meat as long as a stick and as wide as a piece of tobacco. It did not more than get done till we pitched into it and sure it was the best dinner I ever ate. I have had several kinds of pies and tarts but none as good as that. Butter is worth one dollar and twenty-five cents per pound.

Molly, I have not seen William Darnell for some time but think I will go to see him soon. I heard that he was well yesterday. There are a great many of our regiment sick. We have lost another one, George Conkle[22] died at the hospital in Richmond. Colonel Doyal[23] is and has been sick ever since he has been here. Colonel S[loan had] command of the regiment all through the fighting and is a man in every respect but whether Doyal is or not I shall leave for the future to decide.[24] All of our officers are good to me though I

---

[22] George Conkle has not been identified.

[23] Colonel Leonard T. Doyal, 44 years of age and a Griffin resident, recruited Company A of the 53rd and was elected the first colonel of the 53rd Regiment. In 1860, he had a wife and several dependents with different family names. Prior to 1854, he was a McDonough lawyer and Baptist minister. About 1854, he moved to Griffin as did many McDonough merchants and professional men due to the bypassing of McDonough by the railroad.

[24] Lieutenant Colonel Thomas Sloan, a 31-year-old bachelor, was second in command of the 53rd. He was elected captain of Company F on 2 May 1862, and elected lieutenant colonel of the 53rd on 4 June 1862. Prior to the war he was a lawyer in Columbus GA. He

am not under their control. I go over to the regiment every day to see the boys. They all appear glad to see me. I think I have got the goodwill of all. I am glad to hear there are good crops making in Georgia for there is nothing making here. Oh, how bad I want to have some roasting ears and peaches to eat. Send me one in a letter. There were a good many letters came for our company today and I want to go over and hear the news. I think I will surely get a letter from you before I write again though if I don't I shan't blame you for it. I will continue to write as heretofore. Molly, I shall have to close though I could write all day but paper is scarce though I can get it yet. If I get a letter from you in a few days I shall write again shortly. Tell Uncle [William Foster] and Aunt [Penelope Foster] and all to write soon. I am as ever, your faithful husband.

W. R. Stillwell

Direct to Richmond, Virginia, care Captain S. R. Brown, Company F, 53rd Regiment, Georgia Volunteers. It will come.

––––

After two or three month's service, most Confederate units were decimated with communicable diseases, measles probably being the most devastating. This is usually attributed to the fact that Southern boys were raised in rural, sparsely settled area and were not exposed to the usual childhood sicknesses while children. After a term in army camps with close living and poor sanitation they began to drop like flies.

Headquarters First Brigade, 2nd Division, Army of the Potomac, July 24, 1862

Dear Molly,

I would not write so soon but I have an opportunity of sending it to Griffin by hand which will go free of postage. I have been sick for two days and not able for duty but am better, I think, this morning. I hope I will be well in a few days again.

––

was the son of Henry County pioneer Adam Sloan and brother to William Sloan, who initiated the McDonough mercantile empire.

We are still east of Richmond and no sign of a fight. I am induced to believe that the war will not last much longer though it may. I would be very glad it wouldn't, you may be sure, though I am seeing a very easy time myself. I have been to the regiment every day since I left it and am here now. It makes me feel bad to go to it and see so many of the boys sick and dying. There is nearly one third of the regiment sick and a good many have died. The principal sickness is measles and flux or diarrhea which goes very hard with them. John Parker is very sick.[25] There is a call for regulars to serve for five years and a good many of our boys speak of joining them. They give them one hundred dollars bounty, sixty days furlough, and thirty dollars per month. As for my part I don't care to engage at present for I regard it as a good sign of peace, for what do they want with regulars when they have all of the men here to fight as long as they please anyhow, every man may do as he pleases, I shall have to stay here three years if the war lasts that long but, sure, I am not going to volunteer to stay any longer.[26] I don't believe the war can last at farthest twelve months longer but time alone will decide that. I am for my God, my family, and my country and I don't think any harm will befall me though I have to suffer and bear hardships and may have to die in Virginia.

Thomas Harper is here and sutler of our regiment.[27] He is acting the part of a gentleman in every respect and we will fare better now. Robert McDonald has a substitute here, old man Guest,

---

[25] John Parker was a private in Company I. In 1860 he was age 20, and one of seven Parker children living with Mr. And Mrs. Kicker in Unionville of Monroe County, not very distant from Foster residence in Butts County. Mrs. Kicker had probably been the widowed former Mrs. Parker who later married Mr. W. G. Kicker, a modest farmer but a most generous man if the supposition is correct and seven or more children came with Mrs. Parker. John deserted in 1865, taking the oath of allegiance to the US and was furnished transportation to Philadelphia. Nothing further is known of him.

[26] The usual term of enlistment was "three years or the war" (whichever was less).

[27] Thomas Harper cannot be identified precisely. Most likely he was a grandson of Henry County pioneer Thomas Bibb Harper. There was a Thomas Harper, age 26, listed in the 1860 Henry County census in the household of A. W. Turner. Harper listed his occupation as "merchandise" with a personal wealth of $12,000.

Uncle John's overseer, but I don't think he will get off this month.[28] They won't receive but one [substitute] a month. I will send some letters with him when he does go. You tell Pa to look in the soldier's box for letters. This box is a box kept for letters that are sent by hand and are called "drop letter." By this means they don't lose anything.

I seen W. D. Darnell the other day. He is in good health. He told me that he would draw his money in a few days and would send home one hundred dollars. I have not drawn any money yet and don't think I will in some time. I will give you a list of the prices of some of the things that are sold here which you know I want very bad some times and if we are sick. Coffee is $1.00 lb, sugar $1.00 per lb, butter $1.25 lb., cabbage per head very small 50 ct, chickens unweaned $1.25, and everything in accordance.

Molly, I have not received any letter from you yet and am very uneasy about you. Why don't you write and write often. You know you requested me to write often. I have written twelve or fifteen letters since we left and have not got any. Most all of the boys have got letters but me and why can't I get them? I watch the mail very close and eager and if I don't get one in a few days I shall get out of heart. I think surely you have written before now. Molly, I must close. Give my love to all inquiring friends and tell all howdy for me. Kiss my boy all over and over. Direct as I told you to. No more at present but ever remain your loving and affectionate husband until death.

W. R. Stilwell

Goodbye my Molly for this time. Good-by Tommy, my baby

———

WRS now has the measles, but having had a previous case, he is not seriously threatened. Southern soldiers learned quickly that army hospitals and most doctors were to be avoided if at all possible.

---

[28] B. F. Guest was a 55-year-old unmarried Spaulding County overseer.

Near Richmond, Virginia, July 30, 1862
Dear Molly:

I received yesterday the first letter from you. It was the first you wrote dated the 8th. I have not strength to write but very little for I am very sick with the measles. I have had them about a week. I will give it up now, Molly, that a man can have the measles twice. I have not had them as bad as some of the rest for they have been very bad and some have died. Our orderly sergeant, C. A. Crowell is dead.[29] He died Sunday evening last. I lament his passing very much. John Tobens died a few days before he did. Just about one third of regiment is able for duty.[30] George Ross has a discharge and is going home. I will send this letter with him to Jonesboro.[31]

Molly, you wanted me to send you a [news] paper. I can not do it. I made inquiries about it and find that you would not get it half the time. I want you to take the Atlanta Intelligencer. It will be the best paper you can get. I believe it costs two dollars and fifty cents a year. Molly, I can't get up much longer though I am not in danger I don't think but am very weak. When I get well again I will go back to headquarters.

July 31st—Molly I began to write yesterday and was not able to but I feel a good deal better this morning. I am able to eat some. The boys are very kind to me. We have nothing but tent flies to keep us dry. The boys hang up blankets to keep the rain off me. Bob McDonald is a whole soul fellow and waits on me like a brother. You need not be uneasy about me. I think I will be up again in a few days. As for medicine, I don't take much, only a few pills from Knott who is a very good doctor.[32] I don't pay any attention to

---

[29] C. A. Crowell was appointed first sergeant in June 1862. He was a 31-year-old potter with a wife and two children. In 1860, he was residing in the Rocky Plains post office in Newton County. He died 27 July 1862.

[30] John Tobens has not been identified.

[31] George Ross has not been identified.

[32] James J. Knott was assistant surgeon of the 53rd. In 1860, he was a 21-year-old Griffin physician. In 1870 he was again practicing in Griffin, now with an 18-year-old wife.

Saunders,[33] he is an old hog and always drunk. I wish he would go home.

I am continually looking for a letter from you. I think I will get one soon. I read your letter over and over though it is very old and I can read it very well, yet I keep reading it over.

Tell Tom that Pa will kill three Yankees if he can. God bless his little soul. I would like to see him. Molly, I will have to make my letter short for it is raining very hard and our tent is crowded. Molly, you must be sure to write every week. I write more than any one else here. Tell Margaret [Stilwell] to write and Aunt Penelope [Foster], Uncle William [Foster], all to write. Tell Pa to sell his land for me a substitute and let me come home. I will pay him his price for the land. Molly, I close for the present. I remain your loving affectionate husband.

W. R. Stilwell

―――――

Back home, rumors are flying about the behavior of Colonel Doyal and the regiment in general. The reports are not good. But Stilwell defends the regiment by pointing out that their record was no worse than other regiments, and, in any event, what could be expected of men driven into service to avoid conscription. This last remark seems to mark the main difference between the 53rd and earlier regiments. Most of the men of the 53rd had volunteered at the last moment in order to save their honor. But this demonstrates that the similarities between the 53rd and lower numbered regiments are strong in that honor must be maintained above all else.

---

[33] Simon H. J. Saunders was the 44-year-old regimental surgeon. In 1860, he was living alone and practicing medicine in Griffin where he is listed as a founder of an early medical academy. WRS got his wish on 2 January 1863 that Saunders would just go home, when he submitted his resignation. The division chief surgeon forwarded the resignation with the following comment, "The good of the service demands that the within resignation be promptly accepted. His presence with his commission is so very demoralizing that he is more injury than benefit." In 1870, he was boarding with a family in Indian Springs, Butts County and he still listed his occupation as "physician."

Camp near Richmond, Virginia, August 5, 1862
Dear Molly,

I have an other opportunity of writing you a few lines. Bob McDonald will start home in a few days. Old man Guest takes his place. I have been sick for two weeks with bilious fever and measles but thank God I am again most well but very weak. It is a bad thing to be sick in camp but I have fared as well as could be expected in camps. Bob sent off and bought straw for me to lie on and hung up blankets to keep the rain off. Bob is a good friend of mine and I hate for him to leave me but he must go. He says he will visit you shortly after he gets home and he can tell you things which I can't write.

I received your letter of the 20th and was sorry to hear that you and Tommy had been sick. Be sure to be careful and don't let Tommy eat too much fruit. Peaches the smallest kind are worth one dollar per dozen, melons from five to seven dollars a piece. Isn't that huge? William Darnell has been over here with me all day. He is in good health and tolerable good spirits. He thinks the war will close in a short time and so do most all the people here though they don't know any better than I do. I think now is as good a time as they will ever get in this world. Darnell drew sixty-six dollars the other day and sent home sixty. He has not drawn near all his money yet and don't know when he will. We have not drawn yet and I don't suppose we will in some months yet. I bought several things when I was sick and it cost a great deal to buy a little. Butter is a dollar a pound. If I don't get sick again I will have money enough to do me. If I was not bound down I could make lots of money. Thomas Harper, our sutler, would give me fifty dollars a month to clerk for him. If the war lasts long I would do well to hire a substitute as I am not able to stand camp life now. I could soon make it back at fifty dollars a month and could buy and sell a great many things of my own.

You wanted to know about Colonel Doyal. I say that it is not so [that] he was with the regiment in the fight on Sunday but was sick and when he got to Richmond and before the fight on Tuesday he was so sick that he had to leave. Now the question is was he sick or not? I don't know, but about his running off and not being heard from, when Jack Hail write is not so and Jack knew it when he wrote.[34] The truth is, Jack never wanted to come to the war and he is mad at everything connected with it. It is also reported there, so I learn in a letter from John [Stilwell], that our regiment ran and that they could not get it in the fight. That is not so also. Our regiment did run on Sunday though it was caused by a regiment from Mississippi firing into the Tenth Georgia and our regiment fired on the Mississippi and our officers ordered a retreat so as to get the thing straight.[35] I don't intend to undertake to defend Doyal or the regiment but simply state facts and then I am done. There is one thing I know and that is that there were lots of regiments that did as bad as ours and old ones at that. I don't believe myself that the regiment is a good fighting one for I knew that before I left home. They are, as the most of them, men that were driven in service by the conscript but as far as I can see they, that is, all the troops North and South are getting very tired of the war. I think it must close shortly and God grant it and grant it shortly. I very often think how happy we will be if I ever get back and I think I will. It is my daily prayer that we may meet again on earth. You must not suffer yourself cast down, be in good spirits and let us trust in God for the rest. I think it must close sure and if it don't, God says, "My grace is sufficient for thee on land or on the sea. I will be with thee." If God is for us who can be against us? Trust thou in God and many other words of consolation.

---

[34] There are three possible "Jack" Hails in company F. (1) John Hale, (2) Josiah Hale, and (3) J. H. Hale. If the offender was J. H. Hale, he spread no more rumors after 3 May 1863 when he was killed near Chancellorsville.

[35] Private John L. G. Wood of Company B reported this incident and stated that the regiment did run but was quickly re-formed. He stated that the only harm done was the killing of Major Simms' horse. Letters of John L. G. Wood, typescript version, GDAH: *UDC bound volumes of Letters from Confederate Soldiers*, 12 vols. 4:117. However, Semmes, in his official report, reported that the 53rd fired on his courier, Lt. Redd, hitting his horse 3 times and perforating his coat with a bullet. Why Semmes put such a trivial incident in his OR is not known but one explanation could be that he was building a case for replacement of the regimental commander and/or his assistant. *O.R.*, 11/2:721.

I enjoy myself very well when I am well but when I get sick I want Molly, but I resign myself to fate. I forget to say when I was writing about Darnell that Jug had deserted and gone off without leave. I showed William your letter about his getting home and he is very uneasy about him. He says he shan't never run roust about his house anymore. If any of them mistreats Jane, that when he gets home he will send them all off. Elie Norman died in our Company the other day.[36] Out of three brothers Dobbins that lived above McDonough, there is but one left and he is bad sick.[37] There have [been] about thirty six men died out of our regiment since we come to Virginia, mostly with measles and a great quantity [are] sick now. I will go back to headquarters in a few days if I keep mending. I don't have much to do there. Captain Brown will start home after conscripts in a few days.

Molly, you never say any thing about crops. I suppose that Pa saw my corn when he was up there. I want to know how they look. You must write long letters so that it will take me a long time to read them. I never stop under four or five pages and postage is high and you must write a heap to get your money back. Notwithstanding, I would give ten cents to get all well, still the more the better. I can't finish on this little piece of paper so I will write on more.

[Remainder of letter missing]

------

[36] Alexander Norman was a 25-year-old Locust Grove (Henry County) wagoner. He married Rachael Gibson in 1859 and by the 1860 census they had one child and there were three other Norman children in the household, probably from a previous marriage. His death was officially recorded as occurring on 1 August 1862.

[37] The three Dobbins brothers were farm laborers living in 1860 with their mother, Mary Dobbins, a 53-year-old seamstress. John F. Dobbins (age 23) died 26 July 1862. Robert R. Dobbins (age 20) died 31 July 1862. Moses B. Dobbins (age 18) was discharged on 25 August 1862. He survived with good health. In 1867, he married Susan Stephens and by 1870 they had a one-year-old daughter and were living with his mother, Mary, now 62 and listed as "retired." Let us hope that the discharge of Moses had an element of compassion in it "a la Private Ryan."

Stilwell's regiment has been left behind to watch McClellan, while most of Lee's army has moved north to meet Union General Pope. Thus, activity around Richmond is quiet and the soldiers deal mostly with food, clothing, and the sicknesses that are ever worsening. They are also concerned about when they are to be paid. A private's salary is $11 per month in swiftly depreciating Confederate notes.

Richmond, Virginia, Aug. 18, 1862

Dear Molly:

Thanks be unto God I am permitted to write to you again. I have been sick for three weeks with measles and fever. Was tolerable bad off but I have got stout again. I hope I will have good health now. I received your letter that you sent by Jim Russell and, oh, how glad I was to hear from you though sorry to hear that your health was not good.[38] I read your letter over and over until I most got it by heart. It was the first you had written that was half long enough and yet you could have written a great deal more that would have been of interest to me though I know that you were in a bad place to write. I was glad that you were going to Tom's and to the old place to dry fruit. You must dry some apples and peaches and send them to me the first chance for we don't get any sweet things except we pay very high for it. Green apples are selling for fifty cents per dozen, peaches one dollar. I had to buy most all that I ate while I was sick for you know I could not eat fat bacon and little flat cakes that we baked, and everything was so high that it took most all my money and we have not drawn any yet and don't know when we will. You must be as saving of your money as you can though I know you will but if you get out of money let me know. You shall have the last shinplaster that I have got. If we draw all that is due us I can send you some but if we don't, I can't.

Get lining for my coat, get strong coarse grade, put plenty of pockets in it. Tell Pa to try to get me an overcoat of coarse goods

---

[38] There was a James Russell on the roll of Company H, 27th Regiment, William Darnell's outfit. James R. Russell, 26, was an unmarried farmer living with his father James Russell, a prosperous 81-year-old farmer who owned 17 slaves in 1860.

before winter if he can. I was cold last night standing guard but that is nothing for we will have some very hot weather here yet. I will want one more shirt this winter but I will let you know when.

I am still at General Semmes' headquarters and seeing a very good time, plenty of meat and bread and but little to do. I have been perfectly resigned to my fate and leave the rest with God. He says, "Grace is sufficient for thee." Reckon I enjoy myself as well as any man away from those that he loves. I try to keep in good spirits all day and when evening comes I steal off in some secret place to offer my evening sacrifice to my God and can feel that it is good to be there even in a strange land. I pray for your and Tommy's health and that you may live right and feel assured that you pray for me. I know that you do. Molly, if it was not for the grace of God I don't believe that I could stand it but I feel that I can rest all I have and am to his care.

You wrote about brother John being ordered into camp but did not say where. I suppose you did not know. If he has to go I want him to come to our company but I don't think he will, he is so much attached to the fourteenth.[39] If he don't, let him go like colen's ram.[40] It is rumored here that as sure as Congress meets, which is today, that they will call out the men from thirty-five to forty-five and I have no doubt it will be done ever long if the war don't close and it don't look like it will, though we don't know.

There is still a heap of sickness in our regiment. We have lost about one hundred and twenty-five men. We have lost twelve in our company I believe. We don't mind seeing a dead man here though I never pass one without a mourn and a prayer for their family. I have not seen our company all together since the next day after we got here nor never will anymore. It don't look like the same men, but

---

[39] John F. Stillwell had been the second sergeant of Company C (Jasper County) of the 14th Georgia. He was discharged due to disability at Manassas VA on 6 December 1861.

[40] This is apparently a literary allusion that the editor can't trace. However, it has been observed at least once more in an unpublished contemporary letter written by a Henry County surgeon.

Vandergriff[41] and Simpson[42] are both sick and gone to the pesthouse.

I saw William Darnell and stayed all night and day with him last week. His health is good. Jug got back the same day and I got some of Jane's [Darnell] and Margaret's [Stilwell] cake, very good but not enough. If any one should be passing I want you to send me a jug of butter, melt it and pour it in. I can break it here. There is a lot sent that way but be sure to send the dried fruit to make pies.

Molly, you wanted to know what to do with our sow and pigs. I would like for Grannie[43] to let them run in the pasture for if the war should break we may need them and if you have to sell them after while she can be paid for her trouble. But let Pa do what he thinks best though I hate to have them sold but will be satisfied anyway. I reckon you went over our crop and when you write again, I will expect to hear how it looks and all about the potatoes and garden and etc.

I am writing a very long letter where I have to pay a dollar and half for a quire but I will write if it was five [dollars].[44] I want to know if Pa has got Tom spoilt. God bless his little soul. I would give Virginia to see him. Tell Margaret [sister] that things look dark when I have asked her to write so often to me when I have read some very lengthy letters to Darnell. She can use her pleasure about writing now as I am not particular about it now. I got a letter yesterday from Uncle John [Stillwell] and it surprised me so much I don't know what to think of it yet. I shall have to answer it soon but will make him pay the postage sure. I will write a little on

---

[41] James W. Vandergriff was first lieutenant of Company F. He was 26 years old in 1860, unmarried and living in the household of his father, John Vandergriff, a small slave owning farmer in Locust Grove, Henry County.

[42] John Simpson, Jr., second lieutenant of Company F, would die of fever in a private home in Richmond on 22 August 1862. He was a McDonough farmer who owned one slave in 1860 and was married and had six children.

[43] WRS usually applied this form of "grandmother" to his paternal grandmother, Elizabeth, who was 85, cannot be found in the 1860 census but was likely living independently next door to John Stilwell.

[44] A quire was a bundle of 24 or 25 sheets of paper.

another sheet for you privately as this is a public sheet. Give my love to all.

[No private sheet survives]

W. R. Stilwell

2

ANTIETAM

WRS and his unit begin moving north and he has adopted a pessimistic view of how and when the war will end. On a personal note, he acknowledges that he knows that Molly is pregnant but he doesn't seem very excited by the prospect.

Hanover Junction, Virginia, August 22, 1862
Dear Molly:
You may think strange of not getting any letter from me in some time but you will soon see the reason why. You will notice that one of the letters was written the 18th while the other was written 22nd. I wrote the first last Sunday and thought I would write you a piece to its self afterward but we were ordered to march the next morning at four o'clock so I had not any chance to send it off. We marched down James River until we came to Malvern Hill where the great battle was fought but found no Yankees. Our pickets were eight or nine miles below. It was then found out that they [the Yankees] were leaving below Richmond and going to pop into the valley so we were ordered here, twenty-seven miles north of Richmond. How long we will stay here I don't know. I don't think long. General Lee commands the army in the valley now though the hero, Jackson, is there. I think that the Yankees will try for Richmond soon again or they will leave the state of Virginia and try

some other state.[1] I tell you now they never will take Richmond in five years.

Molly, I have never got your letter that you wrote to me before you sent that one by Russell nor don't suppose I will as we have been moving so much. Our boys are very much fatigued marching so much. I don't have to march with them and I get to write some. Both of the drivers that haul the baggage that I guard are from our company and I can ride pretty often. I have not heard a word from brother John. I don't know what is the reason he don't write. Molly, my health is very good at present. I think we will have better health here than we did below Richmond, but one thing I see that I don't like. From all appearances we will have to spend the winter in northwestern Virginia and that is pretty hard sure, though can't help it. That is a cold country up there.

The first thing that Congress did was to offer a resolution to call out the men from thirty-five to forty-five. It has not yet passed but they will have to come sure, and I think it best, for we are going to need them, I am afraid, before we can get them. There is going to be lots of fighting this fall yet. This war has got to close in the next twelve months or last until both nations are ruined forever. It must close by that time, I think, but not before then, I am afraid.

The other side is for yourself. Molly, I am sorry that your health is not better. I think maybe you had better get some medicine from Wright and see if he can't help you.[2] I am sorry if you are in a family way but you must be careful of yourself and may God protect you safe through. I was afraid of it when I left but did not say anything about it. You must let it be a girl to play with my Tommy. I think it will be a girl sure. Molly, you must not do anything that would hurt you and don't be scared for it will be all for the best. I feel like I will get home some time and if so we will be a happy people once more. I can enjoy myself better than I ever

---

[1] The legendary "Stonewall Jackson."

[2] According to the narrative of Butts County History, there were twin Wrights serving as Butts County physicians. William Coleman Wright and Thomas Sharpe Wright were born in 1819 and educated at the University of Pennsylvania. However, they have not been located in any census or other source data.

thought I could though that is not so good but brace up and go ahead and hope for better days to come. Molly, you must direct your letters to Richmond as heretofore until I know where we will stop. Your letters will be sent to the brigade no matter where it goes. Molly, write often and long. Give my love to all those that ask for it and no one else. Live right and do the best you can. I am your loving and affectionate husband now, henceforth and forever more. May God spare us to meet on earth again and in heaven.

W. R. Stilwell

Mr. J. T. Stilwell, my dear baby, You must be a good boy and love Pa and Mother and Granpa. Pa wants to see you very bad and hear you say "To ranks!" but I expect you can talk right smart now. Farewell, my sweet little boy. Kiss Ma for me.

Goodbye to all,

W.R. Stilwell

———

The army is now at Manassas Junction near Washington where a great battle was fought on 29 and 30 August. Stilwell's unit did not participate. Even though the army has been marched almost beyond endurance, Stilwell's mood is considerably more optimistic and the Southern army now consists of super-heroes who can endure any thing and are always victorious. There is good reason for this mood. In less than three months, the Union army has been pushed from the doorstep of Richmond to the outskirts of Washington. Stilwell hints that he knows that the Southern army is headed for Maryland.

Manassas Junction, September 2, 1862

Dear Molly,

You will not only be surprised but almost alarmed to see the captain [heading] of this letter. I have not been to Manassas yet but am in a short distance of it. Molly, I have seen so much and passed through so much since I last wrote to you that I have news enough to fill a dozen sheets of paper and therefore I am at a loss to know what to write but I will commence at Richmond. We left there some time ago, not knowing whither we goeth. In a northwest direction we traveled twenty-seven miles and stopped for two days and then started again and thus we went for eight days. Thus we traveled from Malvern Hill sixteen miles below Richmond to Manassas above, a distance of one hundred and thirty miles by land. I need not say that we suffered for you know that an army of fifty thousand men to march that distance in eight days would tire anyone and besides the troops having nothing to eat hardly but green corn and not much of that. As for my part I have fared tolerable well. My feet are blistered some and my legs are a little stiff but having all of my baggage hauled, I did very well and as for provisions I have enough so far. The reason is when I draw rations, it is hauled but if the troops can't carry theirs they have to throw it away. Molly, we are not far from the Blue Ridge Mountains and you know what a man I am to study the works of God and here I had a great feast, something that was beautiful. One day we stopped at four o'clock in the evening on a large mountain in full view of the blue mountain and after I got through with my work I took my little bible and got off in a lonely place and thinking of the scripture which says "Lord, thy righteousness is like the great mountains." I had a good time here. You could see the hills commence like potato hills and the farther they went the larger they got, until they would rise up almost to the heavens. Thus it was as far as you could see in the west and from north to south. I was so much delighted with the scene that I forgot the toil and trouble of war and enjoyed myself very well until the sun was about to bid adieu to earth when it was just throwing its last glittering rays on the huge mountains behind which it had to go. It was then that I thought of myself and it was then that I wanted to retire to my little cottage as I used to do but, alas; I can do very well all day but when the sun sets I get lonesome and many tears have run down my cheeks at that time of day but I will turn from this sad part of my letter to something else.

Next morning the old drum beat the long roll and we knew that our tale was not done, so off for Mason and Dixon line we went. That day we passed Cedar Mountain as it once was called but now called Slaughter Hill like Jacob of old because there is where

Jackson slew the Yankees, I passed over the battlefield and the many little mounds of dirt told that death had done its work on many a poor boy.[3] This is where the battle was fought since the battle at Richmond, called in the papers, Cedar Mountain, but Jackson called it Slaughter Hill, because he killed ten to one. But leaving this battle brings me to the great battle that was fought at Manassas last Saturday.[4] It seems that there it [was] where the hard fighting commenced and I hope to God that there is where it will end. But we whipped them again and while we lament the death of the men on both sides of it we thank God for giving us the victory. The Yankees fought desperately but it was no use. God will defend the right. I learn that we have driven the enemy beyond Centerville and farther and that we are in possession of both. What our intention is I don't know, most all think that our intention is to go to Washington. Some say that we took fifty pieces of cannon and some say seventy but they say that there is no mistake but what we took small arms enough to arm the rising generation in the Confederacy. They got all their big dogs whipped, Burnsides[5] and McClellan, Pope[6] and Fremont[7] and they all had to toddle. I guess they will learn after while that we are in earnest about this matter. God grant that this may be the last blood that will be shed.

Molly, this war can't last at the rate it is going on now. We are not going to stop as long as there is an army on Virginia soil and we may invade their country. They are in a good deal worse fix now

---

[3] The battle of Cedar Mountain was fought by Jackson's forces against Union General Nathaniel Banks on 9 August 1862. While a clear Confederate victory, the loss ratio was considerably below 10 to 1. It actually was less than 2 to 1. Mark M. Boatner III, *Civil War Dictionary* (New York: Random House) 102.

[4] Ibid., 105. The battle of Second Manassas was fought on 29-30 August 1862 and was a resounding Confederate victory. Casualties at Second Manassas were 16,000 Federal and 9000 Confederates.

[5] Major General Ambrose Burnsides was commanding a corps at this time but was not significantly engaged at Second Manassas.

[6] Major General John Pope was the Union commanding general at Second Manassas. After his resounding defeat, he was replaced by McClellan who became Commander-in-Chief for the second time.

[7] Major General John Charles Fremont refused to serve under Pope so he was relieved of command of his corps, thus he was not involved in Second Manassas.

than they were twelve months ago. I am impressed that when we drive them to Washington that they will stay there and never come back again. If they carry on this way any longer I think they will carry it to some other state but I think they will have to give it up before long. I have not had any chance to hear who was killed or wounded that I knew for none of our division was there. We were left at Richmond to guard it until we were certain that the Yankees were all gone and that accounts for our not being in the fights. We didn't run jack trail.

Molly, I will have to write the blank side of this sheet for paper is very high and, in fact it is almost impossible to get it at all but when I get to Washington I will get some that is good and get it cheap. I have just heard that we have to continue our march in one hour and will have to write fast. Molly, you must not be uneasy about me and about my not writing for I don't expect I will have much chance to write. You know we can't get nor send any mail hardly while we are on the march. I could not send this if I had not got a chance by hand to send it to McDonough so I feel pretty certain that you will get this. I wrote to you at Hanover Junction but don't know whether you will get it or not. I hope you will. I got your letter that you wrote before the war [?] that you sent by Russell and could not help shedding tears while 1 read about you being so sorry for me to stand the hardships of camp life. It does me good to know that somebody feels for me. I have to take the broiling sun and the drenching rain but I take it all easy and can sleep all night in a wet blanket. I have got so I don't mind it at all, just go ahead like I was a hog and big pig, little pig, root hog or die, I don't care much. We have moved from twice to three times a week ever since the first of August and by the time you were dragged and hauled about like I have been you wouldn't care either. I am not satisfied now to stay in one place more than twenty-four hours. When we start from here we will go in the direction of Fairfax Court House but where we will go I don't know any more than you do, and when we will stop this march I can't tell, and what is more, as long as the Yankees are running I don't care. They have not laid up baggage yet so I will write more.

[WRS was at the bottom of a page at this point. No additional writing is available]

Lee's army is moving fast Into Maryland and Stilwell's morale is very high. God seems to be favoring the Southern effort. Many accounts have been written about the excitement and spectacle of the Confederate armies crossing of the Potomac River. Stilwell's account may be the best of all—more poetry than prose. After [the crossing] "we were in a foreign nation."

Near Fredericksburg City, Maryland, September 10, 1862
My dear Molly:
We have stopped this morning to rest and I thought I would write a few lines though I have no idea when I can send it off but it is the best I can do to have one written and should there be a chance I will have it ready. I have had the diarrhea for several days and having to march it has made me very weak but I hope I will be well in a few days again. Molly, it makes me feel very bad to think that we can not write to each other, not but that I can do myself but it makes me sorry for you as I know that you are among friends and I am in a strange land among enemies and amid dangers but I still hope in God and trust that he will preserve us both. I have written and sent off several letters to you but don't know whether you have ever got them or not but I hope you have. I will continue to write anyhow whenever I get the chance. If you know of anyone coming here you must be sure to write and send it but unless you do you need not write until further orders. We will have mail just as soon as we stop this march, I reckon, but that may not be until we take Baltimore and Washington. We are in possession of the Baltimore & Ohio Railroad; that is, our division is about forty-five or fifty miles from Baltimore. I think it is very doubtful whether we have any fight in taking Baltimore but if it is our intention to attack Washington we will have hard fighting I think. But be of good cheer for I believe that God will deliver them into our hands. Molly, I

think God is going to stop this unholy war before long and God grant that he may and do it speedily. I will try to write on the other side if I can. The reason that I use this paper is that I don't want to use my good paper unless I was sure it would be sent off.

Molly, it would be impossible for me to give you an account of what I have seen in my travels, tired, worn out men almost broken down. I was in no fix to take many notes but I must mention a few things which come under my knowledge. In the first place we left Leesburg on the sixth for the Potomac and for Maryland. We traveled up the river for some time before we come to the ford but at last [arrived] over the big mountains which rose up to where we could see the great monster along whose banks there has been so much precious blood spilt. Here it was, the great river about half mile wide but not more than waist deep at this time of the year. The water being limestone, it was as clear as crystal, but now comes the best of all, to see about fifty thousand men pull off their socks, britches and hold up their shirt tails and "Forward!," the different commands being plunge water, kick water, slip off rocks, get up when you fall down but on they went knowing that men that had waded through Pope's whole army could wade the Potomac and to add to the scenes, the many big brass bands stayed on the banks and played Dixie as if sorry to leave old Dixie but when they got on the other side such a yell was never heard which rent the air and echoed down the long extending banks of the river, and here the band struck up the tune of Maryland which has become very common at the present day.[8] So the sight was closed and we were in a foreign nation. Directly we bivouacked for the night and slept and slept in the beautiful moonlight which shone down through the tall trees on the bank and on the morrow "Onward!" was the cry and off we went until we got here.

It is enough to make ones blood boil to see the ladies who had gathered on horseback along the road with Confederate flags flying

[8] *Maryland, My Maryland* in Stephen W. Sears, *Landscape Turned Red: The Battle of Antietam* (New York: Tichnor & Fields, 1983) 82.

and cheers for the Southern army.[9] The people where we come are mostly friends to the South though we have found some that is not. We treat them with due respect and don't have any of their property interfered with. Molly, it looks strange that ten months ago the whole Yankee army lay in front of Richmond and now they have been driven out of Virginia and have been driven back to defend Washington. God is surely with us, we never could have whipped them so bad. We have just heard that our army has whipped them bad in Tennessee[10] but whether it is so or not we don't know, for we hear so many things here that we don't know what to believe. How long we will stay here I do not know. We may leave in half-hour.

Molly, I want you to keep in good spirits and not be cast down but trust in God with cheerfulness for while I am sorry that we are so far apart and can't correspond, still I assure you that I am in better heart than I have been since I left home because I know that the war can't last long the way it is going on at present. I never seen a hard storm but what it was soon over. I try to live right and to trust in God and I believe he will protect and direct me safely through to the last but if it is his will that I should fall and I put my trust in him as I should do, it will be for best but if it is his will for me to return to the embraces of my family again I shall feel very thankful for it, but his will be done, not mine. Let us pray much for his protecting grace and guidance.

Molly, you need not bother much about my clothes without you can find out someone that is coming here for I don't expect that I can get them. I am very sorry but can't help it. If I could draw my money I could buy them cheaper here anyhow. Every thing is very cheap here but we have not got any money hardly. I haven't got but four dollars and most of the company is without a cent but I think I can get along somehow as I don't expect they would take our money here nohow and of course if they don't it will do me no good to

---

[9] This does not have the modern connotation of being angry but instead seems to mean being excited.

[10] General Kirby Smith with two Confederate divisions advanced from Knoxville TN toward Kentucky on 14 August 1862. On 30 August, the battle of Richmond KY was a smashing Confederate victory.

have it. I reckon the government will make arrangements about our clothes, they know we can't fight without clothes. Molly, I feel just like I will have to throw this letter away and of course can't take the same pains as if I knew you would get it anyhow. I will have to close it for the present. I hope to be able to write and to receive letters from you in a short time but if I don't, so must it be. You must give my love to all inquiring friends and reserve a double portion for yourself and one third for Tommy.

Molly, [if] I could see you I could tell you enough to interest you for some time but can't spare paper to write it. I have not a word from William Darnell, don't know where he is, only he is in Maryland somewhere I suppose. Haven't heard anything about our friends that was in the second Manassas battle. Some of Flint's company[11] was killed I know, don't know who.[12] I must come to a close. I remain your loving and affectionate husband until death as ever. Kiss my baby all over and over. So goodbye my ever worthy wife and baby and friends.

W. R. Stilwell

The master strategy of the Confederacy seems to be working: Simultaneous invasions of Maryland and Kentucky designed to bring the two states into the Confederate camp. Contrast this with the position of six months earlier when the fight in the east was on the

------

[11] Company G of the 19th Georgia Volunteer Infantry (Henry Guards) was the first regular Confederate unit to be organized in Henry County. The first muster occurred at Shingleroof Campground on 19 April 1861. Tighlman W. Flynt was the company commander. In 1860 he was a 32-year-old lawyer, married with two children. He had no real estate but possessed personal property of $4600 that included 3 slaves. He was living in the household of his father-in-law, James B. Turner, a farmer and Methodist minister. James Turner reported real estate valued at $3000 and personal property of $7000, including 7 slaves. When the company was formed, Flynt was living on Cotton Indian Creek near Moseley's mill (now Miller's mill) at a home known as the Madison-Maddox place.

[12] A review of the roster does not reveal any outright fatalities but mentions several wounded including one fellow who lost a leg.

peninsula near Richmond and the line in the west ran through northern Alabama and Mississippi.

Camp Near Frederickstown, Maryland, September 11, 1862
My dear Molly:

You will see that I wrote to you on yesterday and did not know then when I could send it off but after I had written who did I see step up but William Darnell. He was camped in about half mile of me. I went back to his camp with him and took tea and stayed till bedtime. I have come over to his camp this morning and have an opportunity of sending my letter and I thought I would write a little more. Darnell is in good health and good spirits. He is of the opinion that the war will close in a short time and I think six months will decide the fate of the war one way or the other but let that be as it may. We have to wait until it comes.

I thought when I wrote yesterday that we would start on this morning but we haven't yet. Molly, I can't take time to write much nor write that good. I am better this morning. It is a little cool this morning. It feels like winter is coming on soon. Molly, I am very anxious to hear from brother John. I have written to him and can't get any answer from him. I think that the conscript has taken away his understanding so that he has forgot his absent brother. In fact I think all of my relatives have treated me with a great deal of coolness in not writing to me but I am as independent as a woodchuck. I don't want to task them with writing to me if they don't want to.

Molly, we have just heard cheering news from General Kirby Smith's army in the west.[13] I think they had better give it up to Mr. Brown.[14] Molly, we have a large army here and still they come. I think the war will all be carried to this state if it lasts much longer and we will fight them on their own grounds. Some think that

---

[13] General Kirby Smith conducted a very successful advance into Kentucky, capturing Lexington on 1 September 1862 and the state capitol, Frankfort on 3 September.

[14] This may be a jest referring to the inept invasion of Harper's Ferry by John Brown's ragtag "army" in 1859.

Maryland will secede in a short time. There are a great many men joining our army now and they say we will get thirty thousand as sure as we get to Baltimore. Let them come, we may need them all yet. Mr. Lincoln has called his congress to meet in Cincinnati so they say.[15] I don't know whether it is so or not. Molly, I want you to ask Uncle William [Foster] or Aunt Penelope [Foster] what regiment Cousin Margaret Glass's two boys belong to and I will try to get to see them and let me know the first chance.[16] I think maybe you can send a letter by Colonel Doyal when he comes. If you do, send as much news as you can for it may be all the chance in some time. Molly, I think that I will get to write to you every once and awhile by watching my chances but if you should not get any more from me in a long time you must not be uneasy because it is uncertain when I can write and if anything was to happen to me and there was any chance to write I have plenty of friends to do so. Again I say be in good heart. We are by their help going to end this war some way soon. Molly you must take good care of your health and not do any thing that would hurt you in the least. Molly, I want you to write to William Edmons and tell him that I am gone to the war and that you need that money and I think that he will send it to you.[17] Tell him to send Confederate notes. Be sure to do so for we will need the money if I get back and if I don't you will anyhow. Molly, I will have to begin to close my letter and I do it with sorrow, though I am getting to be like Paul in whatever condition of life [I] am placed, be there with content. This is the time of great affliction in the land and I should bear my portion though it be hard. Pray much for me as I know you do. Give my love to Uncle William, Aunt P. B. and Granma [Foster]. Tell her I hope she will live till I get back. Tell Bob and all the rest of the servants "howdy" for me.[18] My love to all the family. Write if you can. I

---

[15] All of the preceding was wishful thinking.

[16] Margaret Glass and her two boys have not been identified.

[17] William Edmonds has not been identified.

[18] William Foster owned 23 slaves. Note that convention dictated that they be referred to as "servants" and not "slaves." "Howdy" seems to have been the universal greetings for "servants."

close with pen and ink and tears. Kiss my baby and may the God of peace, love, mercy, goodness be with you all now, hence-forth and forever more is the prayer of him that remains yours until death.

W. R. Stilwell

––––––

The following letter was written on tiny note paper about 2 x 3 inches. This is the first of several letters written during an actual conflict that reflect the true reality of war. Lee's Maryland campaign of 1862 began with a risky and complicated plan to isolate the Union garrison at Harper's Ferry located on the south bank of the Potomac. McLaws' Division was assigned the task of capturing the Maryland Heights that dominate Harper's Ferry from the north bank of the Potomac. Part of Semmes' Brigade was in a sharp fight at Crampton's Gap on South Mountain, though greatly outnumbered, they held up the Union Army for several hours, thus allowing for the capture of Harper's Ferry on 15 September 1862. The 53rd Regiment was guarding wagon trains in the rear and were not in any of this fighting.

Stilwell does not know where the unit will go from here but he senses that more hard marching is ahead. Both armies are already concentrating near Sharpsburg, Maryland on either side of Antietam Creek. By sunup the next morning, after a ten-mile night march, Stilwell will be in Sharpsburg and his unit would be preparing to enter the battlefield at Lee's command.

Harper's Ferry, Sept. 16, 1862
My dear Molly:
It is with great pleasure that I attempt to write to you after a long laborious, dangerous, and tiresome march of over two hundred miles over mountainous country and through an enemy country. Fought three hard battles, took Harper's Ferry with the loss of one man killed and one wounded. We took fourteen thousand five hundred prisoners and artillery wagons and in fact every thing that it takes to arm and equip a large army. I am now about three miles from the Ferry and they have been hauling captured things by here

all day. Some of the best artillery that I ever saw. I crossed the Potomac at the ferry the same day that they surrendered the fort. I saw all of the Yanks and their arms stood on the hill all around them. I am so much delighted at our success and of the hope of getting to write and receive letters from you before long that I am in no fix writing as I am only writing this to keep from forgetting Molly.

I went up to the company just now and an old man Hambrick is there.[19] We will leave here in a few minutes. I had been writing the above for [in order to] past time, not thinking that I could send it off and I thought I would write until we started.

I am well, still at Semmes' quarters. We are now in Virginia. Don't know how long I will stay in the state. We have been fighting for four days and whipped the Yankees bad. I have suffered much from hardships but thank God my life is spared until now. This is the greatest marching I ever knew. None of our regiment killed yet. I hear that Jo Manson was killed.[20] William Darnell well. We hope to start. Goodbye.

W. R. S.

———

17 September 1862 was the bloodiest single day of this or any other American war. Twenty three thousand dead and wounded soldiers of both armies were left on the Antietam battlefield. Survivors are in shock and disbelief over the magnitude of casualties. The

---

[19] The only Henry Countian listed in the 1860 census who meets this description was Thomas Hambrick, age 59 in 1860, who was a substantial planter, owning real estate worth $6500 and 36 slaves.

[20] Joseph A. Manson was a McDonough youth and a student at Emory College before the war. He joined Cobb's Legion which suffered dreadful casualties at Crampton's Gap on the South Mountain on 14 September. But Joseph was not killed. After the war, he moved to Tennessee and in 1885 he was elected speaker of the state house of representatives. His father was a prominent Henry County pioneer who was a physician, clergyman, and farmer. In the 1860 census, he was listed as a farmer with his present wife, Mary J. and 11 children living at home. He reported values of $6000 in real estate and $17,500 in personal property, which included 23 slaves.

Regiment did its duty and "it will be said no more that the 53rd Georgia will not fight."

Ten miles above Harper's Ferry on the Potomac, Virginia side, September 18, 1862

Dear Molly:

I am in good health this morning so far as my body is concerned but in my mind I am perplexed. Great God, what awful things I have to chronicle this morning! One of the most awful battles that was ever fought was fought yesterday, commenced at daylight and continued all day until dark. It is hard to find out which side got the best of it but reports say we did.[21] The battle has not been continued as yet this morning though they seem to be preparing to fight. I was not in the fight myself though our regiment was. General Semmes left me at his headquarters to guard his things. Our regiment went on to fight about twelve o'clock[22] in good spirits, Colonel Sloan at the head, waving his sword and cheering the men on but, alas, for the noble person, he fell severely wounded and it is thought will die. He was doing the part of a brave man. As soon as he fell, the regiment called for him but he could not answer. They then asked who would lead them to the charge when Lieutenant Redd[23] of Semmes' staff said he would and they said, "Go on!" Off he put with his bright sword flying in the air and the men after him with yells like demons. They fought and fought like men and while other regiments have straggled off. They, that is, what is left of them are there ready for them again. It will be said no more that the 53rd Georgia Regiment won't fight. Molly, I have not heard who was killed and wounded in my company though

---

[21] The vastly outnumbered Confederates fought the Union army to a virtual standstill. The battle was considered a draw; however, in strategic terms, it was a major defeat for the South.

[22] Actually, about 9 A.M.

[23] Lieutenant J. K. Redd was a volunteer aide-de-camp to General Semmes. He entered the war on 31 October 1861 as a private in Company G of the 2nd Georgia Infantry, organized by Semmes. After the death of Semmes at Gettysburg, Redd disappears from history. A volunteer position automatically ended with that of his commander.

I learn that the regiment was almost cut to pieces. I will try to find out and if I ever get to send this off I will send you a list of them. I have no doubt but some of my friends is lying cold on the ground now. How long we will continue to follow up the Yankees and how much more we will fight before we stop, I know not but it looks like they are going to kill all the men on both sides before they stop. This war will have to stop before long or all the men will be killed. Oh God, grant that it may close and close now. Molly, I have not been out of the hearing of cannon for half day at a time in a week, I have been hemmed in or surrounded once with my wagons. We are between large mountains in the Blue Ridge. The valley was about one mile wide and a large mountain on both sides. They held the gap behind us and Harper's Ferry was in front but God who does all things well, gave Jackson the power to take the Ferry and we got reinforcements and were safe.[24]

Molly, I know that you are very uneasy about me but you know that it will do no good to grieve. It is for the best to be cheerful as you can for we ought to be willing to say "The will of God be done and if it is his will that your best friend should die away from home, let us submit to it but at the same time let us pray the father of mercy to spare me to return to your fond embraces again." I don't see any more hope of the war closing now than six months ago, only there has been so much fighting that I think both sides will be glad to stop it soon. I think it will close this fall and winter. I don't think our generals are going to stop until the thing is settled one way or other and that is just what I want them to do.

Molly, I have managed so as to write back to you several times since we left our own country but don't know whether you got them or not. I think I was smart in that when we would stop and other men were asleep I would be writing and then no matter where I was, if I saw anybody that was going back I was ready. Just so with this, I don't know now that I will ever get to send this off but will have it ready. It is hard enough for a man to be taken away from his

---

[24] General Stonewall Jackson commanded the successful effort to capture the Harper's Ferry garrison.

family a long ways where he can hear from them by mail but it is too hard to be taken where he never can hear from them at all, though by the grace of God we can do all things, therefore I have stood it like a good soldier and have not suffered myself to be cast down but have hoped for better times and still I live in hopes and will, if I die in despair.

The last letter that I received from you was the one that you sent by Russell. It was dated the 11th August I believe or July I don't know which, some times I don't know when Sunday comes until it is past. I never thought that it would be so but you march for weeks like I have and have no almanac and get no chance to study and you are sure to forget to. I could not tell what day of the week this is now. I just ask the date of the month, that's all I want to know. I don't know when I washed my face last. The truth is you can't get the water. All we think about is for the present day's comforts, provide for itself. We have got some very good apples all through this country but that is all the fruit that I have eaten this year, apples, but I have had plenty of them since we left Richmond, in fact we have lived some days on raw, baked and roasted apples, some times on green corn and some times nothing. Molly, after summing up the whole matter I think our independence ought to be worth a great deal for it cost enough, but thank God men fighting on corn and baked apples were never subdued yet, nor never will be I don't think. I have suffered much since we left Richmond but think I have fared as well or better than a great many others for I have all my clothes with me and the rest haven't. I have fared much better by being one of Semmes' guards and will be glad if I can stay here until the war ends. Sometimes I think that it was my lot to get here for I could not have marched this far with the troop to have saved my life.

Molly, I don't know what to say about my clothes. I suppose you may just have them ready until the future will decide what to do for no one knows what a day may bring forth but you may be sure of one thing, that is, I will keep you posted if it lies in my power to do so but when I can't, I can't. I will bring this letter to a close before long but if I don't get to send it off before I get the particulars of the battle I will give them to you [later].

I have forgot heretofore to mention that Elb Farrar was elected in Lieutenant's Simpson's place after his death.[25] You can tell Mrs. Kicker[26] that William Lemmond[27] is with the wagons, he is driver for Foster.[28] Tell her also that Sandy [Parker] and John [Parker] were not in the fight I don't think though I won't be certain, I think they are left behind sick. I saw both of Mrs. Evans sons the other day but not since the fight.[29] As soon as I get the particulars I will give them. I heard that Joe Manson was killed the other day but don't know for certain.

Molly, I had a very pleasant dream the other night. I thought that I was at home and I could see you and Tommy so plain. Oh how I would like to feel of their little golden curls and see their little bright teeth shine and little plump feet paddle around the house. I reckon he can talk plain now and is most large enough to carry wood for his ma. I hope to see him soon yet. Surely this war won't last much longer but if it does let us do the best we can and trust to God for the rest.

Molly, if you know of anyone that is coming to our regiment be sure to write but you need not write unless you do at present. Remember me in love to all my friends and neighbors. Molly, I

---

[25] Absalom Farrar was elected junior second lieutenant on 4 September 1862. He was a married, thirty-one-year-old with three children and was a Henry County farmer with five slaves in 1860. Severely wounded at Gettysburg, he returned to the company to be elected captain in January 1865. By 1870 he was a modest farmer in Henry County.

[26] The relationship between Mrs. Kicker and William Lemmond is a great mystery.

[27] William A. Lemmond was a private in Company I of the 53rd. In 1860 he was a Butts County overseer with wife, Emily and one child; he lived close to Alexander Parker. He would survive and serve until the bitter end in April 1865. In 1870, with two more children, he was relatively well-off as a farmer in Indian Springs of Butts County holding $1700 in real estate.

[28] Foster has not been identified.

[29] Mrs. Evans is presumed to be the wife of David Evans. Two sons were in Company I of the 53rd. John B. Evans was second lieutenant. In 1860, he was a twenty-six-year-old shoemaker with wife Nancy who was twenty. They lived next door to Mr. and Mrs. Evans. David Frank Evans was a private. In 1860, he was an 18-year-old schoolboy living with his parents. Both sons were among the few survivors who surrendered at Appomattox.

think of you while the cannon roars and the muskets flash. Never have I been so much excited yet but what I could compose myself enough to think of you and I have often thought of having to die on the battlefield, if some kind friend would just lay my bible under my head and your likeness on my breast with the golden curls of hair in it that it would be enough. Molly, I shall have to close for my eyes are bathed in tears till I can't write. May the God of mercy and goodness be with and bless you, preserve and protect, guide and direct you and yours always is the prayer of your ever disconsolate husband as ever, Goodbye.

W. R. Stilwell

Goodbye, Tommy, my son

————

Stilwell had adopted a melancholy mood as the horrors of the battlefield sinks in and the casualties are counted and named. He is particularly upset at the death of B. F. Guest, the substitute for his friend, Griffin dentist R. A. McDonald. This situation reflects the absurdity of the substitute system; that a 55-year-old man could replace a 31-year-old man as an effective rifleman and suggests that the Confederacy was only interested in individuals as "cannon fodder." Stilwell is very bitter about the treatment of the dead and wounded. Stilwell's melancholy mood continues right to the end of the letter but in a postscript he acknowledges that he is venting his bitterness and now that it is off his chest, he feels better.

Bunker Hill Virginia, September 20, 1862—15 Miles from Winchester, NW Va.

Dear Molly:

I will write another letter and enclose it in one that I wrote the 18th as I have had no chance to send it off. There was no fighting on the 18th but there was all day the 19th without any result except killing and wounding men. We have been pushing back for the purpose of drawing them across the river. The greatest battle that was ever fought on this continent was fought on the 17th in which my regiment took an active part and suffered very bad; though there was but one man killed dead on the field out of our company and that was old man Guest. Poor old man; he sold his life very dearly. I think he was shot through the head and died without a word and I am sorry to say that he was never buried. All that I can say in regard to his life is that he was a brave man and a good soldier and died in defense of the rights of his country. There was about eighteen or twenty of the camp wounded though, I have not been able to get all their names but will give the ones to you that you know, Israel Sowell and his brother, Joseph Sowell, these are the only two that you know.[30] Every thing is about as usual as far as I know at present. Quin Cames was killed dead.[31] Colonel Sloan was shot through the left breast seriously. Brave man, the last word, that he said to his regiment was "Forward, forward, men, forward," and he in front of the regiment with his sword flying in the air. Molly, I can't give many particulars as I have to write in a hurry for we never stay long in one place. Colonel Smith[32] of the 27th was killed and Lieutenant Colonel Zachry[33] was mortally wounded. Some of the boys saw Darnell since the fight. They have been fighting today and God only knows when they will stop. I think they have determined to fight it out at once and be done with it this fall and winter and that is what I want them to do.

---

[30] Israel and Joseph Sowell were privates in Company F of the 53rd. They were two of the seven brothers who served in the Confederate army from a large family living in Bear Creek (now Hampton) in Henry County. Curiously, they were entirely missed in the 1860 census. Both survived to surrender in Virginia in April 1865. Israel had been disabled with gangrene and was detailed to the Quartermaster Corps but was present at the end in that capacity.

[31] Quin Cames has not been identified.

[32] Levi Beck Smith was the first colonel of the 27th Georgia Infantry. He was killed on 17 April 1862 at Antietam. Before the war he was a lawyer in Talbotton, Georgia.

[33] This report of his mortal wounding was false. Charles T. Zachry was the first commander of Company H of the 27th Infantry. The company (and later the regiment) bore his name-Zachry's Rangers. In 1860 he was a Henry County farmer with real estate worth $400 and personal property of $11,000, including eleven slaves. He had married Frances Turner in 1853 and they had two children. He survived the war and later became one of the most prominent citizens of Henry County. He rebuilt and further developed the mill complex at Peachstone Shoals, served in the Georgia legislature and was perceived as the most distinguished of Henry County veterans.

Molly, you can tell Mrs. Kicker that her sons were not in the fight. Also tell Mrs. Evans that her sons were not in it. There was not half of the regiment in it. There were so many sick and some cowards. Captain Brown stood like a man and so did Elliott and Farrar. Vandergriff not here.[34] The fight on the 17th was five or six miles across the Potomac into Maryland. Monday we are in that state and the next somewhere else. I am here this Saturday evening but I don't know where I will be tonight at twelve o'clock. Some time we march most all night and get so tired that we go to sleep on our feet. God save the nation. That is, it was to see men marched on rocks and briers bare footed and almost naked, to see wounded men walked twenty-five miles before they can get to a hospital is something that is often seen here and worse. Men that has left their homes and family to fight for their country and put in battle and after they are shot dead their body left to the fowls to consume with a little clay thrown over them. Again I say "God save our nation." I am a man of sorrow and acquainted with grief but it almost breaks my heart to think that while a many a loving wife and mother sits watching the embers die out on the hearth, and thinking of husband or son they may be lying cold and lifeless on some bloody field. Oh this wicked world. God have mercy on it and that speedily or we are all going astray. Molly if it was not for you and Tommy and my relatives I don't think I could ask God to lengthen my days for I have become convinced that this world is no friend to grace but as long as you live I want to live also and where you die there let me die also.

Molly, I will have to begin to draw my letter to a close as the sun is now setting. Don't be uneasy about me for if I die in a foreign land, I hope that all will be right and well with me in the morning of the great day. Molly, let us both live so that if we never meet on earth that we may meet around the throne of God. Oh what a

---

[34] Baylor S. Elliott was the second lieutenant in Company F of the 53rd. He was the 23-year-old youngest son of Robert Henry Elliott of Henry County. In 1860, he was a "student" living in the household of farmer P. W. Merritt and he was tallied in the census as "attending school this year."

meeting that would be, to meet where parting would be no more, where wars and fighting will be no more, where our tears are all dry and God shall wipe them all away and where we can forever live around the throne of God and of the lamb forever and bless God, the promise is to us and our children and you must remember that the training of our precious little boy all remains on you and I hope you will discharge the duty faithfully. I want him trained right and I have every reason to believe that you will do the best you can. Molly, I must close as it is getting dark. Give my respects and love to all the friends and now, Molly I pray that God by his spirit may uphold and sustain, bless you and console you in your affliction and keep you under his care. Now I commend you to God and to his grace and may the God of peace be with you all now henceforth and forever and ever, amen, is the prayer of him that remains true to you, true to his God and true to his Country. So I close for this time. I remain yours until death. Kiss my baby all over and over. Goodbye Molly.

W. R. Stilwell

P.S. I am in good spirits. Don't be uneasy from the way I wrote. I done it for good–goodbye.

Stilwell cites a comic episode that occurred at Harper's Ferry as soldiers who had marched for several days surviving only on apples and green corn "liberated" a Yankee sutler's syrup and butter. Now that they are back in the rich Shennandoah Valley they are receiving plentiful but monotonous food. These deep-south boys are used to their beloved pork but they're receiving a steady diet of beef.

The problem of adequate clothing is becoming critical. Remember that they dropped their baggage at Richmond in June and have been marching and fighting since, most with only the clothes on their backs.

[The first part of the following letter is missing. It was probably written on September 22, 1862.]

—I am sorry to say that was old man Guest who took Bob's place, poor old man he sold his life very dear. I think he was a brave man and a good soldier. I wrote to Uncle John about it but for fear he don't get it, if Pa has any chance, send him word. I see Sowell and Jo[35] was both wounded. Colonel Sloan was severely wounded in the early part of the fight. Molly, there has been lots of hard fighting for the last two months and I don't know when it will stop but I am still in hopes it will close this fall and winter, If it don't the men from thirty-five to forty-five, if not fifty may lookout, they will have to come sure. As for my part I have become reconciled to the fate that waits us and do the best I can for myself. Let others do the same. I have heard bombs burst and bullets sing until it don't frighten me much. I crossed at Harper's Ferry the same day that it was surrendered and saw all the Yankees and their arms stacked, all their wagons and cannons and lots of blue bells as the boys call them. We took fourteen thousand five hundred there but I didn't pay much attention to the Yankees when I learned that the soldiers was getting some syrup and if they had been firing cannons, I would have had some syrup, so I out with my canteen, filled it up with some of the boys, got butter and we had fine times off of a Yankee sutler's syrup and butter. I would not object to another bite of the same kind. You better believe I sopped both sides of my bread. For several days I have eat beef until I can almost low like a cow though we get the finest kind of beef but it don't shorten bread much but take all things together I get plenty most of the time. If I can continue so, I will never perish during the war.

Molly, I was never bothered as bad to know what to do in my life about my clothes. I will need them this winter but if we keep marching like we have been doing for some time I can't get them nor I could not carry them with me. So I reckon you had better hold on for the present unless we get stationed somewhere. You may send my coat anyhow if you can but nothing else unless it is the pair of drawers and they are bad to keep clean of lice unless they can be

---

[35] This apparently refers to the two Sowells already footnoted.

boiled every week but send them along if you have a good chance with my coat. If I need the rest or get where I can take care of them I will try and let you know some way or other if I can. I will write more in the morning as I have to get a bite of supper. I will have to quit for the present.

Morning—Molly, I have just eat a hearty breakfast of beef and set down to write a little more. I am well this morning. Molly, we have just heard that there is a mail for us at headquarters but I suppose it is an old mail and as I have just heard from you I don't care much though if I was to get a letter that was six months old it would interest me. I hope that we will have mail regularly. I think that you may write now and if I don't get it or if the mail don't continue to come I will let you know. I think we will be stationed somewhere before another month, for winter will be here before long. Our army is most in need, having only one suit and how they will live this winter I don't know. The government don't furnish them clothes nor pay them their money either. We have not received one cent yet and I have got three dollars and that's all but I don't need very much nohow. I don't have any idea when we will draw any money. Not until we get settled I know and I don't care for if we was to draw it now we could not buy anything and it would just be in our way, though I don't suppose we will draw much nohow, as they never pay anyone all they owe at a time. I don't know how much I will get but if I ever get any, I will try to send you part of it as I think you will need it about buying shoes this winter. Oh, Molly, I had like to forgot, if you send any of my clothes, try to send, if they can be had easy, me a pair of shoes no. 7. I did want boots but as I have not drawn my money I can't pay for them and I don't want you to spend what little you have. It makes me feel bad to think that you have but ten dollars but I can't help it. You know I wrote you some time ago that I wanted you to write to William Edmons to send you that money but you did not say anything about it and I suppose you did not get the letter, if you did not and have not written I want you to write. Tell him that I am in the war and that you need the money and I think he will send it to you. Tell him to send Confederate treasury notes. You remember that his post office is Decatur, be sure to write to him and I think you will get it. Be sure to tell him to direct his letter to Griffin so you will be sure to get it. Tell Pa and Uncle William to go and see Mr. Evans and he can tell them all about me that they will want to know. It does me a heap of good to see anybody that lives so close to you though he could not give you much satisfaction nor can he give me much about you, it would do you good to see the boys gather around him to hear from their friends.

[Unsigned]

The determined Mr. Evans has arrived in camp near Martinsburg (now West Virginia) bearing mail from home. A glance at a map will indicate just how isolated and northerly the Martinsburg and Winchester areas are. The last 100 miles of the journey would have to be done without railroads.

Camp near Martinsburg, N. W. Virginia, September 23, 1862
My dear Molly:
This is a day of joy and thanksgiving to me. Mr. Evans has just arrived and I got your letter and you cannot imagine how glad I was to read it, for it is the first that I have got since the one you sent by James Russell though I have written many to you. You seem to think that I had neglected to write because you had not got one from me in three weeks. I don't doubt but what I have written more letters since we left Richmond than all my company put together though you may not have got them for I always keep them ready and whenever I could see any one going back I would send it off. We have not had any mail since we left and you may be sure that I was glad to hear from you once more and also to hear that your health was improving.

My health is still good though I am almost broke down from hard marching. I have suffered a great deal of late. Some times we would march all day and night and I have been tired and sleepy enough to go to sleep on my feet but I still hold up some and go

56

ahead. I have lived on green corn and apples and marched twenty miles a day and stood guard at night but still while I have done this I have fared much better than my regiment because they had to march and fight too and I had no fighting to do nor wont, I don't suppose while I stay on [as] General Semmes' guard. It is a very honorable position, and I will be glad if I can remain with him as long as the war lasts but don't know whether I will or not though its very likely I will stay.

Molly, I wrote you a long letter of five or six pages and just sent it off yesterday and if I knew whether you would get it I would know better what to write as I wrote all I could think of. You must not expect more than six or seven pages this time. You boast of your writing a long letter this time when you made out to write four pages. That is just only half a letter for me.

Molly, I went over to the 17th Georgia Regiment to see if I could find Cousin James Speer but he is no more. He had two brothers with him, one by the name of Jessie.[36] He is here but was absent at the time I went. James and his other brother are both dead, died with sickness, I was very sorry to hear. I was going to go back this evening to see if I could see Jes but we had to move about a mile to a better camp and I don't suppose I will get to see him. I will if I can. Uncle Tom James[37] was not hurt in the battle. I would write to you all about the fight and our regiment but suppose you will get my letter that I wrote yesterday and if you do, it will give you the particulars of the whole affair but for fear that you don't, I will say that our company lost one man killed, and twelve or fifteen

---

[36] Jesse H. Speer and J. A. (James) Speer were privates in Company H, 17th Georgia. James Speer died of diarrhea on 6 June 1862. The third brother remains a mystery. The two identified brothers were sons of a John Speer of Harris County Georgia. Family history lists a John Speer as a possible brother of Molly's father, James Madison Speer. Harris County, Georgia, on the Alabama line seems to be connected with several of the Speers. In 1860, Jesse Speer, age 19 was living with his parents, John Speer, age 65, and Mary Speer, age 63. It is possible that James was older and had already left his parents' home. Jesse was killed at Chickamauga on 19 September 1863.

[37] Uncle Tom James is another unidentified relative.

wounded in the battle of the 17th which was one of the largest battles ever fought.

Molly, I will have to begin to close my letter for I have written so much of late that I don't know what to write. I am not satisfied about Brother J[ohn]. I don't know what is the reason that you don't know whether he is in the war or not. I would have supposed that he would have written to you all whether the conscript had kept or released him. I will have to wait until I can hear what has been done with him.

Molly when you don't get letters from me you may be sure that it is because I can't get to write for you know that I have been very faithful to write but some times I can't. You must write whenever you can for it is very few letters that I get from you of late but I don't blame you for that for I know that they can't come without mail and we have not been getting that. Molly, I would be glad to see you and Tommy. Tell Tommy to save a piece of his chicken for Pa and to be a smart boy and when Pa comes home he will bring him some candy and to carry chips for Grandma [Foster]. Oh, how I would like to be at home to get some good cornbread and milk. It made me feel bad when you said that you had to quit writing to eat supper. It seemed to me that I could see you and Pa and Tommy sitting up on his box eating. Some time I can almost see you and Tommy lying in the bed with [his] head on your arm and when I lie down on my blanket in the broad moonlight and the dew of heaven is far down in my face, have I lay there while tears would run down my cheek but I would get up with my voice ringing through the camp, "On Jordan's stormy banks I stand and cast a wishful eye!" and thus I go along through life. I, like Paul, have learned how to be cast down and how to be exalted. Molly, I did intend to write to Margaret [Stilwell] but it has commenced raining and I have to stay in it so I will write to her some time other. I must close, so goodbye and may the God of love and peace be with you all, Amen.

W. R. Stilwell

PS. Some of the boys saw William Darnell since the fight. He is all right, I have not seen him since myself nor don't know when I will but will as soon as I can. He was in good health the last time I saw him and doing very well. Yours as ever until death.

W. R. Stilwell

———

Straggling and malingering were a major problem for the Confederate Army during the Maryland campaign. Some historians put the number of men who failed to make the battlefield as high as 25 percent. According to the O. R. the 53rd Regiment fielded only 276 men and officers, an astonishingly small number considering that over a thousand men were initially mustered. Those present did their duty, taking 30 percent casualties. But Stilwell is disgusted at the small number of men now present in his Company F. Only 25 or 30 are present, out of the 124 men who received the $50 volunteers' bounty on 21 May 1862.

Camp Near Winchester, W[estern] Virginia, October 1, 1862
My dear Molly:
With thankfulness I seat myself to write you a few lines and am thankful to say that I am in the enjoyment of good health. I feel much better than I have in several weeks for we have not marched but very little in better than a week and you may be sure that I feel better for rest. In fact it has created new life in the whole army for they were completely broke down. No one would doubt that an army that had marched as we did and fought their way through as we did would need rest.

Where we will go from here and when we will go are questions which I will not attempt to answer at present. Everything seems to be done in secret and what is heard in secret is not known until it is thundered from some mountain top and the minions of uncle Abe can say with truth that somebody is hurt. When this war commenced there could not be a skirmish without everybody knowing all about it but now we can fight for three days and nights and no one knows it, only them that are in it. But to the question of our going away from this cold region, I will give you my opinion and then you can

59

wait and see whether I was right or not. I think we will remain here or hereabout until we get all of our sick and wounded off and then go back in the direction of Richmond. My reasons are our army is almost without clothes. Many of them barefooted and none of them have more than one suit hardly and this country is all ready eat out of everything almost that an army wants. We can't get provision nor clothing, and taking all things together [with] the coldness of the climate of the country, I don't think it would be best to stay here this winter. I have already seen the ground covered with frost and it reminded me very much of my boyhood days when I used to go to my traps. But when I would think right, I would think that I was in a trap myself and the bait is not so good as I used to give the jaybirds. But I am going to do or try to do like some of them did me, scratch out if I can.

Our present camp is a beautiful one in a grove of large trees which makes a good tent for a soldier but Red gave me a part of a fly and I have fixed it up to sleep under but there is no such a thing now in the army as tents, not even colonels have them but Bill is an old rat and always has his one hole, and while I see a heap of hardships and trouble at the same time I have some good times with them. I keep myself roused up and in good spirits and hope for better times to come.[38]

Mr. Evans left here on the 25th September. I sent two letters by him which I hope you will find interesting. I don't expect to get many letters from you until you get them but I shall expect you to write often afterwards.

I understand that most all of our sick boys have gone home from Richmond. Some of them ought to be drummed out of every crowd they get into. They don't deserve independence but let them go, they won't do us any good here. We have about twenty-five or thirty men in our company. I suppose they will begin to come in before long. Colonel Doyal has ruined himself completely and the regiment would not care if he would never come back any more. As for my part I am like the little boy that the calf ran over, I haven't a

---

[38] Red has not been identified.

word to say. Molly, you must not expect a long letter from me this time for I have just written one for another man to his wife and am tired writing. You did not know that I had got to writing to other men's wives, did you? It is even so. I wrote her a good letter too.

[Unsigned]

———

This is a long newsy letter for the soldiers have little to do except to write home. They are receiving adequate but monotonous food. They have not yet been paid despite being five months in arrears. The Confederate Treasury printed money without backing but they attempted to slow down the inflation process by simply not paying their bills and payrolls, thus slowing somewhat the rate of inflation. This was the only control they had on the money supply.

On a personal note, Stilwell mentions Molly's pregnancy for the first time since 22 August. It is obvious that he is not at all excited by the prospect except that Tommy will have a little "Virginia" to play with. This remark will return to bedevil Stilwell in the next few months.

Camp near Winchester, W[estern] Virginia, October 10, 1862
My dear Molly:

I would have written some few days ago but for my health which at this time is not good. I have had a very bad bowel complaint for most a week, but [I am] able to be up. I hope I will be well in a few days again. This is a bad place to be sick as I have nothing to eat that a sick man can eat and if I had, Molly is not here to prepare it for me. I have not taken anything for it as there is nothing here. Our army is very near out of medicines and I have no doubt that many have died for the want of it and proper attention. Of all the men now in our army I think that the surgeons are the most unworthy of all the human family. But perhaps I am doing wrong to speak evil of those in authority but let that be as it may be. The Lord rewards them as he sees best.

Molly, it is with the deepest regret that I inform you of the death of Colonel Sloan. He died from his wound received in the battle of the 17th September. In his death we have lost a brave man and a good officer and the country a promising youth but he is no more and his name will only appear with those who died for Southern liberty [39] We mourn his loss. Major Simms is in command of the Regiment, Colonel Doyal gave out. [40] He has not arrived yet and no one waits his arrival with pleasure. I predict that he has ruined himself politically. [41] He won't stand the racket and we don't want such men here. We want men that will face the music.

Molly, I have put up a harness shop at headquarters, that is I have got a peg, an awl, and some shoe thread and needles, and made a bench out of a stump and have got some work to do and more

---

[39] The standard biographical reference for field grade officers of the Army of Northern Virginia is Robert K. Krick, *Lee's Colonels, A Biographical Reference of the Field Officers of the Army of Northern Virginia*, 4th ed., (Dayton OH: Morningside, 1992). In writing up Thomas Sloan, Krick picked up an unfavorable comment written by the regimental drummer boy, John L. G. Wood. "A member of the regiment wrote on 25 August 1862; [Sloan] treats the boys very tyranically and has got the ill will of all the regt. I don't suppose he has a friend in the regt." It is unfortunate that Krick chose to pick up this negative comment when he could have just as well used Stilwell's praise. But these words have sullied for all time the honor and reputation of a brave and honorable man.

[40] James Philip Simms was a member of a family of noted Covington Georgia lawyers. Elected captain of Company E (Newton County) of the 53rd on 3 May 1862. Made major on 4 June 1862 and colonel on 20 October 1862 and later brigadier general. In the 1860 census, he lived in Conyers with his wife Mary L. and a boarder, Gustavious J. Orr, professor at Emory College. He listed his occupation as a farmer holding $5500 in real estate and $16,000 in personal property. After the war Simms resumed his law practice in Covington and served two terms as a Georgia state legislator. He died in 1887. After the war, Gustavus Orr worked to overcome numerous obstacles to the establishment of public education in Georgia. At his death in 1887 he was acknowledged as the "father of the public school system of Georgia." Kenneth Coleman and Charles Stephen Gurr, eds. *Dictionary of Georgia Biography* (Athens: The University of Georgia Press, 1983) 2:766–68.

[41] Possibly this prediction was borne out. There is a severe lack of recorded history about Spalding County or Griffin City and their inhabitants but there is one slim volume entitled *History of Griffin* by Quimby Melton, Jr. published by the *Griffin Daily News* about 1959. Simply a distillation of news items printed in the *Daily News* from 1840 to 1890, it has only two references to Leonard Doyle. In one, he was appointed to the trusteeship of a school and in the other he offered a resolution at a veteran's organization about an upcoming celebration. There is no mention of election to a public office.

engaged. I have got some work to do today if it don't rain but it looks very much like it will. I have not received any letter from you since the one you sent by Mr. Kicker but suppose that the reason is that I wrote to you not to write until I wrote to you to write and will not expect one until you get those I sent by him and have time to write.

Molly, William Darnell came to see me the other day. I was very glad to see him. He is in fine health. The conscript has taken his wagon from him and given it to an old man so he had to return to his regiment He is going to apply for a transfer to our regiment and I am waiting with pleasure to see him come. I hope he will get one though he may not get it. He wants to get with me very bad. By his coming to see me I got to see Pa and Sister's letters that they write together and was glad to read them though they had been written a long time for they were the first they had written to me since I had left. It is still strange that I can get no news from brother. What has become of him? I have written him two letters since I have heard from him and it seems from your writing that none of you know anything about him. If he has to come to the war I want him to come to our regiment and if Darnell gets a transfer we will all be together though it may be if he is a conscript they won't let him go where he wants to. I would like to know what Uncle Richard Everitt is going to do now.[42] He has been wanting to go to the war ever so bad. He can try his hand now and he is not alone for there are a great many men that could fight his battles at home so he can have a chance to do something better in the war and not speculate on the wives of soldiers. Let them come now and see what it goes like.

---

[42] Richard Everitt was Molly's uncle and was guardian of Thomas Sanford Speer and Martha Ann Jane Speer who married Robert Ragland. He was a McDonough harness maker and could have trained WRS and Ragland to the trade. On 15 March 1862, Everitt was elected captain of the 498th Militia, of which WRS was third lieutenant. This unit disbanded with the beginning of Confederate conscription on 1 May 1862. Richard Everitt was over 35 and not subject to conscription at that time. He became a Justice of the Peace on 22 November 1862; this position would exempt him when the age limit was raised to 45. In 1860 he had four children and two apprentices in his household. In 1870, he had only $100 in personal property but had six children at home. He would later move to Conyers GA and prosper.

I am still at my old stand and having a very good time if I just had good health. I don't have anything to do all day but write letters and mend harness and stand guard at night two hours which is a very light job. We get plenty of beef and bread to eat but that is all we do get, not even peas or rice. I am getting tired of beef though we fix it up in many ways, boiling, frying, making soup, and such like. I can make splendid bread though it is not so good without anything to go in it but salt and cold water. This war is a big thing and seems to be getting bigger. If it keeps on it will be large enough to engage us all. It has begun to rain and I will have to stop a while until it quits. Kiss this.

Molly, there are a great many reports around here about our being sent on the coast and about peace but whether there is any thing in them or not we can't tell. I seem to think them all doubtful. It would afford a great pleasure if either was true. If I ever get in Georgia here is one that is going to see Molly. I know my old boss will let me go but getting to Georgia is the worst of all. We will no doubt need men on the coast but whether we will be sent there is the thing. How long we will remain here, I can not tell but think we will leave here before long. Cold weather will soon be here and our army [is] without tents or the necessary clothing for winter and I think that we will be apt to leave here in a short time but in what direction is not known. I still think that we will go in the direction of Richmond. I don't want to stay up here in the country during the winter.

We have not drawn any money yet and don't look like we will. I will send you some as soon as we draw and I have the chance. I think you have made your money last very well. Molly, if you should get out of money and need any, if Pa can sell my sow and pigs, do so or sell anything that we have and get along the best you can. I want to know if you have ever got anything from the county, and if you have not, what is the reason. I told Pa that I wanted him to tend to that and I suppose he would. If he has not I want him to do so. You are as much entitled to it as any one and I want you to have it.[43]

Molly, I felt very lonesome the eighth day of this month. It was that day three years ago that we started to Louisiana. and to think of the difference then and now and to think of the many trials and troubles that I have come through. It makes my heart rise with thankfulness to God for his protecting power and sustaining grace and I think that the same hand that has brought us through this far will lead us through for which let us pray daily and trust to God for health and strength and all will be right in the morning.

Molly, as I have some work to do this morning you must not expect a long letter and I have nothing of importance to write. I want to see you very bad and Tommy. I love to hear of his little tricks and it does me good to hear of his being in good health. I expect he will have a little Virginia to play with him. I am very sorry that you are pregnant but we can't help it and I want you to be very particular and not hurt yourself in anyway whatever. I want you to let me know what time you think you will be sick. I feel very glad to know that you are in such good hands for I know that Mother is the best woman about such a place in the world almost. I don't believe I can finish my letter for the rain.

You must be sure to write long letters and write often, at least once a week whether you get one from me or not as I always write one a week to you when I can. Give my love to all the friends and kiss my baby every morning for me. I must close for the time. Write soon, No more at present but ever remain your affectionate husband until death.

W. R. Stilwell

———

[43] On 24 August 1862, Barbara A. M. Blissit of Henry County wrote her husband, Henry Bluford Blissit of Company A of the 53rd Regiment that "I draw 3 dollars a month from the county." Manuscript, Blissit Family Papers, GDAH, Ref. mf 533, ac 77-365. Henry Blissit died of disease while home on furlough 18 October 1862.

Disaster strikes Molly's Louisiana family. Bob Ragland was a McDonough orphan who married Molly's sister: both girls were wards of Thomas Speer. Bob, like Stilwell, was a harness maker by trade and Richard Everitt, a McDonough harness and saddle maker and brother to Molly's deceased mother likely trained both. This background indicates that the two couples were extremely close. At the same time Stilwell learns of the death of Ragland, he learns that Molly's brother, Thomas Sanford Speer has been stricken with tuberculosis. The Stilwells have received a double dose of bad news.

Camp Near Winchester, W[estern] Virginia. October 19th, 1862

My dear Molly:

I have not received any letter from you since the one I got by Evans and of course I am getting tired waiting but I hope I will get one in a short time. Molly, I am in good health but bad hurt in my feelings. Cousin James Speer got a letter from Uncle Tom[44] yesterday which brought the painful news that Bob Ragland was dead and that T. S. Speer was at Uncle Henry Ware's[45] very low with the consumption. Oh, how it strikes horror to my very heart to think that I have lost one of the best friends that I have and soon will lose another and how bad I feel for Sister [Martha Ann Jane Ragland] to think that she has no one to console her and no friends to take care of her. How much better it would have been for them to come back when we did but it is too late now. Brother Bob is gone and she is left almost without a friend and I fear that she will lose all that Bob was worth. I want you to write to her and tell her that if I live through the war that she shall never suffer for anything as long as I can raise a dollar and that if she wants to come back that I will rent a house for you and her to live in. I think that I can make enough to support you and her if I am in the war. I think that I will write to her tomorrow but I don't know whether she is at home or not but will direct my letters there anyhow. Uncle Tom did not write

---

[44] Uncle Tom is a Louisiana relation not further identified.

[45] Uncle Henry Ware was another unidentified Louisiana relative.

where Bob died nor what was the matter. I hope he was sent home before he died and maybe he fixed up his business before he died. I think I shall write to her to try and keep her house if she can for reasons that I not give her but you can guess, but for fear that she may not get my letter I want you to write to her to keep her house as long as she can or at least until she hears from me. I will try and console her as much as I can.

As for Brother Thomas no one would lament his death more than I but still he is a young man and leaves no family behind him. I hope that his sickness may prove yet to be something else besides consumption though I have told you long ago that he had it I thought. Molly, these are hard trials for us and afflictions but I hope that they may work out for us a far more and exceeding and eternal wait of glory. Let us submit to the will of God without murmuring and still pray that the will of God be done for I believe that our loss is her everlasting gain for I believe that Bob was a Christian. You must tell Sister also that I said that there was so much of any man's estate allowed for his wife in Louisiana and I believe it is one thousand dollars but no matter what the amount is I want her to claim it for she is as much entitled to it as anyone else. I don't know anyone else better than D. W. Dupree to tend to her business though she can do as she pleases about that.[46] He is a businessman and I think would come nearer doing the thing that was right than anyone else. I want her to do as she pleases but I give this advice because I know she must be at a loss to know what to do. I would be glad if I was there to attend to her business for her. I would wind it all up for her and not charge her a cent for it but if she loses it she shall never suffer if I can help it. Molly, perhaps you had better enclose this in your letter and send it to her as you could not perhaps write all that would give her as much satisfaction. So I would just enclose this and send it and I will write to her tomorrow and I hope that she will get one or both. My prayers to God is that she may be protected and blessed and that her affection may be [a] blessing to

---

[46]D. W. Dupree (or Dyue) has not been identified.

her. Sister knows that I am as good a friend as she has got in the world.

Molly, we just heard on yesterday of the great victory won in Kentucky[47] by Generals Bragg[48] and [Kirby] Smith and it is said that the yells that rent the air in the valley of Northern Virginia could be heard for many miles. I hope yet that they will be glad to settle this war this winter but if they don't we will have to put our trust in God and fight on. We must have our independence, if not our way, we must have it another. Our army was never in a better condition in regard to health. There is very little sickness though it is reported that some of the troop here has smallpox and I suppose it is true but I hope it will not progress through the army. We have no tents to sleep under nor nothing but bread and beef to eat but we can live on that a long time. I am still at my old stand and doing finely, enjoying myself as good as could be expected.

When I wrote to you last I only had three dollars and after that I got down to one and a half and it seemed that we were never going to draw any money. So I thought I must make a rise some way or other so I went to buying and selling apples and I have made twenty-five dollars. So I have got money plenty and to spare. I want to send you ten dollars the first chance I get. I would send it by mail if we were about Richmond but I am a little afraid to send it from here that way but will send it the first opportunity. I will send Tom's money by mail. You can tell him that Pa gave four apples for it just for Tommy and that Ma must put a string in it and put it round his neck and he must say "Thank you, Pa, for the pretty money." And if he will talk pretty, Pa will send him another money next time.

---

[47] The battle of Perryville, 8 October 1862 and the major battle on Kentucky soil was far from being a Confederate victory. Following the battle, Bragg withdrew into East Tennessee leaving his dead and wounded on the field. Casualties were 3400 for the Confederates and 4200 for the Federals. Boatner III, *Civil War Dictionary*, 644.

[48] Braxton Bragg was a full general in the Confederate Army. A friend of Jefferson Davis, he was one of the most controversial leaders of the Confederacy since he seemed to always leave disaster in his wake and usually managed to seize defeat from the jaws of victory.

If Mr. Evans comes back you can send my clothes with him or anyone else that you think will bring them. Sure, I will need them before long though I am not suffering for them. I could draw clothes from the government but I had rather have them. William A. Darnell was over here last Sunday and was in good health and is trying to get a transfer to my company. I have not heard from him since but I hope he will get it. I am looking for him every day to come. It will be great satisfaction to me and him both if he does. If you ever hear of John F. Stilwell who is either strayed or stolen or mislaid you will do me a favor by giving me any information that you may chance to get of him and if he is still down in Dixie, just let him rip.

Molly, if you have not written to Edmons about that money you must be sure to write soon and tell him that you need it very bad and must have it and have it now. Molly, this is a beautiful Sunday morning and I expect you are gone to church somewhere, You must not fail to attend church as often as you can. I have not heard a sermon in about four months. Our chaplain went home before we left Richmond and has not come back yet. I never wanted to hear preaching as bad in my life. I intend to take the *Christian Advocate* if we ever get situated anywhere for six months and I think I will send it to you also for six months but can't do it at present. I shall expect you to write often and if you don't do it you will hear my horn for I am like Brownlow, when I commence writing my pen will write what my heart feels so you better look out.[49] Tell Aunt P. B. [Penelope] that I read her letters with interest and hope she will continue them. Margaret has at length broken the ice and I hope the water will rise now. Give my love to all of them and to Mother and Grandma, sure, as they are old and childish. Write soon and often to Billie. Kiss my boy all over and over and may we all meet in the morning. I am yours as ever until death.

W. R. Stilwell

---

[49] William G. Brownlow published the *Knoxville Whig* during the antebellum period. His fiery editorials caused him to be known as "the fighting parson." He was pro-slavery but anti-secession so he was soon suppressed by Confederate authority.

There is nothing like prayer made in faith to God.

———

The regiment is still in far northwestern Virginia and the weather is becoming unpleasant. The men are still without tents or extra clothing but Stilwell seems to be satisfied with conditions. They have finally been issued government shoes.

Camp near Winchester, N. W. Virginia, October 28, 1862
My dear Molly:
I received two letters from you day before yesterday and they being the first I had received since the one that I got by Mr. Evans, you may be sure that I was glad to hear from you. All of them were dated the 28th September which you sent by Doyal and the other by Phillips. I got them both at the same time and ought to have got them long before I did, but not withstanding they were so old, I found them very interesting.

I find myself in very good health this morning and about as well satisfied as common though I am getting tired of staying up in this country for it is very disagreeable. Last Sunday night, Molly, I think was as bad a night as I ever saw. It commenced raining early Sunday morning, rained all day and at night rained, one of those cold dark rainy nights, the wind blew from a pace. I had to stand guard and it came very near freezing me though I had a fire to stay by.

We have a fire all the time at headquarters. I have two men with me from my company here, A. Moore[50] and Ben Adair.[51] Ben is a good fellow. We all sleep together and by doing so we sleep tolerable warm. I need a heavy coat worse than anything else and a pair of gloves.

---

[50] Absalam Moore was private in Company F. Nothing else is known of him.

[51] Benjamin J. Adair was a private in Company F. In 1860 he was a 29-year-old married tenant farmer from McDonough with three small children. He died of a fever in a Richmond hospital on 23 February 1863.

I have been trading some of late. As I wrote to you before I had but one dollar and a half left so I thought that it would never do for me to get out of money so I went to buying and selling apples until I made twenty-five dollars and then I bought an old watch for fourteen dollars and swapped it for a double case silver watch and got five dollars to boot. The watch that I now have is worth at least twenty dollars and was sold two days before I swapped for it for twenty-seven. I think I will sell it before long. I made about fifteen dollars on the rounds of trading. I also drew a pair of shoes from the government at five dollars and swapped them off for a pair of English shoes of the best kind of lined and bound double soled shoes that sell for twelve and fifteen dollars in Richmond and gave one dollar to boot. I was offered ten dollars for them so I am well shod for the present, so you need not be uneasy about me as long as I can find anyone to trade with me. I think we will be paid off or paid some in the course of a month and I will send you some money the first chance I have as I expect you need it by this time.

Molly your letter did not give me any satisfaction about Brother Robert [Ragland]. I don't suppose that you had heard of his death when you wrote. I am looking for a letter from you by John Parker. I learn that he will be here in a few days and I suppose you will write by him and give me the particulars of Bob's death. Oh, how sorry I am about him and for Sister. She must be troubled very much. I wrote you a long letter about it and I suppose that you have got it before now. I wrote to her and Uncle Robert Everitt, too, and will await an answer from all with much interest.[52] You must not expect long letters from me now when it is so cold and, besides you will not write long letters to me. I have not heard from William Darnell since I wrote to you last. I want to hear very bad.

---

[52] Robert B. Everitt was likely a brother of Molly's mother. He also may have been the pathfinder for the Speer orphans who gravitated to northwestern Louisiana. In 1860 he was listed as a farmer in the Vernon post office district of Jackson County, Louisiana with a wife and seven children. Later he was on the rolls as a private in the 28th Louisiana Infantry.

We have had an election in our Regiment lately, which resulted in the election of Major Simms as Colonel and Captain Hance[53] of Coweta County as lieutenant colonel and Captain Sims of Henry as major.[54] I fear they are not such men as Sloan was. You wanted me to write about Sloan treating his men bad but I can't waste paper to sustain the character of a man whom a few cowards tried to ruin. Suffice it to say that I fear we will never get such another.

We have no tents yet and there is not much prospect of our moving but I still think we will fall back towards Richmond this winter and it may be soon or late. You did not write anything about

---

[53] James Washington Hance was elected lieutenant colonel of the 53rd on 27 October 1862. He had been captain of Company D of the 53rd. Prior to that he was commander of Company D of the 19th Georgia. He was apparently a native of the Laurens District of South Carolina and attended South Carolina College. WRS may have assumed that he was from Coweta as that was where Company D was recruited. Hance was killed at Gettysburg.

[54] Thomas W. Sims was elected Major of the 53rd Regiment on 27 October 1862. However, he would resign due to disability on 28 October, the day this letter was written. He was not from Henry County but rather from just over the county line in Rocky Plains post office, Newton County. He had been Captain of Company B from Newton County (South River Farmers). Before the war he practiced as a physician in Newton County and operated a farm (for which he had an overseer). In 1860 he was 42 years old and his wife, Nancy A. was 38. They had nine children ranging in age from 1 to 17. In 1870 he was a prosperous physician still living in Rocky Plains. He had continued to father many children as he and his wife listed eight children at home, the youngest of whom was four years old.

Brother John. What in the world has become of him (don't you know)? He is like old General Johnson, we don't know whether he is dead or alive. I will write a little more. It is hard for me to quit even if I am cold.

[Letter ends abruptly at this point.]

3

FREDERICKSBURG AND
A QUIET WINTER

As Stilwell has predicted, the regiment has moved considerably closer to Richmond. The indefatigable Mr. Evans is back in camp but he has nothing for Stilwell.

Camp near Culpeper, Virginia, November 5, 1862
My dear Molly,
With pleasure I avail myself of the present opportunity of writing you a few lines which will inform you that my health is still good. It seems that God has blessed me in point of health above many of my fellows and in your last seems to be grumbling that others can get sick and that I can't so that I can get a furlough but you must not be grumbling because if I can stay well I can get along very well. So if you don't quit talking so and wanting me to get sick I will box your jaws when I do come. I never had better health in my life except I am bothered some with the gravel and I am afraid that it will get worse this winter but hope not.[1]

You will see by this letter that we have moved back in the direction of Richmond a good long way, some hundred miles. So you see that I was right when I said that I thought we would fall back this winter. We left Winchester the last day of October and

---

[1] Bladder or kidney stones.

marched four days which was very hard marching on a turnpike road. We came from Winchester to Port Royal and here we crossed the Shenandoah river and there I saw the beautiful valley of the Shenandoah but then we struck those huge mountains again and they were much larger than before and much longer across them. We had to come through them for about twenty-five miles and you can imagine the fatigue of such marching. The first day we marched twenty-four or five miles and I had not been walking any for so long that my feet were blistered very bad and you may know how I got along next day with my feel all blistered but I kept up and we got to our present camp and I am all right again and ready for another march. But I learn that they have sent for tents for all of our troops here and from that I guess that we will remain here for some time to come. I am much better satisfied now than I was up at Winchester for we are on the mountains where it will not be so cold and besides that the cars run from here to Richmond and we can get our mail regular and clothes from home and get more to eat. Our present camp is about 2 miles north of Culpeper which is about seventy-five miles from Richmond on the Virginia Central Railroad. The cars run from here to Richmond in seven hours.

I am in hopes that we will draw some bacon. I have not eaten one pound of bacon in three months or more. Mr. Evans came to us on the march and I was in hopes he had brought my clothes but he said that Pa came over to get him to bring them but he would not bring them. He said also that he thought that Pa give him a letter but he could not find it so I did not get it. I have not had a letter from you since the one you sent by Philips but you may be sure that I will get your letters hereafter as we will have mail every day. Evans said that you were all well but that is not like getting a letter from you. I shall not write much this time and will write again soon if I get a letter from you. I wanted to have sent you ten dollars by Mr. Evans but he was gone before I knew it. But will send you some the first chance I get. We will be paid off in a short time. I have been trading watches again, I have now a fine double case silver watch and a gold chain worth fifty dollars that cost me only seventeen. If I knew that I would get home soon I would not sell it and I don't know whether I will or not.

Give all of my love to all the friends and write soon to your Billy. I am still anxious to hear about the death of Robert [Ragland] and about Brother John. Molly, let me know if Pa has got any money from the county for you and if he has not I want him to get it for you as you are as much entitled to it as any one else I close. Kiss my baby and tell him all about Pa and write to him that he remains as ever your true and faithful husband until death. Goodbye

W. R. Stilwell (Kiss this)

Stilwell is expecting to move closer to Richmond at any moment and seems fairly satisfied with conditions. He does not remark on how the Southern army, by moving south, has again conceded Northern Virginia to Union occupation.

Camp Near Culpeper, Virginia, November 8th, 1862

My dear Wife:

I wrote you a letter the other day but have not sent it off yet and I thought I would write a little more at present. On yesterday we had a very pretty snow which covered old mother earth and made all the earth look white and made the mountains north of here look most beautiful but when we consider that we are here without tents or anything to keep us from the intense cold but a log hut and a bush arbor it was not so pleasant but notwithstanding all that I got along finely by building me a house out of [fence] rails and pinetops and slept as sound as a bat. But when I rose up this morning I found that we were ordered to be ready to march at a moment's warning so we packed up in the snow and have stood here all day but have not moved and just now the order is countermanded and we will stay here awhile longer, though [I] think, and almost know, that we will still fall back farther in the direction of Richmond. I hear this evening that the whole army is falling back towards Richmond. I think there will be more fighting shortly and who will get the best of it, I don't know. They have a large force here and so have we but Molly, I don't suppose I will be in it as I still hold my old position.

My health is good and appetite better. We have just drawn some bacon and you ought to see me eat "Old Ned." Molly, I can not send this off tonight and will try to send it off in the morning and may write a little more if I can and if not, all right. I think we will leave in the morning. Sure enough we leave, the orders have just come in; in the morning at daylight. I will try to mail this letter as soon as I can. I will write as soon as we stop again and let you know where we are and what we have done.

Molly, as we leave in the morning I will continue my letter a little longer. Molly, I am still without a letter from you and it looks like I will still be [in] the same way when I get one letter and then another that will be two since the sixth of last month. I have got so when I don't get a letter from you that I just go without it and will continue to do so hereafter. I cannot write longer as it is late and the sun is setting behind the Blue Ridge Mountains and this is the time of day that always affects me most as I have often written to you. Molly, I love you as I ever have with my whole heart and soul and I feel that God will let me get home sometime to see you and my dear little boy. I want to hear from him very bad and to roach up his little curly head. You don't know how bad it makes me feel to think what a sweet wife and child I have so many miles from me and can't get to see them but, Molly, you know my feelings about such things, and how I take such things. I always look ahead and forget the things that are behind and look forward to the future and trust in God for protection. I always pray every night that God will guard me and you and Tommy, and I feel that he will do it so you must pray for me often and let us trust in God. I must bring my letter to a close. Give my love to all the friends and inquirers. I am your loving and affectionate Billie, and honey, Goodbye, write soon to Billie.

W.R. Stilwell

———

Still at Culpeper, Stilwell is expecting a general battle in the next few days but this will not occur.

Headquarters First Brigade, 2nd Division, Army of Northern
   Virginia, November 10, 1862
My dear little wife

With pleasure I send you another letter and am glad to say that my health is very good, so you will have to complain again that I don't get sick and get a furlough. I hope I will continue so. I can eat more than ten men ought to eat and am glad to say that I get plenty to eat. I am as sassy as a big house nigga. Got money and tobacco a plenty for the present. We have not drawn any money yet but think we will in a few days or a week at most.

I received a letter from Uncle John [Stilwell] a few days ago, which gave me the first news where Brother John was.[2] He said that he was at Savannah but did not say what he was doing there. He did not say whether he was in service or not and of course I could not write to him. I have not had a letter from him in four months.

Molly, I will have to close without finishing my letter, I expect. We have just received orders to be ready to march at a minutes warning and I expect to the battlefield but Molly I will not be in it I don't expect as I am always in the rear. I think it will be a general battle and this may be the last letter that you may give from me in some time but don't be uneasy about me. I have just learned that the mail for today is gone so I will quit writing for the present. I may write more and I may not, so goodbye. Yours as ever until death.

W. R. Stilwell

Molly, the order has been countermanded and I thought I would write a little more. We have not heard the result of the battle

---

[2] John F. Stilwell was a private in Company A of the 32nd Georgia; this company was composed of Jasper and Jones County men. Stilwell was appointed a regimental musician. The regiment was organized in April and May 1862 and assigned to the Department of South Carolina, Georgia, and Florida in June 1862. As noted previously, Stilwell was earlier a member of the 14th Regiment but discharged due to disability in 1861. In 1860 John was a 25-year-old clerk, living in a hotel in Monticello, Jasper County.

but suppose it is all right by our not having to go. If the returns come in tonight I will let you know the result.

P. S. I have not sold my fine watch yet. It is worth $50. I made it by trading. Lookout boys, I must make money.

———

This is the first letter of the collection to someone other than Molly. It is to his brother and is a recapitulation of Stilwell's army experience to date. WRS also reveals that he is in correspondence with his Uncle John.

Camp near Culpeper, November 12, 1862
Mr. John F. Stilwell:
Dear brother:
I have not had a letter from you in about four months and not knowing where you were I could not write to you and think that you have treated me with a great deal of coolness in not writing to me.

Since my last letter to you I have gone through scenes most severe and through many dangers seen and unseen but thanks be to God I have been spared to the present time. I left Richmond with the army and have been with it through all the march from Richmond through Maryland. I was at or near the battle of Crampton's Gap and at Harper's Ferry and Sharpsburg, though being still at my old stand of guard, which position I still hold, I was not right in the fights.[3] I need not say that we suffered very much marching so far and so hard, many times without anything to eat. My health is very good and has been for four months past. I weigh one hundred and twenty-seven lbs, twelve lbs more than ever I did in my life and I am still improving daily in health.

After the battle of Sharpsburg which was fought on the 17th September and, was no doubt, the greatest battle of the war, we camped four miles below Winchester where we remained about three weeks and then took up our line of march for this place.

---

[3] The preferred Southern name for Antietam.

Culpeper is about 75 miles north of Richmond. We are expecting orders every day to march farther south and I have no doubt we will in a few days. They fought all day before yesterday but with what result I know not. Some suppose that we will fall back on Richmond and take winter quarters but that, I think, is uncertain. Let it be remembered that we have not had any tents since we left Richmond and you may guess how we have fared amidst frost and snow which we have had in abundance. Brother, I shall enclose this letter in a letter to R. D. McDonald with a request to forward as I do not know what regiment you belong to. I got a letter from Uncle John the other day stating that you were at Savannah but he did not state what you were doing there.

Uncle John writes me some very interesting letters but it is very expensive to keep up so many correspondences. It cost me about twenty five cents every letter I write but that is what I live for, to inform my friends. It is with sorrow that I inform you of the death of R. W. Ragland. He was in service in the west and took sick was sent home and died, poor fellow. I lost one of my best friends when I lost him sure. I received a letter from my little wife yesterday. She was in good health and good spirits. She takes the world as she comes to it and is one of the loveliest things that ever breathed air. Would to God that this unholy war would close and let me get home to her once more.

I employ myself in trading and have made about fifty dollars trading on watches. I got down to one dollar and fifty cents before I commenced trading and no prospect of drawing money so I went to buying and selling apples and from that to watches and now have a watch double case silver and gold chain worth fifty dollars and money a plenty for current expenses.

When you write, direct to Richmond as before and always do that as long as I remain north or at Richmond. How long I will stay with Gen. Semmes I don't know but will stay as long as I can. I prefer it to being with the regiment. William Darnell was in good health the last time I saw him about three weeks ago. No more at present but I ever remain your affectionate brother until death.

W. R. Stilwell

After a couple months of quiet and boredom in northwestern Virginia, Stilwell has moved to Fredericksburg where excitement prevails. Both armies are concentrating on this city located about halfway between Washington and Richmond. Stilwell participates in assisting the evacuation of the civilians. He paints a word picture of the little child that can just toddle and the old mother with her cane and baggage trying to walk the muddy streets. This is a familiar scene to modern viewers of movie and TV news accounts that occurs in the areas of fighting in WW II, Korea, Vietnam, Africa, Bosnia, Croatia, and Kosovo, among other places. But it is a shock to realize that it once occurred in America.

Fredericksburg, Virginia, November 23, 1862
My dear Molly:
Once more I seat myself to write you a few lines though it is in the midst of great excitement. You will notice by this letter that we have moved again about fifty miles to Fredericksburg where the artillery of both sides seem to be concentrated and where I expect we will have a great battle to fight. We arrived here day before yesterday in the rain. We were four days on the march and you can suppose what hard times we saw when an army of 60 many thousand had gone along with wagons and horses. In many places the mud was most knee deep and the rain was very cold. I suffered more than I have at any time since I have been in the army and today while I write I am cold, my clothes having worn thin and no overcoat, but I am still looking for the clothes that you have made me and thinking can do very well then.

I will tell you something about the excitement which prevails here. On yesterday the Yankees sent word in that they were going to shell the city, which is as large as Atlanta, at nine o'clock and for us to move the women and children out at once. They sent the news all over town and the inhabitants commenced leaving their homes as they thought, and may be truth, never to see them any more but in ashes. General Semmes sent me with some of the guard and a wagon to move or help move some of the families out so I had a good chance to witness a great deal. As we got in town the enemy threw some shells at the train as they came in but did not hit any. I was so sorry for the poor little innocent children and the ladies seemed to be scared out of anything like reason, but I told them I had heard bigger dogs bark than that and never had been bit yet. They would cry and then scold the Yankees. They would get scared and then brave but when a bomb would burst they would gather hold of you and hollow. Here was one of the most exciting times that ever I saw. To see from the little child that could just walk to the mother of seventy years old with her cane trying to walk the muddy streets with loads of baggage presented a sight not pleasant to look on.

The day passed off and no more firing was done but it is expected every minute yet. Today they still say that they will burn the town and General Lee says if he leaves the town he will leave it in ashes but I think he is ready for them. I will have to quit for the present. I am so cold I can not write but will write more after a while.

November 24—Molly, I now write more after another day has passed off and the excitement has ceased to a great event. The Yankees have not shelled the city yet but we are still expecting them to do so. A great many families are living in the woods. Our brigade is gone out on picket and the camps look very lonesome. The two great armies are lying very near together and it don't look like they could keep from fighting much longer. I wish they would fight or let it alone, one or the other, so we could get into winter quarters, for just as long as they keep moving about we will have to do the same. They are afraid to fight us and don't want to acknowledge it but they will have to do it before long. I think the war will close by April or May, if it don't there is no telling when it will close. I wish it would close for I am very tired of it and I never wanted it commenced but I can't help it and will have to wait the appointed time for it to close but would be glad it would be done as soon as possible. Molly, It is so cold to write that I don't know whether you can read my letter or not. I do the best I can.

[Unsigned]

———

Stilwell is still without his overcoat and other clothing left in Richmond and he is freezing. He is so uncomfortable that he curses the Confederacy for putting him in this predicament. His morale has hit rock bottom. Again he informs Molly that the new baby must be a girl and her name must be Virginia.

Fredericksburg, Virginia, November 30, 1862

My dear little wife:

Your very welcome letter was received that you sent by Mr. Bell the other day and it was the first since the sixth of last month so you may know how glad I was to get it and was more than glad to hear that your health was good.[4] Surely God has been very good to us. Let us be thankful for my health was never better and I am getting fat on beef.

I wrote to you the other day after we got to this place. It looks like it falls to our part to go wherever there is to be fighting to do. I thought the other day when I wrote that we would have fought a battle before now but we have not and both armies have gone to fortifying and when they commence that I never think there is going to be much fighting done. Molly, my clothes is still in Richmond and may stay there until next summer. They won't let them be sent up here and that makes me think that we will go back to Richmond before long. I am needing them very bad but will have to do without them until they get ready. I wouldn't care much if the Confederacy was broken into a thousand fragments anyhow for they treat the army like so many dogs. It is like Pa says, if God blesses us as a nation it can't be hard to get a blessing, for of all the nations on earth, I think in the course of another year we will be the most corrupted, Yankedom not excepted. But nothing but war would do the people and they have just it in all of its bitterest crimes and truly the way of the transgressor is hard. Just think of a man fighting

---

[4] Mr. Bell is not identified.

for eleven dollars per month and paying from eight to ten dollars for a pair of shoes. But Molly, this war will close sometime and God grant how soon it may be and let us get home to our family. They may talk of liberty and they may talk of me dying in war but I want to live with my family and live in peace. I think this war will have to close before six months some way or other and how it will be done, I don't say for I don't know. I am doing finely. I just do what I am ordered and I don't care whether anybody else does or not. If they do anything that I don't like it is all the same with me. I just eat whenever I please, don't care whether it's mealtime or not, in fact I don't care which way the wind blows anyhow. I have seen most enough of this world anyhow and if it was not for my family I think I would be glad to hear them say, "It is enough, come up higher." All I think or care about is my family. If I can just hear that they are well I am all right. As for anything else it don't bother my mind.

Molly, you need not talk about another boy. War or no war I must have a girl. If you go to talking that way I shall not like it at all. It must be a girl and its name must be Virginia. If it is a boy I will call it Bull Run.

I don't like it about John getting my butter and dried fruit but as he always got the best of everything it seems natural for him to still do so. I don't care much about that though it would have eaten well but that potato that Tom put in, that makes me as mad as blazes. I know they could have let that come but this Confederacy treats us just like a dog. If you want him to obey you well keep him under good command.

Molly, I must close, I have got some work to do for the old general on his saddle this evening. Write soon and often. That last letter was great for length. I close for the present. Give my love to all. Kiss my boy. I am yours until death.

W. R. S.

———

Stilwell is still so cold and miserable that he declares that he prefers bondage to independence. Perhaps his current low morale influences his decision to reject an offer to become a courier for General Semmes. The reason given by Stilwell for the rejection was the expense of obtaining and maintaining a horse which would be required should he accept the position. Most of a brigade commander's couriers seem to be lieutenants. The difference in duties and responsibilities between officer and private couriers is not known to this editor but as indicated in later letters they don't seem to be very great and the position is a very honorable one for a private.

Camp near Fredericksburg, Virginia, December 7, 1862
My dear Molly,

I avail myself of the present opportunity of writing a few lines which will inform you that I am in good health and doing very well. I should have written to you some few days ago but from the fact that my mind has been bothered and I thought I would not write until I decided what to do but have decided at last. I could get the appointment of courier for General Semmes. I thought at first that I would accept it but after thinking about it for several days I have declined the idea of taking it. It is a very good position but the reason that I don't take it is that it would take all of my wages and [I] have to have about one hundred dollars more to buy me a horse. The boys of the company said I should have the money if I wanted it but that would not leave any money for you and you know that that don't suit me for to take my wages to buy a horse when I know that you will need it. So I thought I had better stay right where I am if I can and let do well alone.

We are still at the same place and no fight yet but don't see how long we will remain here. Yesterday we had a tremendous snowstorm which lasted all night last night and you may guess how the men in camp suffered from cold weather. Just think of so many thousand men camped in the naked woods without any tents and some barefooted, some without any blankets and living on a little beef and bread. God only knows what will become of us. If this is independence [I] don't want it. I had rather take bondage. I shall have to close for the present. I am so cold that I can't write.

December 9th—Molly, it has been so cold that I could not finish my letter until now. Today is the third day since the snow fell and the ground is still covered and still very cold and now while I write my fingers are so cold that I can hardly write. My health is still good and I sleep in a shed of a barn on some clover and sleep as sound as I ever did. Our clothes are still in Richmond and I don't suppose they will be sent to us as long as we stay up here. The government is not treating us right in this matter.

Molly, I have not yet drawn any money but suppose I will in a week or two. I don't know how much I will draw but I want to send the most of it home as soon as I draw it if I can and I want you to buy some things as you need for you and Tommy. Don't suffer for anything for I think I can make enough money to get along with while I am in the war.

Molly, I am looking for a letter from you every day, I think surely that you will write often after you get my last letters. If you don't, I will always think you ought to. I have done my best in writing to you and then to think that I don't get a letter from you once a month is very hard but if you don't write, I can't help it. You must not expect long letters [during] this cold weather but I will try to write once a week. Honey, I hope I will get to wear those fine clothes that you worked so hard to make for me some day. I am fairing tolerably well but would fare better if I had them.

Molly, I will have to close as it is so cold I can't write hardly at all. If it was not that I am writing to you I could not write any. Give my love to all the friends and reserve a double portion for yourself and Tommy. Kiss him for me and write soon and often to your affectionate husband until death.

W. R. S.

———

No Confederate soldier was ever satisfied with the letters he received from his home folks. Much about the mail delivery was not under the control of the originators or the recipients. The soldiers understood this but the complaints were still vociferous. Thus, Stilwell gives Molly some mild and good-humored chastisement about not writing enough. Then much of this letter is given to talking about Tommy. Stilwell takes a very peculiar and detached position to the unborn child. He is positive that it will be a girl and states that she will belong to Molly.

Fredericksburg, Virginia, December 11, 1862
My Dear Little Wife,
Not with standing that you will sit up in the corner of the chimney by a good fire and don't write when others do, yet I will not forsake you, yet you sit up there and read. Pretty thing you are and not condescend to write. Never mind, when I get to be General Stilwell, then you will want to be writing to me and I won't notice your letters, ha, ha. Gal, you know me, but as I have given you some pretty good letters about not writing I shan't fight you any this time as it is a very good plan for me to write on Monday and the other on Saturday and that would give me two letters a week instead of one every two months. And what is twenty cts a week? Why I would give that to hear that you had eaten butter and milk for supper.

But I must tell you about one [letter] which one of the guard got last Saturday and what do you suppose it contained. Why it contained some butter, large yam potatoes, dried fruit and on Sunday, what do you think we had? Why we had an old fashioned sliced pie, yes, a great big sliced pie. I was chief cook and bottle washer and when it got done you ought to have seen me. I ate pie until I had to unbutton most all my clothes. I thought of A. Gray and his pudding and then we ate fruit and butter. It makes me feel good till yet to think about it. It made some of the boys sick, C. B. Smith for one, and I think it will get him a furlough, that very pie, but, no, it did not get any furlough for me so if I can get some more potatoes I will try it again and if it is found out that Georgia potatoes will give furloughs I want you to offer your whole crop for sale for you can get a fine price for them.[5] I believe I would take a few myself.

For a little I was afraid that Tom's money had got lost as it was sent at Winchester, and I had never heard any thing from it but am glad to hear that he got it and as I promised if he would talk pretty I would send him another one, I will send it in this letter but don't know whether I will ever get another one for him. When sister wrote about him being in the bed with pa and mother I could almost see him in my imagination. I would give half the Confederacy to see him and the other half to see somebody else if they would write. Sister says he was smart. That was nothing new to me. I have always known that he was smart and I tell you now Tom will fill a page in the history of the world yet and I want to live to educate him. I will work him all night to do it. I want him to have all the education that his mind is able to bear and that is one thing that pains me. If I die in the war I can't leave enough to do that and if I do I want you to give him to John and let him give it to him or any other good man that will do it. Always teach him that an education is worth more than fortune. But you may ask what is to be done with Jinney [the unborn child]. Well, that is for you to say as she belongs to you. You must choose her life to satisfy yourself. Perhaps she would make a good weaver but anyone that will look at Tom's head will say at once that he was destined to make his mark in the world. I don't say what he shall follow for he ought to choose that himself but give him an education and he is ready for anything and be sure to give him for his first book the bible and for his

---

[5]Charles B. Smith in 1860 was a McDonough tailor aged 32 with a 22-year-old wife and two small children. He came into Company F of the 53rd as a substitute for J. M. Harris who was a Henry County farm manager. In 1860, Smith and his wife, Sarah Guest (married 1853) had 4 small children. He owned no real estate and had $1225 in personal property. What qualified Smith to be a substitute (he would have to be exempt from conscription) and how a farm manager could raise the substantial sum required to purchase a substitute is not known. As an experienced tailor, Smith was a valuable addition to the 53rd. He appears on the last roll of the 53rd on 28 February 1865. He does not appear in the Henry County 1870 census. Harris appears in the 1870 Henry County census as a small farmer.

second the life of Joe Brown and if he never sees any others these two are enough.[6]

Molly, I did not think that I would write much when I commenced but after I get started I don't know where to stop. I don't know anything of Darnell, only his division is about ten miles below me nearer Richmond and I suppose he is there. Molly, I will write a letter and put it in to Pa. Write often and believe ever I am your faithful husband until death.

W. R. Stilwell

———

What follows is an account of the Battle of Fredericksburg for which Stilwell had a birdseye view and reported in his "you are there" manner. The outcome of this battle was probably the most one-sided victory for the Confederacy during the entire war. The 53rd was stationed on Marye's Heights, a key but very protected site and their losses were small. With the excitement and decisive Confederate victory, Stilwell's attitude had gone through a dramatic shift. Still frozen, unpaid and unclothed, he has adopted a "so what" attitude.

Fredericksburg, Virginia, December 14, A. D. 1862
My dear Molly,

It is with the most profound gratitude that I avail myself of this opportunity of writing to you and to inform you that I am well, in fact enjoying better health than common. Again I have to record the clash of arms. On the morning of the eleventh, I was awaken from sleep by the roaring cannon and the bursting shells in the city. It seems that about five o'clock in the morning the enemy had attempted to throw pontoon bridges across the river. Our men knowing their plan gave them to understand that they would have something to do and the battle began at once, it being the plan of General Lee to fall back and let them cross after firing. It was

---

[6] Joseph E. Brown was the controversial but widely popular wartime governor of Georgia.

accordingly done and they commenced shelling the city which they continued to do all day, our batteries not firing on them but holding out the idea that we did not have much of an army there. They set the city on fire about three o'clock. I went out and got on a high hill where I could see all the city and the huge brass cannon of the enemy and see their shells burst in the city and thus fire on many houses. Here I stood in full view of the enemy though at long range. I enjoyed myself as well as you could suppose and perhaps better. The firing continued all day Thursday and Thursday night they crossed the river and next day the ball opened at daylight with increased energy. All day the firing continued with great fury and progress. Again I stood on the hill to see the conflict which continued all day as the day before but with little result so far as we know. That night General Semmes sent for the guard to go to his headquarters to guard him. That night I volunteered my service to go, and went down with my old musket all right. He wanted us to watch for any signs that the enemy might give of an advance during the night and wanted his own guard quiet and here to confer with us but the night passed off without any alarm and we were ordered back to camp next morning to take charge of his baggage and again Saturday, the thirteenth, the conflict commenced with more fury than ever. All up and down the river for ten miles you could hear nothing but the roar of cannon and after awhile the musketry began and it seemed as though you had set fire to a canebrake of a thousand acres. Again I visited my elevated spot and here I stood viewing the whole affair. Here you could see the Yankees charge our batteries and could see them run back as often. One battery [was] charged seven times but were driven back as often with great slaughter and here I stood regardless of the now and then bursting shells that came from the enemy's guns. Now and then you could see our shells strike in their ranks and see them skedaddle. All day the battle continued all along the lines and no doubt the enemy were badly whipped. The firing continued all day and up to nine o'clock at night and opened this morning at sunrise and now while I write I can hear them fighting and think I will lay down my pen and go to my hill as I don't think of sending this off until the battle is over but thought I would write lest I would forget something that would interest you.

Just now they brought by a squad of twenty-two prisoners. I almost treat them with kindness and try to heap coals of fire on their heads. I have recorded good news up to this hour but the battle is not ours and we may have to mourn over defeat yet. All ready some of the noble sons of Georgia have fallen, among them Gen. T. R. R. Cobb was killed on yesterday.[7] I go and take my stand to witness the fight, some of our boys were in the heat of the battle and of course did suffer much. I reckon there never was a battle in which men fought more desperately than our men did.

Cobbs' Brigade was stationed behind a rock fence. The Yankees advanced twelve columns deep. The first would fire about ten minutes and lie down and the second would advance on them and fire and lie down, likewise the fourth, etc. but before the last column got over our boys got too hot for them and they skedaddled like scared bucks.

I saw most all of the fighting the five days, more than I ever expected to see again but believe me many a good and brave women could say "husband" last Saturday morning when they rose, that were widows when the sun set and many children that could say "father" were orphans. Oh, that God would intercede and give us peace once more. But his will be done and not ours. I have given you all particulars that I now remember. For further accounts I refer you to the papers. Let us be thankful to God for his favors and pray for a continuation of the same.

Today is very cold and accounts for my bad writing. Our clothes are in Richmond yet. Don't know when we will get them, Whether ever or not. We have not drawn any money yet. Don't know

---

[7] Thomas Reade Rootes Cobb, a prominent pro-secessionist before the war was a significant force in taking Georgia out of the Union. In August 1861, he organized a composite unit consisting of infantry, cavalry, and artillery that was named "Cobb's Legion." The unit's first colonel, Cobb was promoted to brigadier general on 1 November 1862 and given command of a brigade. He was serving in this capacity and defending the sunken road at Fredericksburg on 13 December 1862 when he was struck by a musket ball and bled to death. Warner, *Generals in Gray*, 56.

when we will. Our quartermaster is gone home on sick furlough. Don't care whether he ever comes back or not. I have got plenty of money to answer all purposes yet and if I need any more I can get it. It is a good thing to have friends but I always have them everywhere I go.

I am very anxious to hear from William Darnell. I hope he has come out all right. I don't know that he was in the fight but suppose he was. In what direction we will go from here will depend on the movements of the enemy. I am in hopes they will go home and stay there always. I think their next attempt at Richmond will be at Petersburg, Virginia by water. If so let them come on.

Dec. 17 Dear Molly, it is with profound gratitude to almighty God for the privilege of completing my letter that I commenced the other day and thanks be to God that I am able to inform you of a great victory won over our common enemies by our brave boys. Their loss is said to be fifteen thousand, ours about twenty-five hundred.[8] I have witnessed the whole affair. On the evening of the fourteenth I went to guard the old general as usual, his headquarters being in the edge of town and about one hundred and fifty yards from the Yankee pickets. I knew I was in great danger and kept a sharp look out. I had been on guard and just at one o'clock I was sitting by the fire and thinking of the hundreds of dead men that were lying in a hundred yards of me when a shower of bullets came over and around me, sip, sip, sip, right at my head. I thought the ball had opened and at once sprung to my rifle and cartridge box and took my stand and was going to make the best fight that I could when the firing stopped and I never got a chance so I lay down and went to sleep notwithstanding their pickets kept firing increasingly all night but without much damage to any. The fighting continued for five days and ended in the complete rout of the enemy who retreated across the river under the darkness of the night and left their dead lying on the field as usual for us to bury which will be done today. They had been lying on the field since Saturday and

---

[8] Union killed and wounded were 12,700; Confederate losses were 5300. Boatner, *Civil War Dictionary*, 313.

many of the wounded had been there all the time and nary side could get them. I could not help feeling sorry for them though they were our enemy. We lost several of our best men and among them General T.R.R. Cobb of Georgia who was killed in five hundred yards of where he was born and where he was married.[9] What strange things will happen some times but the ways of God are past finding out.

W. R. Stillwell

———

There has been a dramatic shift in Stilwell's mood and morale. Just a month ago he was cursing the Confederacy. Now, after the great victory at Fredericksburg, he is most content. Despite all the grumbling about army food or lack thereof, we must note that he gained 20 pounds, from 115 to 135, in the eight months of his army experience.

This letter contains two items that reflect dramatic shifts in taste and manners from 1863 to today. Stilwell refers to Molly's coming delivery as a "time of sickness" probably indicating a delicacy about any thing sexual or the results thereof. The other matter is about society's view of ideal personal weight. Stilwell states that Molly used to weigh his present weight (135 pounds) and he wonders who weighs the most now considering that Molly has likely "improved" some since then. To improve was to add weight. It was certainly a very different time.

Camp Fredericksburg, January 1, AD 1863

Oh, magnify the Lord with me for his mercy endureth forever. Let the hills and mountains and all the inhabitants praise the Lord for he is good and his mercy endureth forever. Oh, let us praise the Lord for he has brought us safe through another year. Yes, he has brought us through dangers seen and unseen.

Molly, my dear, I am glad to say this morning that I am in the best of health. Never in my life have I enjoyed as good health as I

---

[9] This is not true. There may have been some connection with this spot to his mother's life.

do at present. I have just been vaccinated a few days ago and have a very sore arm. We have had a good deal of smallpox in the army, a good many cases in our regiment but I have never been alarmed. There are many who die with it here. I may have it but I am not uneasy. I think that if the war would last about twelve months longer and I can have good health and good luck it will make a man of me yet. I weigh now one hundred and thirty-five lbs. You use to weigh as much as me but I think I can beat you now though I suppose you have improved some yourself.

I have just returned from off picket downtown. I love to go down there on picket for we get a good room to sleep in and the people are so kind, more so than any place I have been.

The other day when I was down there a lady sent to us as to know if we would go and assist her in getting her granma out of a cellar and in the carriage. She stayed down in the cellar all the time of the fight and cannon balls passed through the house. She was near a hundred years old and her niece could not get her away. I got all the boys and went. I found she had to be carried up a flight of stairs through a very narrow passage. She could hardly speak but when we had carried her up which we did in a chair and laid her in the carriage, she could not speak. Looking at us she burst into tears and you could see that she was thankful. Her niece a very nice good girl, was the most thankful person I ever saw. The old lady was the widow of old Judge Lumbus of Virginia.

My dear Molly. When I remember that your time of sickness draws near, I can not help but pass some very gloomy evenings. Oh, how I want to be with you in that day of trouble and sickness, but, my dear, I can do no better than to put you in the care of God and I feel that you will be safe under his care for God will take care of those that are afflicted. You must trust in him and pray much and may he spare you and bless you. I do hope that you may have an easy time. Take good care of yourself. I know that you could not be in better hands than you are in now. I know that you will be well cared for, but at the same time it is not like having Billie. Be sure and do the best you can and take care of yourself for if I lose my Molly I lose my all. If I was to lose you I would not want to fight any more for what is life or liberty to me without my Molly. But I know that your love for me, if nothing else, will keep you in good heart. Oh, what a blessing it is to have a loving wife. I don't know whether Dr. Wright is at home yet or not but will leave you to choose any doctor that you want and when you are sick remember that I will be thinking of you and praying for your safety and once more I say trust in God and all will be well.

Give my love to all Uncles' family. Tell them to write to me, also Pa and Ma, Margaret she must write. Kiss my little baby. Oh, how bad I want to see him but want to see you worse than all, my dear. I long for the day when I shall be permitted to return to you in peace. I believe it will come but, oh, how shall I wait for it but wait, I say, on the Lord. I am about to finish my first letter for "sixty three." You will see that I have numbered it so I will know, and so will you, how many letters I write and whether you receive them or not. Give my love to all and a double, yea, triple portion for yourself and may God bless and preserve you is the prayer of your ever true and faithful husband until death.

W. R. Stilwell

My Dear, I got some more of the best books when I was in town you ever saw. Among them was one *The Young Christian*, a very good book. I get more books than I can read and study my grammar too amongst them. I have a very nice little prayer book captured from the enemy. My bible, though I have taken the best care of it I could, is damaged right smart. I always carry it with me everywhere I go and your picture through hard usage is becoming smartly worn and I have to look at it every day. My pants are smartly worn, more especially the seat but I have patched them so I think they will do me until I get my new clothes. It was a mistake about any clothes coming some time ago as I wrote to you but I think I will get them the last of this week. C. B. Smith has gone after them. I have good shoes yet, my socks will do tolerable well. I have darned them with saddle thread. I will have a set of metal buttons to put on my coat when I get it. I am going to get Smith to cover my hat and I am going to quilt it myself. I have not sold my watch and don't think I will soon unless I get a good price for it. It is one of the best of watches. We have not drawn any money, some of the company have. Two companies have been paid off and I reckon the rest will in a short time.

Molly I heard from Darnell. I saw Lyles Harkness from the 44th in the same brigade as the twenty-seventh.[10] He said he saw Darnell a few days before and that he was in good health. I wrote a letter to him by Harkness.

Every thing is quiet here. We are still fortifying and another fight is expected here and will no doubt be another victory. God send that we may whip them at every fight until it will bring the war to a close. I have nothing of the regiment or company to write. Just staying here in the camp. There is a general review this morning in sight of me while I write but I have seen so much that I don't pay any attention to such things of late days.

No letter from you yet nor don't expect to [hear] soon. I shall never grumble any more, write or not.

[Unsigned]

———

Stilwell is enjoying several incidents of good fortune. He has a new job that brings better conditions and less boredom than the old job of brigade guard. He has been paid and has received a set of government issue clothing. He describes his present condition as living in luxury.

---

[10] Elias A. Harkness was a private in Company I (Henry and Morgan Counties) of the 44th Regiment. In 1860, he was living with his mother, Mary A. Harkness and five siblings in the Locust Grove area of Henry County. He owned property of his own valued at $850 in real estate and $210 in personal property. His mother owned three slaves. On 6 March 1862, he married Harriett Benton. He was one of few men of Company I who would remain in service until the surrender in Virginia in April 1865. Practically all men still present in the company were captured at Spotsylvania VA on 10 May 1864 and incarcerated in Fort Delaware for the rest of the war—or until they died. Harkness was a small farmer in the 1870 Henry County census. He and Harriett had four children.

Camp near Fredericksburg, January 8, 1863
My dear Molly,

I am blessed with the present opportunity of writing to you and to inform you that I am well and doing well. I have changed my occupation since my last letter. I am now acting courier for Major Davis.[11] He is quartermaster for our brigade and belongs to General Semmes' staff. So I am at the same place. I am furnished with a horse to ride in carrying around orders to all the regiments in the brigade. I am very glad that I have got the position for it is much better than standing guard and having to get up all times of the night and [in] all kinds of weather. As it is now I can lie down and sleep all night. I tell you there is nothing like being a man and if a man will be a man he will always get along though he be in the war and my getting a good position in the quartermaster's department is not all the good news. I got my new clothes yesterday and you just ought to see me. Oh hush, but in order to let you know how I look, I will give you some particulars. When we were at Winchester I drew a pair of shoes at four dollars so I sold my old shoes that I wore from home for two dollars. You know they cost only three dollars at first. Well, I swapped the ones that I drew for a splendid pair of English shoes and gave one dollar to boot. I have worn them ever since until I got them that Uncle gave me and I sold them for eight dollars. I put on them that Uncle sent me and wore them one day. They fit well and were good shoes but one of my mess had a splendid pair of boots and he said he would swap for fourteen dollars to boot so I swapped with him so I am prepared to give you a look at me as I now write. If you could only look sitting in the door of a comfortable tent surrounded by a nice bush arbor, comfortable fire and dressed out in a fine suit of jeans and fine

---

[11] John E. Davis was appointed major and quartermaster 10 July 1862 to rank from 1 June 1862. No background data on his pre-war history has been found. According to his service record, in August 1863 he requested post (as opposed to field) duty. In October, he was assigned to quartermaster duties in Columbus, Georgia. The last entry in his very incomplete service record notes that, as of 25 August 1864, someone has applied for the post of paymaster in Columbus, which position has been made available by the death of Major John E. Davis.

boots with a fine watch in my pocket and fob and chain hanging down, and sitting on a cushion chair with a gold pen to write with, plenty of rations, a pocket full of money, a heavy beard and mustache on my upper lip, plenty of good books to read, now who wouldn't be in the war? This is a fact. It is true I can't help but think of my "poor kin." I have bought me a new jeans vest for three dollars and a half and sold my old one for two and a half so you see I am all right. I drew seventy-four dollars yesterday and I want to send you fifty or sixty dollars the first chance I have. I have no use for so much here. Molly, I have to carry off some orders and haven't time to write any more hardly for the mail will go off shortly. I got a letter from William Darnell the other day but will send it in this. Give my love to all Uncle William's family and all the rest of the friends. Give my thanks to Uncle for his present of shoes and to all for their kindness of helping you. My clothes fit like a bug's shirt, everything just right. I will write again before long when I have more time. Kiss Tom all over for me and to you I would say my heart and prayers are with and for you. Oh Molly, let us love God for that will enable us to be strong under all the affliction. So goodbye and may God bless and sustain you and keep you now and forever more and may we all meet in the morning.

W. R. Stilwell

———

Stilwell is very homesick and he writes a very tender letter to Molly.

Headquarters Second Brigade, First Division, Army of Potomac,[12] January 15, 1863

My dear Molly:

I hope you will excuse my shortcomings in not writing to you before now but I know that my excuse will be availing. I have been very busy of several days. We have moved our camp about three

---

[12] WRS has reverted to the obsolete designation.

miles and are erecting winter quarters and that accounts for the delay of my communication. My health, dearest is very good and when I am dressed in my fine suit I look well. My clothes fit so nice and they are so warm and comfortable, all just right except my drawers, they were most too small. I suppose you did not think I had fattened so much. I am ready for old winter and snow. We have had a very moderate winter so far.

My dear, I have not received any letters from you later than the twenty-third in which you wrote about old Sandy Claus but your old Sandy was not present but he was thinking about the past, present and the future. It was a sad day for me to be sure but it is past and gone, dear, and may we pray for better times the next time it comes. Oh, that me and you darling may be together then, I fear that I am loosing the best part of my life by being absent from you. Oh dear, was there ever love like ours and to be torn from you is so wicked and to think of you being sick! Oh Molly, I could not stand it at all if it was not that I know that your love for me will bear you up in your affliction. I know that you will have to suffer and suffer more, but I know that you will bear it with Christian fortitude. I know that when you are sick and think of me it will ease your pain. Think, oh think, that the prayers of your humble husband are being sent up for you, and for your safety. You must bear up and be cheerful. Let us be thankful that we are blessed as we are for I assure you that your darling is blessed above a great many others. I am thankful for it but I am seeing a very good time, If it was not for your large blue eyes that always haunt me everywhere I go, I could enjoy myself finely, but no matter where I go or what I do you are always before me, but you may haunt me as much as you please as I like to be haunted by such. I had like to have said an angel but maybe that would not be right but I won't take it back for if there are such persons that inhabit this earth you are one of them but as you are very sensitive about flattery, I had better quit lest you accuse me of being guilty.

Molly, I confess that I am in no fix to write. My mind is not composed but what I fail in writing I reckon Darnell will tell you. He appeared surprised to see me look so well. I went to see him the other day. He had sent for me stating that he was sick. I tell you he looks bad. I expect he has a furlough by this time and gone home. He had a certificate from the board and I have no doubt he will get a furlough, I was very glad to think he was going home so you could see him and he could tell you all about me

I sent fifty dollars by him, which money I want you to use as you think best. If Father needs any you must let him have it as he is so good to us. I also sent you my little book that I prize so high, the *Pioneer Preacher*. He said that he would give it to you, I know that it will interest you very much as I prize it so high. It was given me by a friend and as soon as I read it I told him that I intended to send it to you. I have a book of the title of which is the *Hidden Path*. I wish I could send it to Sister Margaret and I will if I ever get a chance. So you may tell her that I have a present for her when the war ends and I hope that will be soon. I think that Darnell will get his transfer to my regiment by the time he comes back. If he does I will write to him where to come to. I think that we will stay here all winter if the enemy stops where they are. Darling, I received a letter from Bob McDonald the other day in which he stated that he had received a letter from Brother John from near Wilmington, N.C. It surprised me, I thought he was at Savannah. I don't know what is the reason he don't write me. He must know that I can't write to him when I don't know where he is but he has treated me so lightly that it don't bother me much. I have not received a letter except the one he sent in my clothes, in six months. So I don't expect a letter from him.

Molly, it is very cold to write to day and I can't write much. I shall look for a letter from you from now on until I get one. You must be sure to have Sister write often to me for the next two months, and, dear, you know how bad I will want to hear how you are. Give my love to all the friends and my thanks to them for their kindness towards you and Tommy. Oh, how bad I want to see him. His little curls would be so nice but no chance for me but no doubt it is for the best. Molly, I can't write. I try but forget what I am writing about and find myself sitting with my pen in hand and looking into the fire and not thinking what I was writing about. As I said awhile ago my mind is not composed. You must forgive me but I can't help it. Molly, when you write again say that you love me. I want to hear that word once more.

My dear, I put you in the hands of God and I pray that he may take care of you and bless you, and may his grace be bountifully showered upon you. So I can feel that you are safe and may he bless us both early with his love. So goodbye, my darling. Kiss my boy and my little Virginia and believe me ever to be to you true and faithful. So goodbye again.

Yours until Death

W. R. Stilwell

———

Stilwell finally learns that his Brother John is a musician in the 32nd Regiment Georgia Volunteer Infantry, currently stationed near Wilmington, North Carolina. John thinks his regiment might be sent to Virginia but WRS doubts this, "I would more think that troops would be sent from Virginia to North Carolina." We don't know where Stilwell was getting his intelligence on the strategic situation in the eastern Confederacy but he was right on the mark. In February, Longstreet with Hood's and Pickett's Divisions would be moved to southern Virginia and North Carolina.

Pine Grove Camp near Fredericksburg, Virginia, January 21, 1863

My dearest Molly,

This morning finds me with pencil in hand to write you a few lines which leaves me in the enjoyment of excellent health and spirits except I can not hear from you which gives me some uneasiness. I have not received any letter from you since way last month, the 23 I believe, and this makes the fourth letter I have wrote without getting any answers. I am not grumbling at you dear but think it is hard that Margaret or Pa or some of them don't write for you; when they know that I am uneasy about you and when you don't feel like writing I think they ought to write for you, but nevertheless, I will wait as patient as I can until I get one knowing that you will write when you can but darling a month is a long time to be without hearing from you. My ink is froze and I have to write with pencil and I am afraid that some of it will rub out.

Molly, I am still at my last occupation and well pleased with it. I received a letter from brother John [that he] wrote the twelfth of this month, it surprised me very much when I received it. He was sixteen miles northeast of Wilmington, N.C. in good health except a bad cold. I thought he was at Savannah until I got his letter. He thought that his regiment might be sent to Virginia but I think its very doubtful myself as they need all the troops they have there. I would more think that troops would be sent from Virginia to North Carolina than to think they would be sent to Virginia. I would be glad if he would belong to our regiment but let him have his way. I was very glad to hear the other day that William Darnell was gone home. I suppose he has got home before this and has given you some of the dots of a solder's life. I can almost see you as you question him about me and how I look. I have no doubt but that you would be surprised to know how well I do look. Darnell can give you any information you may desire to know about me. I sent you my book the *Pioneer Preacher*. I know you will be delighted with it. I also sent you fifty dollars by him which you must use in the way that you think best.

Molly, I am at a loss to know what to say about you being sick. I can only say do the best you can and trust in God. I believe he will take care of you if you will only trust in him for he said that they [who] will trust him shall be comforted. Molly, you know how I love you and how bad I want to be with you, but there is no chance if I was to get a furlough and come to see you, it of course would be great satisfaction but if I could and did so it might throw me out of a good position and I think that while I am in a good position that it will be best for you and me both in time to come and I know that you will think it best if you know that I was doing well for me to stay there as long as I can. I know it is bad for me to be away from you and you to be confined to a bed of sickness but let us trust in God and do the best we can. Molly, I would write more but the mail will leave directly so I must close and I will write again as soon as I get a letter from you. Oh how bad I want to see you and Tommy. Kiss him for me, write when you can. My love to all the friends. I remain yours until death always and may God bless and preserve you.

W. R. Stilwell

———

Stilwell is relieved as he finally receives a letter from Molly.

Camp near Fredericksburg, Virginia, January 28, 1863
My dear Molly:
Your long looked for letter came to hand last evening as you beg so pretty I shall not grumble at you. I believe that you would have done better if you could. I had got very uneasy about you and many nights while the moon was throwing its dim rays over the vast extending plans of Virginia found me walking all through the pine grove in which we are camped and as I would think of home and those dear ones at home often would the tear of loneliness fall from my eyes thinking that something was surely the matter but thanks unto God for his grace safe to you thus far and I pray God that he may continue his blessing with you to the end. My health was never better in my life you would hardly know me if you could see me, you would be surprised to see me look so well. Molly, I have to write with a pencil, I have no ink, thought I would get some as soon as I can. I have no news of importance to write, you need not be surprised to hear of another fight here at any time. It was thought the other day that the enemy was going to cross the river again and the plan was if the Yankees did try to cross that a house was to be set on fire at a certain place. So the other night just before day while the wind and rain was blowing very hard, in fact it was one of those cold winter nights, orders had been given to cook three days rations all ready, just waiting for the signal cannon to be fired and this house caught on fire near the one that was to be set on fire in the event that they want to cross and General McLaws give orders to fire the

signal guns which was done when the poor soldiers had to rise out of their warm beds, put on their vestments and prepare to meet Yanks in a few minutes.[13] All was ready and we formed in a line of battle and started toward the battlefield. The roads was from ankle to knee deep in mud, the cannon booming. All thought that the deadly conflict had commenced when a courier arrived and informed them that it was all a mistake, so they right about faced and marched back to their camps all satisfied that no battles was to be fought. The question may present itself to you and what was Billie doing all this time? I can tell you what he was doing, he was lying in his tent warm and comfortable listening at the old drums as they beat the long roll and hearing them hollow, "Fall in, fall in." Well did he know that he did not have to fall in and besides that, he has heard so many cannons that it don't alarm him no more than an old popgun. So all the excitement wore off and nobody hurt yet. I hear some firing this morning but don't know what it is for, but don't suppose there is any fight up. I think we will have peace by the fourth of July though it is all guesswork but I hope we will, but if we don't—fight on.

Molly, I have got back and think I will write a little more. Molly, I have just read of the peace meeting held in New York.[14] I think it is a very good symptom. I think we will have peace in four or five months but God only knows. I shall wait his time without murmuring. Molly, it hurts me to think of being so far from you and you in such a condition, but Molly, I never lie down to rest of a night without asking God to protect you and Tommy and I believe he will take care of you, only put your trust in him and he will be sure to take care of you. I would be very glad to come home and stay while you are sick but there is no chance and besides nothing

[13] Lafayette McLaws had been a lieutenant general and division commander in Longstreet's corps since 23 May 1862. He was born in Augusta GA and was a graduate of West Point, class of 1842, married to a niece of former president Zachary Taylor. Warner, *Generals in Gray*, 204.

[14] While there was much discontent in the North about the course of the war, the editor knows of no significant peace activity in New York at this time. This was a case of over-optimism by WRS.

could afford me more pleasure than meeting you but I don't never want to part with you any more. I can see the tears flowing down your eyes just as plain now as I could the day I left and God forbid that I ever should have to part with you again. Only live right and God will make it all work out for our good. I am trying to keep my garments unspotted from the world. I want to live so that when I fall either [on] the battlefield or not, all will be well.

My duties are confined strictly to camp and as long as I hold my present position I will not be away from camp. I won't have to go on picket nor do none of the duties of the feetuge [?].

My dear, don't you be uneasy about me, if you can get along yourself I will be very glad. Molly, if you need money very bad let me know and if I don't get no chance to send it by hand I will send you as much as ten dollars by mail anyhow. I must close. I am yours as ever until death.

W. R. Stillwell

――――

Now in winter quarters, with many of the officers on furlough, Stilwell is temporarily living in a general's tent. The outlook for the Confederacy is now so good that he is beginning to think of what he will do post-war. Evidently he has no intention of returning to Louisiana.

Camp near Fredericksburg, Virginia, February 1, AD 1863
My dear Molly:
On this beautiful Sabbath morning I seat myself to write you a few lines. I have been very unwell for several days with cold. I think I have the worst cold that I ever had in my life though I am still on duty and hope I will get well in a few days. I think the weather being so bad is what caused me to take cold. We had a powerful snow about a week ago and my duties required me to be exposed a good deal. It was so deep that my coattail would drag on the snow when I would walk in it. It is not all gone yet but we have beautiful weather now and it will all be gone in a few days.

I am sitting at General Benning's desk while I write and in his tent. General Semmes has been gone home over a month and General Benning came in his place and he got a furlough and started home this morning, to be gone one month and he left all his things in our care with the privilege of occupying his tent with a good stove so I will have a good time for some time to come.[15]

The weather has been so bad that there will not be likely to be any fighting here soon. In fact I don't know whether there ever will be any more fighting here or elsewhere. Molly, I think that the war is going to close in a short time, at least by the fourth of July, and on, what a happy day it would be when husbands, brothers and fathers would return to greet their long absent families. On roll, on roll, sweet moments, roll on and bring me to my home but what would home be without you to bedeck and beautify it. Oh home, name ever dear to me, when shall my labors have an end and I my Molly see? And there is my boy, my baby boy, darling ever dear to me. When shall my absence have an end and I my baby—baby see? My dear Molly, you must forgive the poet this morning for you know when the mind of a poet gets full it's obliged to run over. So it is with me. When I get building castles about getting home I get almost wild but there is one thing that pains me very much and that is that I can not be at home with you while you are sick but I feel that God will take care of you for I have placed you in his hands and I feel that you are safe though it' s very painful to know that you have to suffer and I cannot be there to soothe your pain. While I know that no one else can comfort you like myself, yet I know that you will receive all the attention that kind friends can bestow and while this may be the last letter that you will get from me before

---

[15] Henry Lewis Benning, "Old Rock" had been promoted to brigadier general as of 17 January 1863. He was evidently at this time acting as a temporary replacement for General Semmes before getting his own brigade in Hood's division. Now 52, Benning had been a Columbus GA lawyer, statesman, and planter. He was active in pre-war politics and had voted for secession at the 1861 convention. In 1860, he had a 35-year-old wife and six children, the youngest of which was four. Very wealthy, he owned 90 slaves. After the war, he resumed his law practice in Columbus. After World War I, the post on which the new infantry school was established would be named in his honor—"Fort Benning."

you are sick, know ye therefore that my daily prayer is that you may be restored to good health again. Therefore, I commend you to God and to his grace. Trust thou in God and all things shall work for our good. Wait on the Lord, wait I say on the Lord and he will bring it to past. My dear Molly I have many things to tell you. I don't think you will ever have to complain any more at the silence of my tongue. As some of the boys said when we were at Griffin that they wanted something to tell their grandchildren.[16] I think I have got enough of dots to spare a few to my children's children but as I can not write them as I can tell them, I will wait with the hope that peace will soon come and I can lean back in the corner and tell you of things past, present and things to come. I can almost in my imagination see your large blue eyes as you listen to my story. I can tell you of the terrible battle of Malvern Hill and the battle of South Mountain, of Sharpsburg and last of all, though not least, of the great battle of Fredericksburg. I can tell you of the dead bodies that lay on the plains of Manassas.

Molly, if the war does close soon you must have some nice place selected for our future home. I think of returning to my trade and would like for you to pick out some nice little village wherein we may dwell though you need not commence business until I come but only make ready.[17] I have gained a great deal of useful knowledge about my business since I have been in the war so if you can think of any place where you would like to live let me know and I will put it on the list of places that I think of looking at.

You stated in your last letter that Tom could or was learning his letters. Perhaps he can write Pa a letter by this time so I would like to get one from him but in the letter that I wrote in answer to that one, I said that you did not say whether he could say his prayers. Now if he is old enough to learn his letters he is old enough to learn his prayers and I exhort you therefore that first of all things prayers and supplications be made. That should be first.

---

[16]At the camp of instruction.
[17]Harness making.

Molly, you see what a large letter I have written to you. Behold I, W. R. Stilwell, have written it with mine own hand. I exhort you therefore that you endure all things as a good soldier of Jesus Christ ever looking forward unto the coming of our lord Jesus Christ and now may God who at Sunday times spoke unto us by his prophets but who has in these latter days spoken unto us through his Son, keep you unspotted from the world. I write no new commandment unto you but an old commandment, that we love one another. My love to all inquiring friends. Write when you feel able. Kiss my baby boy all over and over and believe me ever to be your affectionate true and loving good, little, and best faithful, devoted, and unchangeable old Billy.

P.S. My last letter I directed to Unionville, Monroe County and will send this also. Goodbye my dear.[18]

W. R. Stilwell

———

Stilwell writes Molly a long letter to "pass off the time." Winter quarters were very boring. He concentrates on the risk of Molly's dying during childbirth. The risk was significant and people in those days lived with untimely death and were not reticent about talking about the possibility. It was a culture very different from today's where the discussion of the possibility of a healthy person's dying is a taboo subject.

Camp near Fredericksburg, Virginia, February 10, 1863
My dear Molly:
Your kind letter of the 27 January has been received and you may be sure that I was very glad to hear from you once more, but oh, how shall I write tonight when I remember that tomorrow all that I hold sacred, yea, all that I have on this earth may be taken

---

[18]Unionville was in northern Monroe County just south of Butts. It was one of those rural villages once big enough for a post office but which now has completely disappeared. Knowing the location does assist in locating Molly's abode at William Foster's farm as being in extreme southwest Butts County. The spot where Unionville once existed is now in Lamar County.

away from me. Oh God, deliver me from having the pain of mourning for the one that I love with love stronger than death. Molly, I hope you will forgive me and I know you will, but when I remember the condition that you are in and through what affliction you have to pass, it makes my heart ache. Oh God, shall her whom I love so dearly be taken away from me without ever these eyes being allowed the privilege of beholding her again. God forbid, God forbid. Molly I went off this evening to pray for your safety and may God grant to deliver you and restore you to health, but Molly when I begin to weep and lament your condition it seems to me that God says my grace is sufficient for thee. If it was not for the faith I have in God's goodness, I could not stand it.

Molly when I wrote to you last I was not well, was suffering from a bad cold but I have got well and am in the enjoyment of good health again. I was very glad that Darnell had got home safe but sorry that his health was not better. I was afraid that his health was gone for a long time, if not forever and I fear he will never have good health again. I want him to stay at home until he gets well. I would stay just as long as I could get my furlough extended. I don't think his transfer has been completed nor I don't think it will be until he comes back. I was glad to hear that you did not need any money. To be sure you are a very saving person. You are a wife worthy of King William and not this little old Billy that has the blame but nevertheless I am so jealous that I would not be willing to give you up to him. Yes you are mine and though I know I am unworthy of such a woman, I never could give you up.

To all my friends I would say that I may not live through this war but I would say this much; that if the US should, as it seems they are determined to send negroes to fight the South, just as sure as they ever do, I intend to make wool fly if I ever get a chance. Their congress has just passed the Negro bill and I intend to get me enough of negroes to settle me a plantation down in Dixey. Aha! Poor Yankee who is afraid to face the music themselves, they think they can send the poor nigger down south to get killed. I think they are nearly played out when they want to fight the South with Negroes.

Molly, I think the war will close in five or six months though I think that we will have very hard fighting to do before that time. I don't know, I may never live to see the end of it but where is the man that deserves the name of a man that would not fight a nation who would try to raise insurrection among women and children. But God will never bless such a nation, I know he will not, but let us as a people worship God and pray him to bless us and give us peace. Oh, what a happy day it seems to me that it will be, somewhat like the morning of the resurrection for many shall come from the east and the west and so many meeting with their friends it will be most like that great morning. Oh, may it soon come and let me get home to see my Molly and my Tommy and I don't know what, I reckon my Virginia [unborn child]. You said that you thought I never would want to hear of Virginia [the state] again. If I ever get home, if I could live to be grandfather to Methuselah, I could never forget Virginia. Molly, I was in hopes when I saw the paper that you sent me in your letter that you had sent a list of the circuit preachers. I want you to write me who is on the Butts and McDonough circuit. I want you to send me John W. Speer's post office.[19] I have forgot it and I want to write to him and can't until you send me his post office. I have forgot what I once knew but you.

Dear Molly, I commenced writing to you last night but did not finish. I thought I would finish tonight. I am so uneasy about you that when I go to write I can't think of any thing but you and of course I can't write much of a letter when I am thinking of something a thousand miles from my pen. I do hope that I will get a letter soon informing me of your welfare. Oh how can I wait until I can get a letter from you but I know that you will have them to write as soon as you can. Oh, shall I not have a letter from my Molly any more in a long time? Oh God, save me from the sorrow that dwells in my heart. I can't stand to be absent from you when

---

[19] John W. Speer had some connection with local Methodism. Whether he was a blood relation is not known. There is a John Speer, age 43, with wife Louise, 36, and three children, the youngest age one living in Bear Creek (now Hampton) in the 1860 census of Henry County.

you are to be sick. Molly, I thought I had a heart like a man but I confess that I am nearly ready to give up. Oh, I would give anything to hear from you tonight The more I study about you the worse out of heart I get. I had studied about it until I thought I could stand it pretty well but when the time has come, I find that I have not got the firmness that I thought I had but God grant to save you for if I lost my Molly I am undone forever.

Molly, Abraham Farrar started home on a furlough for twenty-nine days. Two men from a company is allowed a furlough at a time now and one officer but there was no chance for me. James Speer is still under guard for not going in the fight at Fredericksburg. He will be court marshaled. We are looking for Captain Brown every day. I want to see him very bad. He has had a good time. I hope he will have better health hereafter. I got a letter from Uncle [Richard] Everitt. He says he has been mustered into service and detailed to make government work. Molly, you said that you wanted Uncle William [Foster] to take that money that I sent you and keep it for you. If you do not need it nor Father don't, why you can make any arrangement that you wish to make but if you need it, I want you to use it. Molly, I have not received any letter from Uncle Robert Everitt and I don't suppose that sister Meg [Martha Ann Jane Ragland] ever got the letter that I wrote to her. I want to write to them again just as soon as you write me her post office. You must send me something good by Darnell if he ever comes back. I can get a fellow to go to his regiment most any time. I have not written to him yet. I have been waiting to hear from his transfer but can hear nothing and will write in a few days, maybe tomorrow. Now Molly, I must close. I have tried to write a long letter to pass off the time but I believe it is the poorest letter that I ever wrote in my life but I know that you will forgive me as you know under what circumstances I wrote it. Give my love to Uncle William and all of his family and tell Pa and Margaret to write often until you get so you can write. If they don't I don't know when I will forgive them. Oh, [that] my baby should be an orphan. I fear I can never live to get home. While I love him as dearly as I could do I confess that if my Molly dies I have little hope of ever getting home and now may the God of love and mercy keep you and sustain you, Molly. I shall pray for your delivery. So goodbye, goodbye, my darling. I am yours as ever until death.

William R. Stilwell

———

Another long and newsy letter, mostly about homefolks. The winter around Fredericksburg has been especially snowy and the principal recreation activity has been snowball fights.

Fredericksburg Virginia, February 17, 1863
My dear and affectionate wife:
Your letter of the 12th was received today and oh how glad I was to get it! It came and to my surprise you were still up. I thought that you would have been confined before this but it seems that you hold up very well and now I am almost as uneasy about you as I was before for I know that you have to be sick yet and although you say for me not to be uneasy, yet I cannot help it. You know that I cannot rest easy when I know that my Molly is sick. You said for me not to take on so. Why if I was to even express one half that I think I would not think of trying to write my feelings. I don't say much but you must forgive me for you know that out of the abundance of the heart the mouth speaketh. The reason that I said I wanted you to say that you loved me, I thought it would sound like it used to but I find that that loving voice cannot be written on paper. Those loving eyes which once met mine cannot make the expression on paper.

I was very glad to get Brother John Speer's[20] letter. I was very glad to hear from him and all the rest. I shall write to him in a few days. I was glad to hear that Sister [Martha Ann Jane Ragland] was there and doing so well and [you] all there together. Molly, when we lay down last night it was clear as crystal and warm and pleasant but when we rose this morning the ground was covered with snow and has been snowing all day. It is about six or eight inches deep

---

[20] "Brother" has a religious connotation.

and I don't know how deep it will be before morning. Snow, snow, I am tired of snow. There has been an unusual amount this winter. It would divert you to be here and see the boys throw snowballs. I have seen one regiment form in line of battle against the others and some times their whole brigade forms and it looks like the sky and the whole element was made of snow and a hole had broken through the middle and it is no rare thing to see a captain or colonel with his hat knocked off and covered in snow. General Longstreet and his adjutant took [chose] regiments the other day and had a fight with snowballs but the general charged him and took them prisoners.[21] As for my part, I generally command instead of fighting. Molly, I think that it is a good thing about changing your post office. I think you will get them much sooner than you did at Griffin and I am in hopes you can write to me when you get able at least once a week. It did me a heap of good to hear about Tommy's pockets. Molly, I can't think how he looks. I have forgot most all about him but if I never see him again I know he will make a man.

Molly, I am glad that Uncle Richard [Everitt] is going to get the money on that note of Maxwell's.[22] I don't hardly know what to say about you paying what I owe in McDonough. I know it is not much but something might happen that you or me might need it and as they don't need it, I think that you had better not do it.[23] We get very little rations now, we only get a quarter of a pound of bacon per day and I have to buy a good deal of my rations and can not save much money unless we get more to eat and I think that [you] had better keep what money you have. I have not got any letter from Brother John since my last to you. I suppose he is in N.C. yet. I am still looking for a letter from him. I received a letter from Bob McDonald the other day and also from uncle John [Stilwell]. I sent

---

[21] James (Old Pete) Longstreet was the senior lieutenant general of the Confederate army and commander of the 1st Corps of the Army of Northern Virginia.

[22] James A. Maxwell was clerk of the Henry county superior court and was a resident of McDonough. He was 28 in 1860 with wife Molly (married 1858), 29, and one child less than a year old. His position exempted him from conscription and he was not in service.

[23] This comment is very illustrative of the nonchalant attitude toward debt in the antebellum South.

Uncle John a map of the line of battle here of my own drawing. He was very well pleased with it and wants me to get him a trophy on the next battlefield for him to keep. He wants me to continue to write to him, He seems to be interested in my welfare and says that he is proud of his two nephews John and me.

I think that we will have to march very soon as part of our army is already gone. Oh what a hard time we would have if we have to move in this snow. I don't know where we will have to go to, some think we will go to North or South Carolina, but I don't think we will. A great many think that we will have peace in a short time but I don't think we will before fourth July. Oh, God that we could have peace, oh that the people would humble themselves under the hand of God and then it would close. As for me, I hope to be able for the war to close or [be] ready for it to last a long time. I want to be ready for life or death. Oh, God grant that we may all live for heaven and enjoy the blessings of God. Molly, you said you wanted to see me to see how I looked because I was so fat. I only weighed one hundred and thirty-five about a month ago. I am a good-looking man now, ha, ha. I am very popular among the ladies up here. I dress very neat, that is keep my clothes clean and decent and that is one thing that is not generally done here. Molly, I must close for tonight.

Morning—I am well this morning. The ground is covered deep with snow. I feel this morning like I would give most anything to hear from you but I will have to wait and trust in God for to protect you. I know that you will have all the attention that can be given to you or anybody else. I can not find out about William Darnell's transfer but don't think he will get it until he gets back. I wrote to him the other day. I wrote a letter to Uncle [William Foster] and Aunt Penelope [enclosed] in a letter to you not long since but don't know whether you got it or not. I don't know how to close my letter but will have to do so. Be sure to have them to write soon and often. I am your true and devoted Billie.

W. R. Stilwell

Stilwell thinks they are going to move toward Richmond. He is exceedingly tired of snow and the winter quarter's drill. But he is very wrong about the move toward Richmond. He underestimates considerably the aggressiveness and tenacity of General Lee. The move toward Richmond will not take place for another 15 months.

Fredericksburg, Virginia, February 22nd, 1863

My dear Molly:

I wrote you a letter not many days ago but owing to the fact that we are going to move I thought I would write to you and inform you of the fact so that if you did not get a letter from me for some time you would not be uneasy though I think that I will be able to write from the fact that we will be very likely to stay a few days at Richmond. My health is as good as could ask. Thank God I am blessed with good health. God has been very good to me. I am very sorry about the march as I am very uneasy to hear from you and if I don't get a letter from you before I start I will not be likely to hear from you until I get to Richmond though you must write and if I don't get it there will not be much expense but you must continue to write to Richmond until further orders. When you write hereafter direct your letter thus: William R. Stilwell, Company F, 53 Georgia Regiment, McLaws Division. By doing so it will follow me anywhere I go. It isn't necessary to put it in care of Captain Brown, just so you put Company F, 53 Ga. Regiment. By putting McLaws' division it can't be lost and will be sent to me anywhere. I am greatly in hopes that I will get a letter from you today.

We have had more snow, snow. I am as tired of snow and mud and long to see the beautiful spring and summer and if we can't have peace I want to hear the cannon roar again. One gets so tired lying here in camps and never hearing anything but the same old thing, "Fall in to roll call," "Prepare for inspection," "Form in third relief" and the old drum that is most always rattling and it makes one want to get off into the desert of Arabia where they never would hear the roar of camps any more. But the soldier always looks forward to the time (alas few of them ever see it) when they will get home to where the laurels that they have so nobly won through danger and hardships not a few. Oh Molly, how the soldiers thinks every sun that rises he knows that he is one day nearer his home or his grave. Oh peace, one of the greatest blessings of this world.

But Molly, I must soon close as the mail will soon leave and besides I have written you and Mag [Margaret] a long letter. I have no word from Brother John. I am in hopes that our army will be sent [to] where he is and I may get to see him. Molly I want to know if you have ever got any thing from the county and if you have not, why? You are as much entitled to it as anybody and if I have friends that will help us in this time of distress that is no reason why you should not get your dues. Tell Father I want him to attend to it. Give my love and respect to all Uncle William's family and all the friends and may God bless us all is the prayer of your Billie. Kiss my baby and, if so be, my babies. Yours forever and ever.

William R. Stilwell

———

This letter is largely a recap of items covered in previous communications. The snow is still around and so is Molly's pregnancy.

Camp near Fredericksburg, February 26, 1863
My dear Molly:
Your kind letter of the 20th was received today. Thus you will see that it came in five days as this letter is written the night of the 25 and dated 26. I confess that I was surprised to find that you were still up. I don't want you to be fooling me any longer. I want the thing brought to a close and if you don't stop it I shall come to the conclusion that you have given it out, ha ha. I am just as uneasy now as I was before I got your letter for I know that you have to be sick yet but your letter was very satisfactory. I think it was the best letter that I have ever received from you. I received Brother John Speer's letter but have not written to him yet but will in a short time, if I have time.

I wrote you a letter the other day stating that we would leave for Richmond in a few days but we have not left yet as you will see and it is not known when we will go [or] whether ever or not. If it don't quit snowing we never will leave. I never was as tired of anything in my life. Snow, snow. When you lie down there is snow and when you rise up there is snow. The snow is now from twelve to fifteen inches deep which fell on the 23rd and will be here for days to come and no one can go about to attend to his business without being snow balled. Well even regiment against regiment and through snow from morning until night. I have seen captains and colonels covered up in snow.

You wanted to know what position I had now, I have written to you but I suppose that you have not got it. I am courier for Major Davis, brigade quartermaster. My business is to carry orders to the regimental quartermasters and to assist in giving out clothing and shoes, etc. etc., to the brigade. I don't have any gun. My position is a very easy one and also an honorable one. I have a horse to ride whenever I want to and I take a ride out most every day. Thus you will see that I am doing very well so you need not be uneasy about me and leave that for me.

I don't know what made Darnell think that those books were for Brother John. I sent them both to you but told him that I was not so particular about the large one but The *Pioneer Preacher* I wanted him to be certain to take to you and it is that one that I suppose you have read. It is a great book.

I have not heard a word from Brother. I wrote about him. Don't know where he is. I have written to him but received no answer. If our army leaves here I think they will go between Richmond and Petersburg. At least two divisions that have left our army have gone there.[24] I would be very glad of the change if it was not for the weather. I will close this letter as I wish to write one in it for private consideration. You must give uncle and aunt and granma my best respects and tell them that I want to see them very bad and tell

---

[24] Longstreet, with two of his divisions, but not including McLaws', moved to operations in southeast Virginia and eastern North Carolina. The purpose was primarily two-fold; one to forage for food in a relatively untouched region and secondly to guard Richmond and Petersburg from Union movements up the peninsular.

Pa that I want to take enough of prisoners to settle a plantation in the west. John Parker and Mr. Lemmonds are both well. Give my love to all my friends for their love to you. Tell them all to write to me.

W. R. Stilwell

[No private letter exists in the collection]

Stilwell writes a newsy letter to his Uncle John Stilwell. He is still worried about his brother John. There are stirrings of the religious revival that would be so strong later. Regular prayer meetings are being instituted.

Camp near Fredericksburg, Virginia, February 27, 1863

Mr. John Stilwell:

Dear Uncle,

I received your kind letter that you sent by Captain Brown and I need not say that I was grateful to get it. Yours found me in the enjoyment of good health and I am still enjoying the same blessing. All is quiet here at present although we were smartly surprised on the morning of the 23rd. When we retired the night before it was very warm and pleasant. The next morning the snow was knee deep. About eight o'clock the cannon commenced roaring and all along the lines huge instruments of death could be heard. All eyes and ears were open and all were expecting to hear the ever memorable word, "Fall in, fall in," We at headquarters were looking for a courier from General McLaws but none came. You can imagine with what horror the thought struck us of being pulled out into the snow to fight and perhaps to get wounded but finally we were informed that it was the day on which General George Washington made his entrance into this sin smitten world and was being celebrated by the Yankees. Strange to think that they would celebrate the birthday of the father of rebellion. Oh, what is man that thou art mindful of him. They are all gone a stray, there is none that doeth good, no not one. God have mercy on Adams' race. Oh, for a Clay or Webster.[25]

I am very uneasy about Brother John. I have not had a word from him in a long time. From what I can learn I think that he is gone to Savannah. We are expecting to march every day. I think we will go between Richmond and Petersburg. At least part of our army is gone there.

You spoke about my officers. Gen. Semmes and most of his staff have gone and have been for two months. Gen. Benning is in command of the brigade. Major Davis and my friend Mr. Cleveland are still here.[26] Mr. Cleveland is a young preacher. We commence a prayer meeting next Sabbath evening, to be continued twice a week thereafter. I am still trying by the grace of God to live right and do my duty. David Laney[27] has not been heard from in a long time. It is supposed he is dead.

Uncle, I would write you more but the mail leaves in a short time. Please give my love to all the friends and kiss the babies for me. Oh that God may grant us to all meet again and if not on earth may we meet in heaven. Oh, that I could see my wife and little boy but the ways of God are past finding out. Write me soon and often and believe me ever to be your affectionate nephew.

W. R. Stilwell

----

[25] Henry Clay and Daniel Webster were the statesmen primarily responsible for the compromises necessary in the early 1800s to keep peace between slave and free states.

[26] Mr. Cleveland has not been identified. He does not appear on army rolls and was probably a volunteer chaplain.

[27] David Laney, a private in Company F, had been sent from Winder Hospital in Richmond to the "tent for smallpox patients" and died there 30 November 1862. In 1860 David was a merchant and owned one slave. He was age 27 and had a wife Martha E., age 20, and two small children. They lived adjacent to David's father, John Laney, a farmer with 10 slaves.

The weather is improving, ball games are being organized. The officers are returning from furlough. Stilwell complains about the quality and quantity of the meat ration.

Fredericksburg, Virginia, March 4, 1863

Dear Molly:

I avail myself of the present opportunity of writing you a few lines which will inform you that I am in good health except, while talking again of town ball[28] the other day, I fell down and mashed my nose and upper lip some, but it will be well in a few days more. We have some very interesting games of ball which I think is an advantage to health as it gives exercise of the body and employs the mind.

Gen. Semmes returned last evening from an absence of more than two months. I was very glad to see old Major Paul J. Semmes and also my friend Dol Cody, one of his aides-de-camp.[29]

Dear Molly, we are still lying still and waiting for the enemy to advance I suppose and if they ever are going to fight here I would be glad if they would do so. I want to whip or be whipped this year, and I have no doubt but what we will whip them here if they ever give us the chance. We have sent off all of our baggage that is heavy to Richmond preparatory to a lively campaign, and if the war lasts I hope we will be in a few months in front of Washington but that is only an opinion of my own, I suppose. Major Jeff says that this is the last year of the war and of course he thinks we will whip them.[30] I hope so.

Molly, this is paper that you sent me with my clothes last winter, and it is so mashed that I can hardly write on it but will try

---

[28] Town ball was an early version of baseball. In town ball, a runner was put out by hitting him with the ball.

[29] Dol Cody was a lieutenant and volunteer aide-de-camp to General Semmes. He does not appear on any army rolls. We know of his existence by three mentions of his valor in Semmes' official reports; once for Malvern Hill *O.R.*, 11/2:721, once for Sharpsburg *OR*, 1:876), and also for Chancellorsville *OR*, 35/1:836. In two of the instances, he was indexed as B. H. Cody. No further identification of Cody has been made.

[30] Major Jeff–Probably a reference to Major John Davis.

and write it so that you can read it for it costs me about twenty five cents to send off a letter. Paper very common, small size is worth four dollars a quire. Envelopes are worth from one dollar to one fifty a bunch.

Molly, I wrote to you some time ago that I had fifty dollars to send home but unless you need it I think I had better keep it at least for a while as we may be like we were last summer and not draw any money, and besides that I must have something to eat if I do buy it myself. I know you won't think hard of me for spending some money for such things as I need and you know me well enough to know that I won't spend it foolishly. Just think, I draw one pound and a half of meat to last me six days—take it as it comes, bone and all. Well, if it is lean I can eat it up in two days, if it is old fat bacon, you remember I can't eat it at all. Well that is it, you can do without or eat that or buy something that you can eat and if you undertake to buy it, will cost so much that it will soon take all you get. Just think, beef sausage is worth $1.50 cts lb. Sweet potatoes are 50 cts a lb. Cowpeas are 75 cts a quart. Our last weeks rations of meat gave out in a few days and some of the boys in my mess said that they were going to draw rations on a special requisition. I did not know what they meant nor didn't want to know so at night the commissary being close to our quarters some of them went down and drew about a gal of the best kind of syrup. I did not know anything about it. I did not want to know but one thing. I know I made syrup and biscuit get up and dust, I tell you it was good, but enough said about that.

I sent you a paper day before yesterday with General McLaws' picture which I hope you will get. Dear Molly, since I commenced writing I have heard cannon firing very plain but don't know what it means. I would not be surprised at any time if we had a general engagement but if I hear anything from it today I will write more tonight about it as I can't send this off until tomorrow. If I don't hear any thing I shall send it off as it is as I am looking for a letter from you and will answer it as soon as I get it. Molly, give my love to all the friends and relations. Kiss the children three times apiece for me. Write once a week. I shall not write a long letter this time.

That firing got worse and worse let 'em come, let 'em come. Old Lee is ready for them. If there is any news, [I] will write more tonight. (if [not,] I will not). So a goodbye for this time. Remember, my Dear, I am as ever your affectionate husband as ever until death.

William Ross Stilwell,

I love you stronger than death.

Conditions remain quiet according to the following letter. Stilwell complains that no one in his family is writing to him enough. Stilwell continues to gain weight, despite all his complaints about the food.

[Date and place are missing on the following letter. The context places it in March 1863]

Dear Molly:

Again in my little cottage after all have lain down to sleep and are dead to the cares and toils of this life and are perhaps having pleasant dreams of loved ones far, far away, here I sit all alone writing to my Molly. Oh, who can tell the worth of pen, ink and paper. It is the telegraph which carries the prayers, pleasures and sorrows from an absent husband to an affectionate wife who dwells in distant lands, but as you have no doubt thought of its value I had better not devote my time in speaking of it. I have not received William Darnell's letter but hope I will in a few days. My advice to him is to stay at home as long as he can get his furlough extended or until he gets well. I have never received any answer from Brother yet. I don't suppose he ever got my letter so I will write to him in a few days again. I have written to John [Stilwell], W.S.[?], and T.S.S. [Thomas Sanford Speer], but have not had time to get an answer. I have not received a letter from R.B.E. [Robert Everitt]. I don't know what can be the reason that Uncle William [Foster] and Aunt P.B. [Penelope] don't write to me. I have written them several times and have never got an answer. Tell them that they must tote fair or Brownlow will get after them with a sharp stick, and they had as well have anybody else after them for I will be certain to dust their old clothes, and as for Father, a hint had better be taken.

All other big men are writing letters in this great crisis, but he is as mute as if it was not expected that Joe Brown would be our next president.

There is no news of late here. It is nothing but the calm that always precedes the storm, and we have nothing to revive our dropping spirits but the shrill March winds which blow some times as if they were mad and had no other way to get revenge. I am looking forward to spring when the beautiful vales of Virginia will be covered with flowers. You know that I am a great man for flowers anyhow but, alas for me, I know that every bunch I visit will have one flower gone which would make all the rest more beautiful if it was there. Yes, one flower and a little bud or two, but it is not worth while for me to write love letters now. I believe we are or have been married but I almost forget it some times and I feel some times like writing a little now. I hope that the war will close this summer and let me get home. Why, I had better court you a little anyhow as I don't intend to marry in this country, but I have given you as much nonsense as is necessary at present. Buck [William A] Lemmonds is going to Richmond with his wagon. I do not know what for nor how long he will stay. John Parker was well the last time I saw him. Mr. Martin Rumels is back to the regiment at last.[31] He appears very friendly but no good. Molly, it's getting late and as we will have a heap of work to do tomorrow I had better begin to wind up as it generally takes one page for me to finish on. Oh, I like to have forgot—I weighed yesterday, guess how much? I weigh 140 lbs. I tell you what I'm some man now, and when I get home just add six fried chickens, one doz. eggs too, 1 lb ham, 2 lb. butter, 1 gallon buttermilk, 5 lbs. corn light bread, a few cakes, pies, custards and other little tricks and a big kiss from my Molly and I think I'll go to two hundred (ha, ha) (and that boss who wouldn't be a soldier fighting on half rations for southern independence). Give my best, no not best, for that is yours, but next best love to all our friends and Uncle, Aunt, Granma, Pa, Ma, lock,

---

[31] Mr. Martin Rumels can not be found on army rolls and thus he remains unidentified.

stock and barrel. Never stop writing till I tell you to march or no march. Kiss my boy, you, my boys, and may heaven bless you all. Goodbye.

William R. Stilwell

―――――

Stilwell equivocates about the South's chances of ending the war successfully. His sense of humor is evident as he recites a typical incident of camp life.

Camp near Fredericksburg, March 7, 1863
My dear Molly:
I received your kind letter of 27th. Again I must confess my surprise at hearing that you were well. How long will you keep me on suspense but so must it be. I am very well this evening except I have the bowel complaint caused, I think, by eating syrup made out of sugar, we draw a heap of sugar now and boil it which makes a good syrup. We get plenty to eat now, that is sugar, meat and flour.

I don't think we will move soon as the Yankees are concentrating their forces here again. I expect the spring campaign will commence soon as I have been expecting for sometime to hear the cannon roar again but have not heard it yet. We have just heard of General Van Dorn's[32] success in Tennessee.[33] Thank God for victory, for if God don't help us we are gone sure and certain. Molly, God only knows when this war will close. I have [believed] all the time that it would close soon but I am out of heart now about

―――――――――――――――――――――

[32] A graduate of West Point, class of 1842, Major General Earl Van Dorn held a number of Confederate commands in both the eastern and western armies, but mostly in the west. At the time of Spring Hill, (see below) he was cavalry commander of middle and west Tennessee. On 7 May 1863, he would be shot and killed by a jealous husband. Warner, *Generals in Gray*, 314.

[33] On 4 and 5 March, a strong Federal force of one infantry and one cavalry brigade was sent from Franklin to reconnoiter toward Columbia. At Spring Hill they were surrounded by Van Dorn with two cavalry divisions (one commanded by Forrest). The federal cavalry escaped but the infantry and a battery of artillery was captured. *Civil War Day by Day*, 326.

its closing for a long time, I fear that it will last two years longer until Lincoln's time is out and I think we might just as well prepare our minds for it. I am not one that thinks that the Yankees will whip us but if the end of the war depends on our whipping them it will take a long time. If we don't have peace by the fourth of July which has been my belief all the time, why I think that it will be a long time, but if we can have one more big fight and whip them like we did here I think that it will settle the war but in the meantime if they whip us it will prolong the war. I think that the end of the war depends on the next long battle that is fought.

We will move our camp tomorrow about a mile and a half so that we can get wood. I hate to leave my chimney but can soon build another. You would be surprised to know how comfortable a place I have to live in, a white house and good fireplace and a box chunk on the ground which are all used for seats. Here we all take our seats, some reading, some writing, some talking, some sitting up sleeping and some thinking of home and friends, some of wife and babies. Finally Mr. A. begins to tell where he heard the first boom and how bad it scared him and Mr. B, not to be out done, tells what dangers he had passed through. Mr. C tells his tale, finally Mr. E speaks as if he just rose from sleep and says that he thinks he is the man that ought to have furlough, F can't see why he has any better reason for a furlough, that he has a family and he got a letter today stating that if he did not come home he would never see them anymore. E asked for the letter & F burnt it. E. "You never got it." F. "I did," "You didn't," "I did"—both mad and rise. Corporal, "Stop that boys or I'll report you to the general." G who has been mute all the time says, "Well boys, you both must be fools, neither can get a furlough in six months and now you are about to fight about it. F and G both speak saying, "You need not say anything, you want a furlough as bad as I do." H commences singing "Home Sweet Home" when all the crowd joins in and the whole woods rebounds with the music. Thus I have described camp life, all of which is true and a heap more I could tell you of many such things but this will do for this time, I will have to stop a while to perform some duty.

[Unsigned]

———

Molly still hasn't delivered and Stilwell is naturally worried and in a pensive mood. The religious revival continues as WRS leads prayer meetings The South has a new hero in John Mosby.

Camp near Fredericksburg, Virginia, March 15, 1863
My dear Molly:
For the last week every day I have watched the mail and expecting every day to get good or bad news but Sabbath morning has come and me without any information. I know not whether I have a Molly or not. I can't help but think some of you have written to me and it has got misplaced but in the event that they have not they may expect some sharp words. Of course I did not expect you to write but there are plenty more without you and if they have not, I shall think that I have been treated badly and will make them think so before I am done with them. My health, dear Molly, is very good and I am doing well in every respect but [in my] mind and that will not be any better until I hear from you. Oh, how can I wait longer? Surely the world is turned against me. How long, oh, how long shall the deep waters run over me? So must it be, I have been trying to rest contented but how can a man rest easy under such circumstances, but I hope that the cloud that hangs over me will break with blessing and, with a prayer that all may be well with you and ours. I leave the subject at least for the present. I don't promise to not speak of it again for out of the abundance of the heart the mouth speaketh.

Our present camp is situated in another pine grove, the brigade on the west of headquarters. The pine grove extends about a mile east of our quarters and furnishes a beautiful place for one to stroll off by themselves to secret devotion and times while the sun was setting in the far west and the March winds come stealing through the pines making a solemn sound and all nature seems to be hushed in gems of pleasure Here many times have I bowed to offer up my evening prayer for dear friends at home and to commit them to God's care and mercy. Oh, what a blessed thing it is when bereft of

126

home and dear friends, of wife and children, parents and brothers, sisters and all that is dear on earth, in the lonely grove there to meet with a friend that sticks closer than a brother, yes, to meet his creator and ask him to take care of those loved ones at home in far, far distant lands. Why, Molly, bless God, a man can never be anywhere if he serves God but what he is happy, take life or death, give ease or pain, take life or friends away, but let me meet them all again in that eternal day. I lead prayer meeting last Wednesday night from the 17th chapter of John and made a few remarks on the last verse.[34] Pray that God may bless our meeting. Our meeting was not in vain. I hope Mr. Cleveland will lead tonight if one of the chaplains don't come from the regiment. We hold meeting in a large tent as long as a community school house.

Molly, all is quiet here now. One of our captains of the cavalry disturbed a Yankee general and staff the other night by waking him from sleep and informed him that he was in the hands of Captain Mosby of the rebel cavalry.[35] He made him ride barebacked for fifteen miles. I think there will be hard fighting next month. May God bless our arms. Molly, I sold my watch the other day for fifty dollars and will send that amount home soon but I will write more about that hereafter. I have drawn some but I have to spend right smart, every thing is so high. I will write what to do with it when I get a chance to send it. Molly, I will not write much this time as I surely will get a letter from you in a few days. Give my love to all the relations and friends and may God bless us all and permit us to meet again. Write always to your ever dear and affectionate husband and Billie. Kiss my boys. I love you.

W. R. Stilwell

---

[34] "O righteous Father, the world has not known thee, but I have known thee; and these know that thou hast sent me. I make known to them thy name, and I will make it known, that the love with; which thou has loved me may be in them, and I in them."

[35] John Singleton Mosby was a famous Confederate partisan ranger. In March 1863, he captured Union brigadier general Edwin H. Stoughton in his bed, uncovering the sleeping general and slapping him on the behind. Boatner, *Civil War Dictionary*, 571.

Molly has finally delivered and Stilwell is now father of a girl child but he evidences a peculiar attitude toward her. Tommy is still the favorite. This letter contains the beginning of a humorous episode about the naming of the girl. Stilwell says he will have no part in the naming, which is solely up to Molly. He has forgotten that he has already referred to the child as "Virginia" several times.

Camp Near Fredericksburg March 17, 1863
My dear Molly:
With grateful thanks to God and to our many friends I seat myself tonight with pleasure to inform you and them that I have heard of your sickness and afflictions must needs have come and feel like I had a great load taken off my mind. To be sure we ought to feel thankful. I had written to you the 15th and complained that I had not received any letters in so long but I take it all back now. I reckon I thought the time longer than it was. Oh, dear Molly, you don't know how glad it makes me feel to think that everything is over. It makes my heart almost bleed to think that you had to suffer so but again I say thanks be unto God for his goodness towards us and to father, mother, sister, uncle, aunt and all others who bore such a kind part in your behalf, I would say please accept my thanks and I assure them that their kindness will ever be remembered with pleasure, but it seems to me that there is one name which I have not registered yet who bore a noble part, yes, yes, that is Ellen and I don't know how to express my thanks to her otherwise than for you to give her a nice present for me.[36] Tell her that I shall ever be her friend but I shall have to write a short letter as it is night and I must say something about our gal, ha, ha, and how shall I believe on whom I have not seen; how shall I see unless the war ends and unless we whip the Yankees but I suppose I will have to believe it but you may kiss me if I feel like I have a girl now. I don't think I ever

---

[36] Could this be Molly's younger sister, Elizabeth Frances? Thomas Speer was also her guardian but she doesn't appear in his household in the 1860 census although she would have been only 16 at the time.

shall unless I see it but if you say that I have a girl I will have to acknowledge it. Oh, I'd give my life to be down there but it will be a revelation. Well, well, a gal and you think that it isn't as pretty as Thomas was. Well, I don't know but I wish I could see it, I would tell them. In regard to a name for it, I don't have anything to do with that. I named Thomas and I think you ought to name the girl, therefore, I shall give way and let you suit yourself, as my choice I know would be yours. I shall not mention any end, wait and let you do as you please, I will be satisfied. So I know that you will think that I have acted strange but time about is fair play, and I have had my time in naming J. T.

Molly, although I am writing without being excited yet there has been fighting on our left this evening. The cannon could be heard distinctly. Whether it will be a skirmish or a big battle I don't know. I hope fighting Joe will try us here again.[37] The sooner he fights the sooner his command will be taken from him. Oh, that God may still bless our army. I heard a courier ride up yesterday but I haven't heard what orders he brought, it may be orders to cook up rations and be ready to march. I have great confidence in our army. Molly, I would caution you against being too anxious to be up but you will be better or worse before you get this and now I must close for this time.

The boys have just finished supper and have gingerbread and ginger tea. We draw lots of sugar and can have sweetbread as much as we want. Write soon and often, at least once a week and never quit writing because you don't know whether I will get it or not. My love to all the friends and, oh, my gal, you must kiss her and kiss her, and kiss her, kiss her all over and over, but you must kiss my Tom boy too for he is my boy. I don't know whether I love the gal or not, but I know I love him.

W. R. Stilwell

---

[37] "Fighting Joe" Joseph Hooker took command of the Army of the Potomac on 26 January 1863, replacing Burnside.

The armies are beginning to stir but no major engagement will take place for some time yet. Stilwell maintains great confidence in his ability to survive the hazards of war.

March 18, 1863
My dear Molly:
In my letter to you last night I stated that a courier had just arrived with orders but I did not know what they were. It was orders to be ready to march at minutes' notice. Again at two o'clock another came with orders to march this morning at five o'clock. The brigade is gone, I don't know where but suppose it is gone on to form a line of battle. I think you will be apt to hear of stirring times before you get this from the army of the Potomac. I have not heard from the fighting yesterday. It was at the US Ford.[38] [I don't know] whether we will move camps or not. I have been listening this morning to hear the cannon roar but have not as yet. I tell you everything is in a stir here this morning I will have a chance to send this off but I may not have another chance in some time so you need not be uneasy about me if you don't get any more letters from me in some time, but I assure you as you yourself bear me witness that if there is any possible chance you shall hear from me and I will keep you posted as far as I can. In the meantime you continue to write, never quit unless I tell you to, for your letters will most always follow me anywhere I am.
Dear Molly,
How is little Virginia this morning? God bless its little soul, you must not praise it too highly or I shall have to desert and come home, but there is nothing like being a soldier. I had just finished a letter to Uncle John and as I am his army correspondent, I shall have to break it and give him the news. He and I write some great letters. Again I say don't be uneasy for I hope that the bullet that is for me has never been molded yet. My love to all the relations and especially to Miss Ellen. Write soon and often and when lightning

---

[38] Actually, the fight was upstream at Kelly's Ford. *Civil War Day by Day,* 329.

brings you the news that cannon have been heard on the Raphappanock believe that your Billie is there. So good bye to Molly and the babes.

W. R. Stilwell

———

Stilwell is expressing a sense of duty that disdains furloughs as "foolish." "When the war closes I will try and get a furlough and come to see you." Perhaps he knows that he cannot get a furlough anytime soon and he is trying to make Molly feel better.

Camp near Fredericksburg, Virginia, March 22, 1863
My dear Molly or Sister,
Your very kind letter of the 15th received and was very glad to hear from you and to hear that you were doing so well. You are some pumpkin anyhow, you are. I am in good health and spirits, my health was never better and the reason that I am in good spirits is because I think that we will have fighting here soon, and have had lately. General Stuart gave them something to think about the other day.[39] We thought the other day when I wrote to you that the fight would be a general one but we gave them such a shook that they thought it would be best to stop a while. Still I think that we will have fighting here soon and, if we must, the sooner the better. Our brigade was ordered to the fight but was ordered back before they got here.

In regard to my getting a furlough, that has played out. The time has been when furloughs were granted but General Lee has put a stop to all such foolishness and no more are to be given and as far as I am concerned I don't wish to express my opinion as it would not do any good. It is true I would like to see my boy and my girl and all my friends and especially my Molly but I had to part with them once and besides I will get in money what it would cost me to get

---

[39] The battle at Kelly's Ford on 17 March was a cavalry battle. Both sides claimed victory but the outnumbered Stuart held the battlefield at the end of fighting. Casualties were 78 for the Federals and 133 for the Confederates. Sears, *Chancellorsville*, 90.

home and that perhaps, will do my family more good than I could do by getting home. But when the war closes I will try and get a furlough and come to see you.

I have to lead meeting tonight and it's getting late so I can't write much. My paper is no account and it makes me mad to write on it. I want to send some money home but have no chance as yet. I will write what to do with it when I send it home. I have not had a bite of meat, only some sausage in four days and that cost $1.50 cts per lb. I suppose they were sending troops on the road and could not ship it (rations) from Richmond. I would kill anybody's hog that would try to bite me now. I don't feel like writing this evening. We have had another snow but it is most all melted now and I hope we are done with the snow this winter. Molly, I don't know how our campaign will be conducted this year but it will soon commence and I hope that the war will close before another winter comes. I must close for this time. I hope you will forgive my short letter and badly written. Give my love to all the relations, kiss my baby and don't think about me getting a furlough but remember that I am doing what I think the best. All things work together for good to them that love God, Amen. Again I say, kiss, kiss and keep kissing. The Major wants me, I must close. Write soon. I am yours as ever until death.

William R. Stilwell

———

The armies remain inactive but rations for the Confederates are very short. Stilwell writes a very tender note to Molly about an incident that happened before they were married, perhaps at the moment of engagement. Stilwell wants to improve himself by additional education, and informs Molly that he is studying grammar.

Camp near Fredericksburg, Virginia, April 7, 1863
My dear Molly:
Yours of the 29th was received today just as I commenced eating dinner. We had a chicken pie made out of bacon, and of course I could not eat anymore until I read your letter and by the

time I got through it was all eaten up. So I lost my dinner but no matter if I did, I got the letter and that paid me for my dinner. I was sorry to know that you had the headache and could not help but think that if I was there how I could cure it but I hope it is well long before now. I still have unusual good health and try to keep my head above the waves of trouble and sorrow. I have already had enough to have made me groan under its load and some times now I fear that I can hear the roaring of distant thunder which I fear will bring up a trouble storm but God forbid for I have enough already.

I wrote you a few days ago. I promised to write again soon and lengthy. I have sent you several papers; one was a paper of General McLaws' picture. Did you get them? We had a heavy snow day before yesterday, some of which now lies on the ground. We have no sign of spring or summer here as yet. The forest is as dead as if it was December and not a bud nor flower have I seen this spring. Oh, I sometimes long for summer and then when I remember the dust I dread to see it come. Many times I have seen clouds of dust so thick that you couldn't see a covered wagon six feet [away] but I believe I prefer dust to mud and snow.

Our army is, far as I know, lying perfectly still though I don't suppose it will be inactive much longer. There is going to be hard fighting this spring and many a bright sun will set, never more to rise in this world. It may fall to my lot but duty to you, duty to my country, and duty to God demands that I should act my part and if I fall, I want to fall in the discharge of duty and that foremost among the foemen. I shall never place myself in danger but if placed there I will never leave my post. I shall go forth remembering that not a sparrow falls to the ground without the notice of God. He is a present help in time of trouble.

General Paul J. Semmes returned to his brigade a few days since. The band of our regiment surrounded him. I was very glad to see him return. He knows me personally and he ought to for I have stood square to my duty for him. It will soon be ten months and I have never flinched. I have been with in danger and all. I saluted the general very politely on his return. He thinks a heap of his guard and showed them special favors. I saw Thomas Hardaway yesterday.[40] He said he had got a letter from Miss lately. He says that John Edmons[41] and one of Lige Gardner's sons were both dead.[42] He did not know whether W. M. Edmons was in the army or not. I have no letter from the west yet, no letter from John lately. Most all the friends are grumbling at him for not writing but you know John, they might as well complain at a stump but he will take care of No. 1 and that right.

I find in the army that it's root hog or die, and consequently I take care of myself, seldom studying the interest of others. We always live under suspense, not knowing today what will be done tomorrow and, to a great extent, not caring. Camp life is one that don't suit many. Much discontentment has occurred in the army here on the account of short allowance of rations which is so short that it can't be measured by the foot but by the inch, say two inches square of bacon per day, three inches deep of flour per day all told. If we did not have money to buy rations with, I don't know what we would do. I hate to pay out what little money I drew but I can't help it. I would suffer if I did not but I don't believe it will be worth anything when the war closes anyhow and would advise all my friends against having much money on hand when the war does close. I do hope that it won't be worth one cent. My reason is that speculators who have been making a fortune off the war will have lots of it on hand and I think it would be a good thing on that account. As for my part I want to have all of mine in land and negroes, ha, ha. This letter is a public document for all the friends. Enclosed you will find one for your own tooth. My love to all the

---

[40] Thomas Jefferson Hardaway was a private in Company A (Spalding County) of the 53rd. He was wounded and captured at Gettysburg and later exchanged. He was home on furlough at the end of the war. No data on his civilian life has been found.

[41] John B. Edmonds, a private in Company A (Pike County) of the 13th regiment, was killed at Antietam on 17 September 1862. No other data on him has been found.

[42] William Gardner, a private in Company A (DeKalb County) of the 38th regiment, died in Savannah, Georgia hospital 30 April 1862. He was a 22-year-old unmarried, unpropertied farmer in the 1860 census of DeKalb County. He was living in the household of a C. Gardner, at 30 years of age too young to have been his father. No data has been found on a Lige Gardner.

friends and relations and even tell them that they need not write unless they feel like it.

[Personal message-some of the beginning may be missing]

—that you have one that was thinks of the past and cherished it is the chief metal of my life, whose chief end is to cherish they memory. Happy are the dreams of one so lovely, so affectionate and who has ever been truth to their trust, but Molly, notwithstanding our present condition, is it not happiness to think that you have one that thinks of those things. I can look back to the Christmas morning with pleasure.[43] It is a happy thought to think of the past notwithstanding the gloom of the present. But that morning, oh, what a vast difference then and now, yet God has been with us all the time and he will be with us to the end. God only knows, four years hence we may be in a better condition than we were four years ago but let us not murmur at our condition but do the best I can. Ha, ha, oh, my gal, I made you cry four years ago and I will make you cry now to remember that day for I am sure it will never be forgotten by me. It is as fresh as if it was yesterday. Let us unite in prayer to God on this day to let us meet again to enjoy another day like that one, only there was only two of us then. There will be more if we ever do again but Molly I have suffered cold today to write this long letter to you and want to know what you was doing that day and what you thought of. I don't know that I ever may say any more about that day but if I never forget it so I will close this affectionate but unfortunate letter and exclaim "Oh God, deep waters are run over me, the floods of grief are like the tide of the sea which cast me to and fro." Molly, keep all my letters safe as they might do you good to refer to them some day and might do our children good to read them. I am studying grammar. An old lady living close by my quarters kindly furnished me with some very good books. She remarks that it was a strange thing to have a soldier inquire for good books, such a thing she never heard of before and would do the best she could for me but I must close. I could tell

---

[43] Christmas four years ago would have been in 1858 before Stilwell and Molly were married. Perhaps the incident was about courtship or engagement.

you many things if I could see you that I can't write. Give my love to all Uncle William's family and tell them to write to me soon and often and may god bless us all and guide us in the way of all truth and believe me ever to be your faithful and truth husband until death.

W. R. Stilwell

I forgot to say that Arch Bufford was dead, he died in Richmond. Some men desire to be sick and God gives them their potion.[44] It's cloudy and will be snowing before night. Molly, Captain Briggs on the general's [staff] just passed by and said for me to give you his pious regards and I promised to do so.[45] He is a good fellow and a good friend of mine, he comes round and takes a social chat with me every few days but I can't tell it all at once so kiss my baby and remember your ever loving Billie.

So good bye,
W. R. Stilwell
It is snowing now.

––––––

The much-traveled Mr. Evans is back in camp and has brought several articles of clothing and food, including dried peaches for Stilwell. In this long letter, mostly about family affairs, Stilwell is anxious that Molly establish a church connection and writes about the mechanics of how this could be done. Stilwell reveals that Southern

---

[44] Arch Bufford was a private in Company F of the 53rd. He died 21 November 1862 at General Hospital # 14 of pneumonia. In 1860, he was a 32-year-old Locust Grove (Henry County) farmer with wife Mary R. They were relatively prosperous, owning $1600 in real estate and $3545 in personal property but according to the slave census, they owned no slaves. Mary remarried to S. G. Treadwell on 10 August 1865.

[45] Edmund B. Briggs was originally a quartermaster sergeant of Company G (Muscogee County Columbus Guards) of the 2nd regiment. He was promoted to 1st lieutenant and aide-de-camp to General Semmes 10 July 1862. He resigned 25 May 1863 to become a captain of militia guarding the Columbus GA arsenal. On 12 November 1864, he wrote a letter to the Confederate Secretary of War asking authority to raise a regiment of Colored troops. In a reply addressed to Major Biggs, the Secretary said, "Absolutely not!"

soldiers are so hungry for cornmeal, as opposed to wheat flour, that they sometimes take that which is ground for the horses.

Camp near Fredericksburg, Virginia, April 11,1863
My dear Molly:
Your kind letter sent by Mr. Evans came to hand on yesterday also the things which you sent by him. The gloves were most beautiful and fit as neat as if they had been made to order. It did me much good to know that my Molly could do such work. They are great sure but most too late in the season as winter is most over but however, I don't blame you for that. The socks would have been better if they had been wool as cotton socks will blister the feet much sooner than wool. Molly, I don't say this in any way of grumbling but only to let you know which is best as I always preferred cotton at home. No doubt you thought I had here and, so I had, but the others are the best. But I have no doubt wool is scarce and you need not trouble yourself much about it. The galluses was good and came in good time but, oh, the peaches, they were so good. I am going to have some pies out of them.

The idea of sending brother a box of flour is the last thing that we would ever think of here. If we ever were to want anything of that kind here it would be meal as we get flour altogether, though we, at headquarters, get [corn]meal sometimes by having it ground for the horses and the truth is we want it for ourselves. But I must laugh at John writing for flour but that is all right as we have to do all the fighting we ought to have the best to eat.

Molly, I have just bought this paper and envelopes at the sutlers. The paper cost me five dollars a quire and the envelopes three dollars a bunch. How do you think that a soldier can save much money at eleven dollars per month when he has to pay such prices as that? Every thing is the same way and we don't get enough to eat and must buy some things.

I was very glad to hear that you were getting well so fast but I am somewhat uneasy about the baby. You must take good care of her. You did not tell me what you had named her. I want to know as I named John T. S. I think you ought to have the right to do this so

let me hear what your name for it is. I received a letter from
William Darnell today, he complimented me very highly of my
girl but says that Nep [his daughter] is the prettiest, but you know
that I am a graduate in human nature and of course he has to wag his
own tail like all other Hobbert natives. "Now then Bill, if you
don't want to be hit, don't put out your mouth at me." Nep is a
sweet little girl but must not put her along side with my stock. But
that is enough of nonsense. Molly, in regard to our [church]
membership I have written long, long ago to Uncle R[obert] B.
Everitt about it and I think to Mr. Slaton[46] too but I have never got
any answer.[47] I shall be satisfied anyway. You may speak to Uncle
Dorman[48] about it and tell him how it is, that when we left that the
preacher in charge was gone and that I have written and can get no
answer and if he will receive you into full membership, why all
right, and if he don't, you can use your own pleasure about joining on
probation. I will be satisfied anyway. I would to God that it should
be over. Molly, you must tell Uncle William and Aunt Penelope
and Ganma that I want to see them very bad and I would write to
them but paper and envelopes are so high and besides you can read
my letters to them. When I send a letter, I send it to all the friends.
Of course I had rather see my family than any one else, that is
natural, but aside from that there is no spot more sacred to me than
his [Uncle William's] house and often with a tear in my eyes do I
remember the happy hours we have spent under his roof and when I
remember his kindness to you and my children, it makes me feel
more grateful. So tell them that when I write it is intended for
them as much as anybody.

Molly, this is Saturday evening, the sun is about down, the
solemn time with me as it is the time in the church with you but

---

[46]Mr. Slaton was probably a church official in Louisiana. No further identification
has been made.

[47]WRS is attempting to get a letter attesting that he is a church member in good
standing that can be transferred to a new church.

[48] Alfred Dorman was Methodist minister. He has been identified as the circuit
rider on the Jackson circuit in 1860 and 1863. This circuit covered most of Butts County
and southern Henry County. Intriguingly, one of the circuit stops was entitled "Stilwell's."

God knows my heart and that is enough. I don't suppose that I could join without being there but I consider myself in the church of God. No matter where I go and if the heart is right all is well. I want Tommy baptized, but you know my feelings about that and if the war ends soon I hope we will have an opportunity of having it done by those that we wanted to do it—R. H. W.[49] In regards to war news my supply is some what limited. All is quiet here, the ground is drying very fast and I look for demonstrations of a hostile character soon. We have heard of the fighting at Charleston. We served them their rights, that is the way, whip them at all points and the war will end this year. Some think that the fighting is done at Charleston but I don't think so—I think they will try it again or they may try Savannah next. I don't think that their army will try to advance here unless they whip us at Charleston or Vicksburg, Mississippi and that seems like a hard nut to crack. I have great confidence in our success now more than ever. God will defend the rights.

Molly, I suppose that those pants you speak of will be large enough. If they are anywhere near the size of the jeans pants you sent me they will do. I don't need any shirts nor drawers. If I need anything I will let you know. Molly, I have a fine double case silver watch which I could sell for sixty-five or seventy dollars, but I don't want to sell it unless you want money as I think it will be better than money after the war closes. I may sell it or I may not. I don't know.

I always returned home from work to meet a smile from those that are so near and dear to me. God forbid that I should ever forget those pleasant hours which I have spent with you and God grant that I may return home again to enjoy your company again as I have in days past and gone. I must close. Oh, that I could see my babies. Miss 'em, kiss me. I shall always write once a week whenever I can and you must do the same. Give my love to all the friends. No

---

[49] R. H. (Russell) Waters was pastor of the McDonough Methodist Church in 1858–1859. He married William and Molly.

more at present but I ever remain your affectionate and loving and true husband until death.

Good bye

William Ross Stilwell

———

In another long letter mostly about family affairs, Stilwell finally admits that he is warming up to his daughter even though he has never seen her. But Tommy still takes preference.

Fredericksburg, Saturday the [April] 18th, 1863

My dear Molly:

By the goodness and mercy of God I am permitted to seat myself this morning to write to you. I am blessed with good health. We are still at our camp near the city. We have been expecting a fight for some time and have had some little [fighting]. The Yankees attempted to cross the river at Kelley's Ford fifteen miles above the city, but were driven back five times in succession. They made several attempts to cross but they could not make the trip.[50] Thus you will see that the Army of the Potomac [Army of Northern Virginia], though lying still, is doing good service and, dear Molly, the news from all points is cheering. At Charleston we have whipped the enemy's fleet,[51] at Suffolk, Va. General James Longstreet, formerly of our army, seems to have the enemy surrounded,[52] and at Washington, N.C., General D. H. Hill, also of our army, has them tied up.[53] At Vicksburg, Mississippi they have

---

[50] This probably refers to the fight of 17 March.

[51] The Union navy with eight monitors and one ironclad battleship made an unsuccessful attempt to force the entrance to Charleston harbor on 7 April 1863. (*Civil War Day by Day,* 335.)

[52] Longstreet surrounded the Union garrison at Suffolk VA but had no intention of attempting to take the city. He bottled up the garrison so that he could gather food freely in the surrounding country. Boatner, *Civil War Dictionary,* 917.

[53] Nothing came of this. Washington NC remained in Union hands. (*Civil War Day by Day,* 338.)

found a nut which they are unable to crack. At all points the prospect is good and, if God will bless our arms the next campaign as he did the last, I have no doubt but they will give it up. (So might it be.)

Dear Molly, spring is about to draw on our once happy country again. On yesterday, I went to a sale in our neighborhood for the purpose of buying General Semmes a chair (did so) and there I saw my first peach bloom. There was a good looking lady there too which to a soldier is a never failing cure for the sore eyes. If one ever chances to pass by there is more gazing than there would be if an elephant should pass by. I hope the day will soon come when we can see those delicate forms at least every morning at breakfast. A land without women is as dark as a world without a son.

Molly, I laid down my pen to go seining [fishing] with the boys. We have seined two or three hours and caught nothing so I thought it would pay me best to come back and write to my Molly. I have not received any letter from you since the one you sent by Mr. Evans. I shall expect one tomorrow or next day. All the things you sent me by Evans were received. I have written you before but lest you might not get [the message], I thought I would write about it again. Dear Molly, I have as many clothes as I can take care of except pants. I need one or two pair, otherwise I am well supplied. Molly, I want you to let me know if you need any money or are likely to need any soon. We get so little to eat here that I have to spend a great deal of my wages [on food] and I want to know so that I can save you some. Molly, I have never withheld any news in regard to our hardships nor don't expect to, neither do I desire to make it worse but the truth is that we don't get half enough to eat, that is, of anything except bread and not enough of that. We draw at headquarters seven day's rations on Saturday to last till Saturday again. Our meat, by using as little as possible, generally by Thursday morning is gone. So you see, Molly, that I have to spend money or suffer. You know that I don't spend it foolishly. Last night I bought six eggs for one dollar, the cheapest I have seen. I had not had any meat in two days. I divided them into two squads, three each, and made supper and breakfast. I have just eaten a biscuit for my dinner. I will get some meat this evening, I reckon, don't know, never know any thing in the army but don't be alarmed at this. I assure you that I am as lively and as cheerful as you ever saw me and take [play] a big game of town ball every day. I have got money plenty yet, a fine watch in my pocket which I can sell any day for fifty dollars and as many friends as any boy in the army. Don't be scared about me. If you and the boys can get along, Billie will take care of himself the best he can and I feel the utmost confidence in that for I know where you are.

I received a letter from Cousin Mary Dick Stilwell lately.[54] I have not received any letters from the west. I got a letter from Uncle John the other day in which he stated that I should have bread when I got home if there was any in his crib. He speaks forth the words of truth and soberness and has become one of our warmest friends and says that he is proud of me and John and that he will remember us with pleasure. I love his letters, they always bring comfort and consolation to the weary. Long may he live and success crown his labors.

Dear, I want to know how Virginia is getting along. I have studied about it until I begin to love something that you have got there but you may kiss me if I know what it is. I love it but don't know what but when you say Tommy I know what to love and I do it with an everlasting love and as for Molly, thou art love forevermore. I must close. You see what a long letter I have written you. I, W.R.S. have written it with mine own hand. Give my love to Uncle, Aunt, Granma and Pa, Mother, Sister and all the friends. Lemmonds, Parker, and all [are] well, I see them every day most. Write soon, at least once a week. Oh, kiss my babes, oh, kiss em. God grant that we may soon meet never to part on earth again and may he bless us all and keep us in the good old way of peace. This is the prayer of your true and devoted husband until death. I have a kiss from you.

William Ross Stilwell

------

[54] Both Richard and John Stilwell had daughters named Mary.

Things are still quiet on the battlefront. Stilwell pretends that he is well-contented to be absent from his family. Poor Molly is being tormented about the naming of the baby. Stilwell obviously wants "Virginia" but he is on record as allowing Molly to pick the name of the female child since he picked the name of their male child. So we are going through a little charade whereby Stilwell appears to want Molly to pick the name while the name "Virginia" is the only one he will accept. Stilwell continues to complain about a lack of food but the early spring wild vegetables are beginning to appear and whether the men know it or not, these vegetables will prevent scurvy.

Camp near Fredericksburg, Virginia, April 21, 1863
My Molly dear:
I wrote to you last Saturday but having received a letter from you on Monday last I could not wait and delay writing to you for a long week. I am enjoying excellent health and [am] as lively as a cricket. It is a great mystery to me how I can content myself like I do. If any one should have told me that I could have been cheerful and happy when absent from you and the babes, I could not have believed them but I have prayed to be made happy and contented and I have no doubt that he has blessed me. I never thought that I could live so long without seeing you but I have learned in what ever condition of life I am placed to be there with content, so by that that means I make myself cheerful and happy, but, oh how long, dear Savior, oh how long will this war last and keep me from those that are near and dear unto me. Oh, that happy day when we all get home. Oh, how I look forward with pleasant anticipation [to]that eventful day. God speed it. Roll round, ye days, fly swift, ye months, and bring me to my home never more to be parted from those loved ones until we part to meet on Canan's bright shore.

Dear Molly, as it seems that you don't intend to name the baby without some assistance from me, I concluded last night while I was on guard to devote my hours to hunting up a name for the jewel, not that I desire to have any hand in naming it but only suggest those in order to assist you for I desire that you name it. The names which I request are Madora Jane. Madora, I think is a very pretty name. The other is Emma Jane. Remma I think is also a pretty name. The name Jane is a family name and would do for sister Mot [Martha Ann Jane Ragland], sister Jane [Darnell], Aunt Jane Everitt [Elizer Jane, wife of Richard], and Aunt Jane Foster, or if you like better Madora Frances or Emma Frances.[55] If I thought your choice was Martha I would not say anything but as you say you don't like it I need not say much. You know that I never did admire the name although I shall be satisfied with any name that you see proper to give it. As for my part, names are of little importance anyhow. If I could get to see it I could pick out some name to suit it but anyway to suit the children, let us have a name. I want to know what to call it and if you don't name it I shall hereafter call it "Virginia." You say it is like me, if so it must be good looking and if it has sense like its father it will make a perfect lady, but take care of Tommie, there is sense in his head.

Dear Molly, I have not much war news. I think that the Yankees are about played out. I think the war will end before a great while if we can only be blessed a little longer. The Yankees have given out the idea of taking Charleston, the truth is we whipped them. At Suffolk General Longstreet still holds them pent up, at Washington, N. C., General D H. Hill holds them tight. Here, we whipped them back every time they attempt to cross the river, hence I believe that they will shortly give it up. It's my opinion that General Lee will advance on them before long if they don't attack us, and if he does you may expect to hear of hot times of the Army of the Potomac. Lieutenant Farrar is here at the company and in good health. He has not been sick. All of our officers, captain and lieutenants are all here and well, some little smallpox in the regiment in Company G. Mr. Lemmonds and Mr. Parker are all well. Sam Whitaker has been sick but is getting better.[56] Martin Sowell[57] has got transferred to our

---

[55] Family history records Jane Foster as a sister to WRS's mother. Her tombstone is in the Fellowship Church cemetery and indicates she was born in 1810 and died in 1835.

[56] Sam V. Whitaker was a private in Company F of the 53rd. He was the oldest son of a modest farming family headed by Robert Whitaker (age 47 in 1860) and wife Francis, age 41. Sam had seven brothers and sisters ranging down to age 1. The family lived in the

regiment. Wiley Henley[58] has been elected junior lieutenant in company A. Mr. Gray,[59] sister's beau is a sergeant. William Norman is second sergeant in our company, and I believe could be elected lieutenant if there was a vacancy. Who knows the luck of a lousy calf but he wouldn't get my vote.[60]

Molly, you need not fret yourself about facing those pants. If you have any chance, send them along and if they are too small I can get C. B. Smith to piece them. I don't suppose they will be too little.

I still have to complain of not much to eat. Now that spring has come I want some vegetables and can get none except the wild shallots which grow here in abundance. We fry them and they eat finely. Southern people were never made to starve. We can lie in the woods and whip Yankees. I must close, as I have to cook today and am making some light bread. I wish I could send you a biscuit of my own, it would surprise you very much. I am some pumpkin myself when it comes to cooking so you see I can be a heap of service to you and never will be hungry if you go visiting. Give my

---

Beersheba post office district of Henry County. He survived to surrender in Virginia in April 1865. He cannot be located in the 1870 Georgia census.

[57] Martin Van Buren Sowell of the large Henry County Sowell family, formerly of Company A of the 44th Regiment, survived to surrender in April 1865. He returned home and established a family of seven children.

[58] Wiley S. Henley was a private in Company A (Spalding County) of the 53rd when the enemy at Antietam captured him on 17 September 1862. He was exchanged at Fortress Monroe, Virginia on 16 October 1862. He was subsequently elected second lieutenant of Company A. He was disabled at Cedar Creek VA on 17 September 1864. He was at home at the end of the war. He died in Butts County in 1909.

[59] The identity of Mr. Gray, Margaret Stilwell's beau, is quite a mystery. There are two obvious candidates; (1) Augustus Gray was a sergeant in Company I who would be killed at Cold Harbor on 3 June 1864 and (2) James R. Gray was a Butts County resident who was the second sergeant in Company A, who survived the war. The problem is that both of them were married and had small children.

[60] William P. Norman was first sergeant in Company F. He was the eldest son of poor farmers in Locust Grove in Henry County. In 1860, he was 19 with seven brothers and sisters ranging in age from 16 to 1 Despite Stilwell's opinion he was elected junior second ieutenant in December 1863. He survived to be captured in April 1865. In 1870 he was a landless farm hand, married with one child.

love to Uncle William and Aunt Penelope and Granma and all the friends. Write soon and often to your ever true and devoted husband.

W. R. Stilwell

———

The weather is beautiful and there are as yet no signs of battle. Stilwell keeps himself employed by fishing while reading his hooks at the same time. The spirit of religious revival is still on the rise and Stilwell makes himself into a small player by holding periodic prayer meetings. He still chides Molly rather meanly about the name of the girl child. He now assumes that Molly has adopted the name "Martha" despite the fact that Stilwell doesn't like that name. The charade continues. The subject turns to summer clothes. He seems to be well fixed except for pants "since sitting on the ground soon wears out the seat." Many historians assume that Civil War soldiers, both North and South, always wore woolens. Not so, Stilwell states, " I don't want any woolen clothes this summer."

Fredericksburg, Virginia, April 28, AD 1863

My dear Molly:

I received your kind letter before yesterday but having written to you but a few days before I thought I had as well wait a day or two. Your letter was quite satisfactory on all subjects. I am enjoying the blessing of good health and spirits as far as the circumstances will admit though I confess while I see spring in all of its beauty and the flowers which perfume the air it makes me think of friends and loved ones far, far away, but by the grace of God I am trying to be resigned to the will of my master. To my surprise we are still in our old camps yet though we are under orders to be ready to march at a moment's notice. Though we don't always march when we receive such orders, I am inclined to think that we will have to march before long, in what direction I do not know. Some think that the enemy is going to try the route by the Peninsula to Richmond again, some think they will try it by the way of Manassas again. All I have to say is that I don't think they ever will get there at all unless they go there like they have been doing heretofore as prisoners. There is a heap of smoke in their camps yesterday and today, some think they are leaving but nobody knows.

Mr. Evans leaves our camps in the morning for Richmond. He thinks that he will return again before he goes home though he don't know. However, if I knew he was going home I would not send any letter by him as you can get them much sooner by mail. I am out of heart of sending letters by hand as I have sent so many that I don't think you ever get, though it is well enough for you to send them by hand as they will come to me better if we should be on a march, though you have sent some that I never got, your last letter came in seven days.

We are having beautiful weather now. I go fishing most every day though don't often catch much but it keeps me employed and I can take my books and read and fish at the same time. I have to hold prayer meeting most every week and have to read a good deal. I have to lead next Wednesday night if nothing happens. I shall read from the fiftieth Psalm. There is a good deal of revival feeling in the army, last Sunday evening I saw three persons baptized. They belonged to the Sixteenth Georgia Regiment in Cobb's old brigade, now General Wofford's.[61] If we don't have to march I think of going to General Stonewall Jackson's headquarters and [attending] preaching. He has preaching there every Sunday. Thank God the people are doing better than they did last year I think. May God bless us more and more.

I am glad that you are teaching Tommy his prayers, that's right. I want him raised right and if he is, I feel that he will make a

---

[61] Brigadier General William Tate Wofford was a prosperous Cassville, Georgia attorney prior to the war. As a member of the state convention of 1861, he voted against secession but later accepted the post of colonel of the 18th regiment. This regiment was part of Cobb's brigade and he was brigade commander after the death of Cobb. Early in 1865, at the request of Georgia's Governor Brown, he would be appointed military commander of the North Georgia district with the mission of restoring order to an area that had become disorderly and lawless. Paroled on 2 May 1865, he was forthwith elected to the National House of Representatives but Republican Radicals refused to seat him. Warner, *Generals in Gray*, 343.

smart man and I know that you will do it if you can treat him more by love than anger.

But what will I say about the queen of the South [the new baby girl]. What can I say when I know nothing about it. I don't recollect much about Tom and how will I know anything about it that I have never seen. It seems to me that I will forget everything I ever knew. If I did not write and receive letters from you I believe that I would forget that I was married. I don't feel much like a married man but I never forget it so far as to court any other lady, but if I should, you must forgive me as I am so forgetful. But about the queen or Martha Jane as I suppose its name must be that. You know that's its name, you can't fool me, you had it named two years ago (ha, ha). I didn't forget that. I pride my memory is getting better. Well, Martha Jane or M. J. Stilwell, and you think that it favors me and Tom too. Well it must be very good looking if it does all that for we are sure I am pretty myself and so for Tom. I defy the state of Georgia to beat him though I don't have anything to say against the queen. If it favors us it must be pretty too.

Dear Molly, it is after nine o'clock and I am getting sleepy. I have written a very bad letter but it's done in a hurry. I hope you can read it. Dear, in regard to my summer clothes I shall not need money. I have just sold a pair of drawers tonight for two dollars that I drew from Mare Jeff at sixty cents. I have three pair left. I have four shirts, three pair of socks and the thumb stalls that Aunt Ann [Stilwell] sent me. I don't need anything now except one or two pair of pants and a hat. Still, if you don't get a chance to send them I can make out very well. Soldiers don't wear out anything hardly but pants. Sitting so much on the ground soon wears out the seat. I don't want any woolen clothes this summer. You can tell uncle that I can draw pants that will suit better for summer than woolen and can get them cheaper than they can be made at home and I will need them [the woolens] worse next winter. My coats are both good yet. I think those pants would be long enough, if not, C. B. Smith is here. Give my love to Granma, Uncle, Aunt, Pa, Mother, and Sister, all, all. I would be glad to see them and to you what more can I say than I have already said. Kiss J. T. & M. J. Write soon and believe me ever to be your loving, affectionate and devoted husband until death.

W. R. Stilwell

4

CHANCELLORSVILLE

Now begins the battle known as "Lee's Masterpiece," the Battle of Chancellorsville. The 53rd Regiment would perform some of their toughest fighting of the war at a simple two-story brick church named Salem that held the back door to Lee's troops fighting at Chancellorsville. The Confederates must keep this door closed to Federals attempting to approach from Fredericksburg and assault Lee's rear. The Confederate army succeeded. We learn in this letter that part of Stilwell's duties while guarding the brigade camp is to arrest the "cowards who do not want to fight" and prevent them from fleeing to the rear. Thus we see that Stilwell has developed the sense of duty and devotion to the objective that involves taking hard actions against his fellow soldiers.

Battlefield ten miles above Fredericksburg Virginia, May 2nd, 1863

My dear Molly:

The battle, which has been raging for two days, is still in progress.[1] The result, I know not. I shall not get to mail this until the fight is over which may be a long time, but I write to let you know that I think of you and friends amidst the din of battle. Oh, could you but sit now where I sit and see the sight which I see, it

---

[1] Battle of Chancellorsville.

would present to you an awful sight. While I write there are two dead Yankees within fifteen feet of me, and others nearby. You may think it strange, but anybody that has seen as much as I have does not pay any attention to it. Dead men are so common that I get used to it though I always try to pay due respect to them. I am about one mile and a half from where they are fighting. I have charge of General Semmes' baggage with four other men, and to keep the stragglers from going to the rear by arresting them and taking them to the general. Cowards who don't want to fight. The general knows that I will do my duty and hence he puts me there. I captured many valuable things off the field this morning. I may write more tomorrow.

May the 3rd—Dear Molly, thank God I am still spared and alive in good health. The fight commenced this morning, fought until 12 o'clock, the hardest battle I have ever heard.[2] We drove them back across the river, but while we were fighting them there, they came across at Fredericksburg. Our division was sent down there to attack them and did so. It was most terrible and we lost a great many men. Our brigade lost, killed or wounded, over five hundred, our regiment one hundred and forty. In our company about 17 or 18, only three of which were killed dead on the field, the rest of them wounded, many of which will die from their wounds. The killed were Bill Whitchie,[3] Floyd Dees,[4] [and] Frank Stephens.[5] I

---

[2] This was the battle at Salem Church, sometimes known as Second Fredericksburg. On the afternoon of 3 May, Sedgwick's Sixth Army Corps forced a breakthrough at Marye's Heights against thin Confederate forces, then charged directly at the rear of Lee's forces about six miles away at Chancellorsville. McLaw's Confederate division did an about-face and moved to take a defensive position at Salem Church. Sedgwick must be stopped at all costs. Semmes' brigade along with Wilcox's brigade bore the brunt of the fierce Federal assault and were successful in stopping the advance. Sears, *Chancellorsville*, 378.

[3] Bill Witchie has not been identified. Later, WRS drops him from the list of killed and adds Lend Upchurch.

[4] M. F. (Floyd) Dees—Confederate records are silent as to what happened to Dees after his enlistment. He is listed in the 1860 Henry County census located in the Mc-Donough post office district. He was age 30 with wife Elizabeth, also 30. They had two small children, one 3 and one less than a year. Floyd was a farm laborer; both he and his wife were illiterate.

have not heard who all is wounded but York Hopkins[6], Joe Sowel[7], John Rape[8], [and] Doss Alexander[9]. The rest I do not know. Dr. Hail in Company A was shot and died on the field. He was shot in the forehead and his brains shot out. I have not heard from Mr. Parker.[10]

May the 4th—The fight is still going on. I think I will send this off tomorrow if nothing happens but I am afraid that you would be uneasy about me but I hope that you will not as I am still in charge of the general's baggage and present guard of the brigade. I think I will write more this evening if I can send it off tomorrow.

---

[5] The service record of F. M. (Frank) Stevens ends with his admission to hospital on 3 May 1863. From another source, we learn that his mother (Sarah Stevens) filed for his pay claiming that he was killed at Chancellorsville. No further identification, including any data on his civilian existence, has been found.

[6] W. P. (York) Hopkins was apparently not disabled by his wound that was not recorded in his personnel file. He served on to be fully disabled by bronchitis in October 1864. In the 1860 census, he was a 21-year-old community schoolteacher boarding with Abasalom Farrar, later a member of Company F. By 1870 he was a modest farmer living with a wife and three children in Henry County.

[7] Joseph Franklin Sowell, one of seven Sowell brothers who served the Confederacy was a private in Company F. His compiled service record shows a hospital admission due to a gunshot wound on 9 May (no year recorded) and a return to duty on 8 June (no year). He surrendered in Virginia in 1865 and returned to Henry County where he lived until 1914.

[8] Nineteen-year-old James M. Rape entered service on 2 March 1863. Apparently this wound was minor because he would soldier on to be permanently disabled at Cedar Creek VA on 19 October 1864. No record of his prewar civilian existence has been found but postwar pension records indicated that he lived until 1914.

[9] Willis M. Alexander was 20 years old and was second sergeant of Company F. His wound would not be immediately disabling as he soldiered on until discharged 27 December 1864. In 1860, he lived on the family farm in the Mount Carmel district of Henry County with his parents, William and Margaret, and seven siblings. His father owned one slave. In 1870, Willis was a recently married, modest farmer with a 20-year-old wife and two children age 1 or less.

[10] Dr. A. J. Hail may have been a doctor to WRS, but in Company A (Spalding County) of the 53rd, he was only a private. The army records confirm his death at Chancellorsville. No further information on him has been found.

Stilwell is jubilant about the superior performance of both his brigade and regiment in defense of Salem Church.

Resting Camp, five miles above Fredericksburg, Virginia, May 5th, 1863

My dear affectionate Molly:

Thanks be unto almighty God that I am permitted to address you once more and blessed with health and strength. Molly, we have had some of the hardest fighting ever seen but thank God the victory is complete. We have knocked both the harness off Joe Hooker, drove his army across the river in perfect confusion and disgrace. Oh, the dead and wounded Yankees. It is true we have lost a great many men but nothing like them. Our brigade covered itself with glory, they whipped a whole corps of Yankees, the noble 53rd captured two stands of colors, one national flag and a white flag they raised to deceive our men, pretending that they had surrendered, but our regiment shot down the flag bearer and took the white flag.[11] We lost one hundred and forty,[12] killed and wounded. I hear of no prisoners taken from our regiment—they don't surrender. Had three killed in our company. I will enclose a letter that I wrote during the whole fight and will give you more of the particulars than I now have time to write as we may have to march in twenty minutes. It may be two or three days before I get to send this off as I learn that we have got more of the Yankees surrounded above here and I expect we will have to go and help them. Dear, I think we are ending this war very fast if they will just come over and give us a chance. Thank God for success. While I write I see the Yankee balloon up over the river.[13] Jos Sowell was wounded very bad in the face. None of our officers were hurt though they all stood up like men. Molly, my mind is too much torn up this morning to write a good letter, but knowing that you would be very uneasy

---

[11] The national (US) flag carried by the Second Rhode Island regiment. *OR*, 25/1:836.

[12] The official count was 120.

[13] One of Professor Thaddeus S. C. Lowe's hydrogen observation balloons.

about me I thought I would write. We had our first fight ten or fifteen miles above the city and while we were fighting them there, they crossed at the city and took the heights in front of Fredericksburg but our men sure drove them off and took them back again. I have not seen any paper in some time.

Oh, Molly, amidst the excitement I forgot to say that I received a letter from you yesterday. I was in charge of the general's baggage at the time and the fight was raging at the time but I broke it and read it and I believe I would if I had been in line of battle. I was more than glad to hear from you and that all was well. I was very uneasy for fear that General Semmes would get killed. He thinks so much of me and is so kind to me. I hope I will stay with him as long as the war lasts. He had his hat shot through but not hurt, also his horse killed under him. Lieutenant Davis,[14] one of his staff, got his nose shot off. I must close. I have not time to write more now.

[Unsigned]

This is evidently the letter that Stilwell wrote during the fighting. The first part is missing. This is another in the series of "you are there" pictorials.

I got me two blankets, sugar, coffee, paper and envelopes enough to last me a long time. In fact, I got a great many things on the battlefield, a little of most anything that I wanted. Tell Father and Mother, Sister, Uncle Wm., Aunt P. B., and Granma that I thought of them often while the cannon and minny balls were flying through the air but thank God none of them hurt me. I was in many dangerous places camping almost every night in front of the line of battle with the general. One night they fought most all night and I was inside of the line. I knew that I was in a great danger though I would fight for the general to the last and he knows it and that is the

---

[14] Lieutenant William Davis of Company D, 10th Georgia Infantry was brigade acting assistant inspector general at the time of Chancellorsville. Shortly thereafter he was elected Captain of Company B but would retire to the invalid corps on 24 October 1864. General Semmes, in his battle report (*OR,* 25/1:836) states that "Lieutenant Davis, while bearing an order, received a frightful wound in the face, which will disable him for months."

reason that he won't have anybody else to guard him of a night but his own guard, so you see the reason that I am not with the company and regiment.

Oh how bad I want to see our babies, that is, Thomas and Martha Jane but no chance until we whip old fighting Joe a little more and then I think maybe I will get to see thee and them. I must close for this time. Tell all the friends howdy for me. Don't be uneasy about me. I hope God will take care of me. Write soon and direct as before. I will write again soon if I have a chance to send it off. Don't be uneasy if I don't. So I remain your loving and true devoted husband in peace, in war, in battle, or out of it, so goodbye, my dear, this time. (Kiss, oh, one Kiss)

William R. Stilwell

See figure illustration on page xxviii for an enclosure in a letter of this period—the page included a drawing of the Chancellorsville battlefield and the text follows.

Dear friends, Joe Hooker came over to see us about ten days ago. He stayed here a few days when he found old Bob Lee about this way. We left a few troops at Fredericksburg but the Yankee drove them back and came up in our rear and General Lee ordered our division back to whip them and they did it at the brick church. They crossed first at the U. S. Ford. You will see by the march of our lines that Jackson got in their rear. We were all around them but if they had not crossed an other army at Banks Ford we would have got them all. We got about eight thousand prisoners. Their loss is said to be twenty-five thousand killed and wounded and prisoners.[15] But now, dear friend, Joe Hooker is gone back. He couldn't stay in Dixie, it was not healthy for him. I think he will try and come back

---

[15] Union casualties (killed, wounded or missing) were about 17,000 or about 13 percent of those engaged. Southern losses were only 13,000 but this was 22 percent of those engaged. Chancellorsville was considered to be Lee's greatest triumph but the casualty list (including Stonewall Jackson) indicated the South couldn't afford many more such triumphs. (Casualty figures are from *Civil War Dictionary*, 140).

soon again as he will lose his character if he don't get to Richmond but he can't get there yet.

W. R. Stilwell

———

Stilwell lists all the booty taken by him from the Yankees and then includes a love poem written during the period.

Same old Camp Fredericksburg, May 10, 1863

My dear Molly:

After nine days hard marching and fighting in rain and mud, bomb shells and blood we have driven the enemy in confusion back across the river and to my surprise have returned back to our old camp in good health though very tired and nearly broked down. I was in mud often knee-deep. Tore my shoes all to pieces and had to pick up some old shoes by the roadside. I suffered very much, nobody can tell, only the poor soldiers [know] what it is to march all day and night in bad weather. I never drew but a days ration of meat in nine days, but I had plenty, captured my rations from the Yankee; meat, sugar, coffee, crackers, salt, pepper, even the paper on which I write is captured. I got about fifty or seventy-five dollars worth, that is, it would cost me that to buy it. Now I've got paper and envelopes to last me a long time. I got me needles, thread, hair brush, comb, portfolio to keep my paper in, good canteen, two of the best blankets worth ten dollars a piece. Also I captured books, hymn and testament, by the wholesale, so I made the trip very profitable if I did suffer. We were gone nine days, and I do think I slept twelve hours in all the time.

Dear, I received your letter of the 27th, while the cannon was roaring all around me most. You can't imagine how glad I was to get it, and at that time it seemed to do me good [more] than any other time though I did not know that I would ever get to answer it, but, thank God, I am in good health and spirits. Our regiment suffered very much on last Sunday evening. Our brigade did the principal part of the fighting at the brick church, I believe it is called Salem. If you see anything about it you may know that we were there. I wrote to you while we were on the march, in which I gave you the account of our company. I am sorry to say that Dr. Hail of Company A was killed. He was shot in the head. He was brave and was a good soldier. We lost a heap of good men, but we can't expect to fight and whip the Yankees without some of us being killed. How long we will get to rest I don't know. We will move our camp tomorrow a mile and a half forward. I never expected when I left to come back and occupy my old tent but so it is. I shall not pretend to describe any more of the battle now as you will see it an account of it in the papers. I am very tired and would not write today, but I knew that you will be uneasy about me and I can't bear the idea of you being uneasy. I knew that you have heard about the fight and of course you want to hear so I thought I ought to write. The other part of my letter will be about other things than battle.

The following was a separate enclosure.

"I watch for thee" by W. R. Stilwell, May 9th, 1863

1.—I watch for thee when parting day sheds on the earth a lingering ray when his blushes o'er the rose a richer tint of crimson throws, and every flower's leaves are curled like beauty shrinking from the world. When silence reigns o'er lawn or lea, then dearest love, I watch for thee.

2.—I watch for thee when eve's first star shines dimly in the heavens afar, and twilight mists and shadows gray upon the lake's broad waters play. When not a breeze or sound is heard to startle evening's lonely bird but hushed is even the humming bee. Then, dearest love, I watch for thee.

3.—I watch for thee when on the eyes of childhood slumber gently lies when sleep has stilled the noisy mirth of playful voices round our hearth and each young cherub's fancy glows with dreams that only childhood knows of pleasures past or yet to be than dearest love I watch for thee.

———

As the excitement of battle abates, Stilwell writes a long and newsy letter on mostly non-army subjects. There is always considerable religious feeling in Stilwell and he reports a growing religious fervor in the Army. In response to WRS's frequent reports of shortages of all types, Molly suggests the problem could be caused by "speculation" in the regiment. Stilwell replies that the problems are army-wide and blames civilians who will not offer their goods, which are plentiful, to the army. This is often the case but the major problem is a lack of transportation and inefficiencies in the distribution chain.

In this letter, Stilwell explicitly confirms that William Foster is taking care of Molly. And, of course, his parents are near at hand which supports the theory that Squire Stilwell is William Foster's overseer.

Camp near Fredericksburg, Virginia, May 13, 1863

My dear Molly:

With great pleasure I seat myself this beautiful Wednesday morning to pen you a few lines in answer to yours of the 6th which was received yesterday. I am thankful to say that I am in good health and have enjoyed good health all the time of our fighting except I was very much fatigued marching in rain and mud day and night. But one good thing was I had plenty to eat which I had drawn from Joe Hooker. But it is not my purpose to make this a war letter as I have written you two letters since the battle and have given you all the particulars. I wrote to you while the battle was in progress and one just as soon as it was over because I knew that you would be uneasy about me, but I am all right though I passed through some very dangerous places. You can get an idea as to fighting that we did for our brigade, out of one thousand four hundred we lost five hundred and eighty-one killed and wounded.[16] I suppose our brigade suffered more than any other that was in the fight. Joseph

---

[16] In *OR*, 39/1: 829, McLaws reports 577 killed and wounded plus 26 missing or captured. Thus, total casualties were 603 which represents a casualty rate of 43 percent, evidence of the terrific struggle that took place at Salem Church.

Sowell was shot in the mouth knocking out all of his teeth and part of his tongue. I hope you have got the letter that I have sent you.

Dear Molly, I am so glad about Uncle Dorman receiving us in the church. I have been pestered about it so much and now to know that it is accomplished I am so glad. I feel greatly relieved and am glad that you have seen him and I hope we will be good members. I am still trying to live right and hope that you are doing the same. There is considerable religious feeling in the army. Last Sunday we had preaching in our regiment; and there were about thirty or forty members and among them our old friend and neighbor, Mr. Darnell. If we had a good preacher I think we would [had] have good times. We have a chaplain by the name of Toy,[17] but he can't preach much. However, he and I are on very good terms. Oh, how bad I want to get home where I can attend church with my little family but when or ever that will be God only knows, but I hope for the best and look forward for the time to come. I think we will be very happy if we ever get together again though we were always before. I am glad that you don't need money for if you did it would be impossible for me to send you much at present. I have had to buy some clothing and something to eat and everything is so high that eleven dollars a month won't buy much. The government furnishes clothes but sometimes they have got plenty and sometimes none and I can't march without shoes.

You said that somebody must be speculating in our regiment, but that is a mistake. The whole army is on quarter rations. A lb. and a half of meat for six days—take it as it comes—bone, skin, and dirt, and it was so rank that it can hardly be eaten, and you know that I never could eat old bacon but I could now if I could get it. It is enough to discourage any army to know that there is plenty in the government and can't be bought for them and has to be forced down from them by law. God save such people, they don't deserve

---

[17] C. H. Toy was chaplain of the 53rd Regiment from 27 December 1862 until he resigned on 8 August 1864. As Lee's Army retreated from Gettysburg, he along with several surgeons volunteered to remain to assist the wounded. No record of his civilian life has been found.

liberty. Most all of the army is willing to fight to the last if the people will sustain them but if they don't care if the government sinks to atoms, but as for me I am in the pile and say, "Go it boys." I will try and take care of number one and let all the rest do as best they can.

I want you to give my love and respect to Uncle William and my thanks to him for his kindness. I knew that he would take care of you for he has got a soul as large, as wide, and as feeling as any man. You can tell him that his box of butter would be very acceptable just now, but I know of no chance to get it. I know he would send it if he could but I take the will for the deed. You can tell Mother to bake me a good light pone [bread] next Saturday evening and you can eat it Sunday and that will do most as well. I can bake light bread myself and if you were only at the head of the table, I think it would eat very well. I can make up and bake bread as quick as any body, but it don't eat so well. My washing costs me twenty-five cents a garment. I would do it myself but can't get soap.

Dear Molly, I have got a trophy from the battlefield for you, one of the prettiest things you have seen. Now guess what it is. It is a black velvet pocket worked with beads. Oh, how I want to send it to you. It is so pretty. I reckon it has a thousand beads on it. I will send it the first chance I have if I don't lose it. I wouldn't take ten dollars for it if I can but send it to you. I also captured from the Yankees a fine razor. I don't know yet whether I will send it to Father as a trophy or keep it myself as I need one. I did hear that Uncle John McKibben was coming to see Clark but if he does Clark is in Richmond,[18] and I fear he won't come any farther than there. If he does [come] I can send it by him.

---

[18] Uncle John McKibben and his brother Clark were related to WRS as John McKibben married WRS's Aunt Talitha Stilwell in 1845. John was currently 43 years old. He and Clark were the sons of Alexander who migrated very early to Henry and Butts County with Alexander's brother, Thomas and their mother, Margaret. Clark, currently 34 years old was a private in Company F. He was sent to Chimborozo hospital in Richmond on 2 May for treatment of diarrhea and was transferred to an Atlanta hospital on 25 May 1864. His service record ends there. Family history records that he came home and died.

Molly, you keep writing me to name the baby, but do you mean it? Didn't you name her long ago, Martha Jane? I think so and, of course, that is her name. I never did admire the name Martha much but I reckon it will do as well as anything else. If it suits you it suits me so let it be that. You can't imagine how bad I want to see the little fellow. You wanted to know if I got your letters straight [timely]. I do. I got one most every Tuesday or Wednesday. I got your last in five days. You are doing fine about writing. Now that is right. I must close for this tine. Give my love to Pa, Mother, and Aunt P.B., Sister and all. Tell them to write. Tell Granma I want to see her very bad and hope she will live until I get back from the war. Ask her if she wants me to bring her a pet Yankee. Kiss the children all over. Write often as you do and long letters. I am as ever your loving and true husband until death.

W. R. Stilwell

———

After more than a year's service, the army has been able to issue complete uniforms to all personnel. Stilwell reports that the suits are nice and fit well. He also reports, without comment, that the shoes have cloth uppers. The Confederacy does not have the wherewithal to supply all-leather shoes.

Camp Near Fredericksburg, Virginia, May 18, 1863
My dear Molly:
I am expecting a letter from you and would not write at this time if it was not to inform you in regard to clothing. I wished to inform you that I have drawn clothes from the government. It was ordered that all the regiments should uniform themselves, that is the government furnished the goods but they [soldiers] were obliged to take them. It comes out of their money allowed for clothes. I drew one jacket, pair of shoes, one pair of pants, and will draw another tomorrow, and a cap. It is a nice suit of blue and gray and fits me nice. The shoes are made of cloth, the toe and bottoms leather in Confederate style. I am not able to say what it will cost but suppose

161

thirty or thirty-five dollars. I am well pleased with it, it is good goods and neatly made. You need not send me any more clothes unless I write for them; at least not more than one shirt and two or three pair of socks. I don't need the shirt now. If Pa could get me a hat and send it I would be very glad but I suppose they are hard to get. I would want a light hat for warm weather, size 6 7/8.

All is quiet here, no visible sign of active operations. We gave Joe Hooker such a whipping that I think it will be some time ere he try us again. Some think that General Lee will advance on him but I don't thing he will, at least for some time.

The mail has just come and I will wait and see if I get any. Yes, I received a letter from Brother John F. S. It is the first in a long time. I was very glad to hear from him, he is well and speaks of getting a furlough soon and wants me to get one also and meet him. But, alas poor Billie has something else to do besides lie in camps and get furloughs, but I am glad that he has this privilege and would most gladly meet him there but the Army of the Potomac gets no furlough while the enemy lies in front of the great capital city of Richmond. I can tell another thing, the army of the Potomac is fighting this war and after it loses, it will be an honor to say I belonged to the Army of the Potomac.[19] John grumbles that I don't write but I think I am the one that should do that [grumble]. I have written time and again to him.

Dear Molly, I am very well today and doing as well as any one could in the army. We have a good nice camp and I have a tent and have made me a cot out of hickory bark in the shade so that I do well. Molly, I shall not write much this time as I will get a letter from you in a few days. I am sorry to say that William Chasen is dead.[20] He died in Richmond by sickness. Give my love to all the friends, all of Uncle William's family and tell them I want to see them very bad. Give my love to Pa, Ma, and Sisters. Kiss our sweet

---

[19] Stilwell is using the outdated designation. He means, of course, the Army of Northern Virginia.

[20] William Chasen has not been identified.

little children. Teach them the good and the right way and may we all meet in the morning. I am your Billie until death.

W. R. Stilwell

———

Brother John, home on furlough has stirred up the naming controversy by suggesting "Gertrude." Molly wants WRS to name the baby, and although he very much wants to do so, he keeps insisting that Molly name the child. She knows that he won't like any name she supplies, so she refuses. The charade continues.

Camp in sight of Fredericksburg, Virginia, May 28, 1863
My dear Molly:
I seat myself this morning to write you a few lines. I am quite sick and have been for over a week though I am better this morning than I have been in several days. I think it is principally [a] cold. I have had a very bad cough but it is some better now. If we don't have to march I think I will be well again soon. I had to move yesterday about five or six miles but had all of my things hauled so I don't think that it hurt me much. Our present camp is within one mile of Fredericksburg. I do not know the object of our moving up so near.

We had preaching at our headquarters last Sunday by General Pendelton.[21] You remember that it was said at [First] Manassas that there was a preacher who would sight his cannon and then say "Lord preserve the soul while I destroy the body—fire." This is the same man. We had a good meeting [with] a good many ladies out in the evening. There were eleven baptized about a half mile from our camp, nine from our brigade, and I walked down. The weather is warm, I think, is one cause of my being no better now and besides

---

[21] General William Nelson Pendleton was rector of an Episcopalian Church in Lexington Virginia. On the outbreak of war he became Captain of the Rockbridge Artillery and was rapidly promoted until he was Chief of Artillery of the ANV. Warner, *Generals in Gray*, 234.

there were a good many ladies there and of course I had to put on a good many airs but as I never have said much about the ladies, allow me to tell you of one that showed kindness to your sick husband. I had been sick for several days and not able to eat anything, so I concluded in the cool of the evening one day that I would go out into the country and see if I could not find some old mother that would bake me some light bread. So off I went. About a mile from camp I saw a house. On going up to it I found a lady whose husband was in the war. I made known my business. She said she was very sorry for me, she had no yeast then but she was going to make some the next day and if I would bring my flour out the next day she would bake me some. She went to her dairy and brought me a great big piece of light bread spread thick with butter. It looked so good I thought I could eat it and tried but failed, my appetite was gone. She gave me a bottle of honey for my coffee and would not have a cent for it. That day we were ordered to move our camp and I did not get my bread baked but that piece of bread and bottle of honey will long be remembered by a poor soldier boy.

I received your letter of the 17th yesterday, the first I had got in two weeks. I was very sorry to hear that Thomas was sick, I hope that he will be well in a short time again. I also received the name which John wants the baby to get. I don't like the name Gertrude, it is a novel name which he has got out of some novel. I thought that you had named her long ago and had quit thinking about it, only thought that I had a daughter by the name of Martha Jane but you keep writing to know what to name it. I want you to name it and you say you will want me to name her. If I must give my choice I will give it now, Mary Virginia Stilwell, thus the name would always be written thus, Miss Mary V. Stilwell or M. V. Stilwell. That is the first [choice], the next is thus: Madora V.S., Miss Madora V. Stilwell, but I have one choice above all of these, that is the choice you make that will suit me better than any other. If we call it by the first name of course we will always have to call her by the middle name of Virginia. I want it named and named now. I want no Sis about me.[22]

There is nothing new here. I believe more that William Darnell's regiment is gone to Goldsboro, N. C. We will never get together any more I don't suppose. I can't get any letter from him. I fear brother John is gone to Vicksburg, Mississippi. They ought to send us out there, we would not leave a Yankee on this side of the river. We are the boys to make Yanks get up and dust, cowardly pups. I am glad to say that we get plenty to eat now. Such as it is, old rank pickle beef and bacon. We get half pound a day now. We make greens out of the polk and other weeds. I don't like it much. General Semmes eats it most every day; I say starve the Southern army—you might as well try to starve a black hog in the piney woods.

Molly, I have written a long letter. I did not expect to do so when I began. It is badly done. You said you had the best husband about writing in the war, he has a better chance than most men and besides on a march I always keep one written in my pocket and whenever I see a chance I send it off. I am getting very tired and will have to close. You need not be uneasy about me. You know I never deceive you. If I was in danger from my sickness I would tell you. Of course I am sick or at least not well but I think it is nothing more than a cold. I must close. Give my love to Granma, Uncle, Aunt, Pa, Mother, Sister, and all the friends. Kiss the children for me. I am, as ever, your true and devoted husband until death.

W. R. Stilwell

———

Stilwell supports the war heartily and says he does not want any disloyalists returned to the Confederate Congress but he wants Joe Brown returned to the governorship. Historians have generally viewed Brown as a considerable hindrance to the war effort, but Stilwell

---

[22] In a time when the naming of a child could be deferred indefinitely, it was common to call an unnamed female child "Sis."

didn't think so and apparently most Georgians of the day agreed with him. Are we receiving the correct picture of Governor Brown?

Camp Near Fredericksburg, Virginia, May 29, 1863

My dear Molly:

As I was sick when I wrote last and knowing that you would be uneasy about me I thought I had better write to you again, I am much better now than I was when I wrote. I am now able for duty though I am not very well yet but hope I will be soon. I have not taken any medicine except some cough drops that I got from Knott. Molly, I felt so bad when I wrote last that I forgot to write about my clothing though I have wrote to you about it but you had not received my letter when you wrote last. I am afraid that you have already sent them and if you have, I will be very sorry as I have as many clothes now as I can take care of. I have drawn a full suit of uniform. The whole regiment had to take them, having no other pants all winter but my jeans that were worn out and I thought it best to take two pair of pants and did so, therefore I don't want anything but socks, if you have any chance send two or three pairs of light socks. Light ones will last as long and be more comfortable in summer. The socks is all I need, dear unless I could get a hat and I suppose that's very hard to do now. I forgot to say also in my last letter that I had sent you a present that I wrote about, by Major Robert Sandifer,[23] Pa is acquainted with him. I wrapped it in a paper and backed [addressed] it to you in the care of Uncle R[ichard] M. Everitt, McDonough. He will give it to Uncle Richard [Stilwell]. I sent a testament which I also captured on the battlefield. I wrote a note to Uncle Richard and addressed him to break open the bundle and look at the pocket. It was the best chance I had [for mailing] and I was afraid I would lose it. I hope you will get it safe. Mr. Sandifer is a nice man and I think will do right. The

---

[23] Mr. Robert Sandifer was a 42-year-old McDonough farmer who was a major in the 85th regiment of militia, not on active duty with the A. N. V. He was married to the former Atha Brown in 1845. In 1860 they had six children, ranging in age from one to 14, and three slaves. In 1870 he and his wife were living on a modest farm and now had nine children living at home.

testament is for Thomas and Madora. Molly, this is Sunday evening. I am setting on a rock which forms an island in the middle of a creek. Here I set writing, the water running all around me which seems to beat a lonely time and makes me think of friends far away. Many are the hours which I pass in those lonely places in the day and while I walk my lonely post at midnight and pray God that there may be a better day coming but I confess that everything looks darker now than it did eight months ago. It looks to me now just like this war has no end but let us remember that God moves in a mysterious way his wonders to perform and he can bring light out of darkness.

We have been expecting to march or fight for some time; have had orders to be ready to march and to cook rations time and again. Last night it was reported that the Yankee were about to cross above and below too and caused me to have to watch nearly three hours for signal lights which signals we're to march immediately but none were given and we are here yet.

Dear, only one letter from you in three weeks. I shan't say much yet but remember [unintelligible]. I wish congress would remodel the conscript act again. I haven't heard a word from Pa since they did [change] the last time but I don't want any more copperheads[24] sent back to congress. I want men of sense and reason. I want Joe Brown for Governor again. But this is no time to speak, now is the time to fight. We in our army always keep our armor bright and our powder dry and when they come we let fly and sure to be a Yankee die. We don't do like the army in Mississippi, get run off with a few bombs. I am glad I don't belong to that army, it's a shame on the Confederacy.[25]

---

[24] In the North, "copperheads" were southern sympathizers who wanted to stop the war. In the South, it was the exact opposite: Union sympathizers who wanted to stop the war. We now know that there were a considerable number of the latter.

[25] The beginning of the end for Vicksburg was on 1 May 1863 when Grant shifted to cross the Mississippi south of Vicksburg at Point Gibson, Mississippi. Grant marched to the rear of Vicksburg, taking Jackson in route. The most severe fighting took place at Champion's Hill on 16 May which went back and forth several times but ultimately the Union forces were winners. On the 19 May and again on the 22 May Grant attempted

Molly, I am somewhat uneasy about Tom but hope he is well by this time. Molly, if we should commence marching you must not stop writing, let that be a standing order. Write till I say don't write. I want you to read this letter to Uncle and tell them that they must not think hard of me for not writing to them separately as paper is high and hard to get. When I write to you it is to all of them. Tell Granma I want to see her very bad and often think of her but it is not worth while for me to name all—they know that I love them all and want to see them very bad. We get plenty of meat and bread now but I have no appetite for bacon. I have fallen off very much and look poor and thin again. I want beef time to come again. Molly, I am much discouraged about the close of the war but our only chance is to trust in God and do our duty, let us be cheerful trusting in God. I must close for the present. Oh for one kiss for you and our sweet little children. Remember I meet you at the throne of grace every night to pray for each other. I am as ever your true devoted and loving and lonely husband until death. May God bless us and ours, [this] is my prayer.

Good by

W. R. Stilwell

———

Stilwell writes his brother-in-law who is visiting the family group in Butts County while on sick furlough. Darnell was a member of the 27th Georgia Regiment that was en route to Charleston as this letter was written.

---

assaults of the Vicksburg lines and was repulsed with heavy losses. Subsequently, he forced the surrender by a classical siege. Boatner, *Civil War Dictionary*, 874-77. There was much wrong with the Confederacy's defense of Vicksburg in 1863 but it was mostly a result of lack of leadership and divided command. WRS is unjust in his criticism of the army defending Vicksburg but this attitude was probably typical of the men of the Army of Northern Virginia.

Camp Near Fredericksburg, Virginia, May 29, 1863
Mr. W. A. Darnell:

Dear brother, again I am writing to you. Why don't you write to me? I have never received but one letter from you since you went home.

I have been very unwell for some time past with cold. I think I am some better now than I have been for several days. I am able to be up and about and to go fishing. Our present camp is one mile from Fredericksburg and in full sight of the Yankee's camps. We can see their tents and their balloons go up most every day. I would attempt to give you some particulars of the late battles which have been fought here but you have no doubt seen them in the papers before now. I was at the battle of Wilderness Church at Chancellorsville and at Salem Church, the latter place is where our brigade suffered so much. Out of 1461 men, we lost 581 killed and wounded. In our regiment, we lost 181, [in] my company three killed and twelve wounded, F. M. Stephens, Floyd Dees and Lend Upchurch[26] were the killed. Joe Sowell was wounded very bad. Men never fought better than our regiment did at Salem Church. I was at my same old stand with the general and was very busy picking up coffee and blankets. I captured paper and envelopes enough to last me a long time. I almost got a little of everything that I wanted, even to a razor. I sent Uncle John the razor. I sent Molly a testament and a fine bead pocket which I captured. I know she would not take any thing for the pocket. It is the finest trinket of the war.

William, your regiment is gone to Goldsboro, N.C. I am sorry it is gone so far from us. I fear we will never get together any more unless you get a transfer to our regiment. I want you to stay at home as long as you can honorably with your family. I want to see you and sister and the children and all the friends at home. I don't expect [that] I will ever get to see my family until the war closes and I think that will be a long time if it ever does [come]. Tell

---

[26] F. M. Upchurch was a private in Company F. There are no entries in his service record beyond his first muster on 3 May 1862 and no identification of him in his civilian status is available.

Sister and the children and your Pa and Ma, Sister, all howdy for me and be sure to write soon. I am as ever your brother until death.

W. R. Stilwell

5

GETTYSBURG

Stilwell's unit is breaking camp. He knows that what happens next will be Lee's greatest adventure. But as an individual soldier, he dreads the prospects.

Camp Fredericksburg, Virginia, June 3, 1863
My dear Molly:

I wrote to you a few days ago and would not write today but we leave today or rather tonight, I suppose for a long march and it may be some time before I can write again though you know that I never fail to write when I can. It is not certain which way we will go but is generally believed that we are going to the same direction that we went last summer up in the direction of Culpeper and Winchester. We leave tonight at dark. May God be with and bless us everywhere we go and be with us.

Molly I made a mistake in dating my last letter. I dated it 29th, it should have been 31st. I won't write much this time as I have three days rations to cook. My health is fully restored now, I am well as common.

The object of our going off after dark is to prevent the Yankees from knowing of our movements. I suppose General Lee wants to deceive them. I don't like the idea of marching all night but whether I like it or not I have to lump it. I have got good clothes and shoes or boots. I don't want any clothes except socks. Molly, when we get to marching it may be that I can't get postage after I use up what I got. It will be well enough therefore for you, when you send to the [post] office, to send money to pay the postage for fear that I didn't.

We are trying to make the arrangements to get the mail all the time and I hope that I can get your letters and not be like it was last summer. Be sure to write often, don't fail to write if we go to Washington or Baltimore. I shall write when I can. I think I can or may have a chance to write when we get to Culpeper if we go that way. If we have got to fight, the sooner the better. I hate to start in that direction again, I suffered up there and hope to God that I may be preserved again this time. There is one thing; we got good beef up there last year. We can live well up there and that is what a soldier wants. I must close. My love to all of the friends. I ask a interest in all of their prayers. This is the last letter that you will get from this old camp. Write soon. I am your lonely, lonesome, absent husband as long as life lasts. May god bless us and ours.

W. R. Stilwell

P. S. I love thee always, oh God if it is possible take this cup from me, nevertheless not mine but thy will be done.

As promised, Stilwell has reached Culpeper and writes Molly a long letter. He is apprehensive about the coming adventure and its attendant hardships. But he is resolved to eat better on this trip into Maryland than he did last year. He now knows that the Marylanders are no friends of the Confederacy and if they are not willing to sell food (for Confederate money), it will be taken.

Camp Near Culpeper, Virginia, June 8th, 1863

My dear Molly:

After four days hard marching in dust and mud, rain and sunshine with tired legs, sore feet, and sleepy heads we have at last camped in ten feet of where we camped last November. Culpeper is about sixty five miles northwest of Fredericksburg and is situated on the railroad running from Richmond to Manassas, about 40 miles from the latter place, a beautiful place of about three thousand inhabitants. This place seems very familiar to me. I prefer this country to the country at Fredericksburg notwithstanding the nights are cold enough for frost and the days are hot enough to bake dough almost.

Dear, I expect to suffer a great deal this summer from hardships but thank God my little back has been able to stand many a rough storm on life's uneven sea. I am passing through some very rough scenes of this life, oh that God may still be with me as he has been in many a conflict. My health, I am thankful to say is good except my feet which are very sore. I need socks. My feet sweat and unless I change socks often in marching, [my feet] will blister and when they do it makes me think of Maryland. I don't know, but it looks very much like we are going there again. At least we are going in that direction. There is one thing sure, if I go back there again, I am going to live well. [If] there is anything there, if they don't sell it and this time at a reasonable price, I am going to press it into service. I only took rations and apples last year, but they are no friends of ours and I am not going to suffer while I can find anything there to eat.

I hear troops marching by now while I write. I expect we will have to march again tomorrow but I always write whenever I get a chance. I never fail to write to my Molly but I have to say that I haven't received but one letter from you in a long time, this makes the fourth letter [written by me] since I got any. We have mail [deliveries] all the time, what can be the matter? We got a mail last night and I looked but in vain. I wrote to you on the third, the day that we left camp. James Speer is here at headquarters in my mess. He is the adjutant's clerk and is doing very well now, he sends his respects to you. Molly, I can't write much now for I want to wash my socks and bathe my feet.[1] You can not imagine how bad I want

---

[1] James Speer is Molly's cousin. WRS reported on 10 February 1863 that he was facing court martial for refusing to fight at Fredericksburg while a member of Company G

to hear from you, as Tommy was sick the last account I had, but I have to write and wait and look. We will get a mail this evening and I do hope I will get a letter though if I do this will be gone so I cannot write to you about it if I get one.

As for war news, I haven't got much. A few days after our (Longstreet's Corps) left Fredericksburg, the Yankees crossed, had a little fight with A. P. Hill but I learn are all gone back.[2] I think they will fall back to defend Washington from Lee though I have no idea that Lee thinks of trying to take that place, but I think Lee intends to turn Hooker's right flank and force him back to Washington but what will be done we will have to wait and see. You may expect to hear of stirring events from our enemy soon; in fact, it is most always stirring. Our army ought to be fed on double rations and paid more than any other army for we do a great deal more than any other men in the service but instead of that we get less to eat, less to wear and less money but I hope we will get more independence.

Molly, I must close. You may expect letters from me as we have mails and I think that will be most of the time. Give my love to Uncle William, Granma, [and] Aunt Penelope. Tell Pa to take care of my baby and Ma to take care of you. I would to God that I could see you all but instead of going home I am going further away, though I don't care how far, so I can get letters from my friends, as I can't get home nohow.

I may be in a foreign nation in a few weeks. Of course Maryland is a foreign country, it don't belong to us nor I don't want it [except for] only what I can eat. Tell Margaret that Mr. Grey is

---

of the 19th Georgia. Service records shed no light on the resolution of this serious problem. There are no existing records that confirm the assignment of Speer to the 53rd Regiment.

[2] Ambrose Powell Hill was promoted to lieutenant general on 23 May 1863, and assigned to command one of the three corps of the Army of Northern Virginia created by the army reorganization occasioned by the death of Stonewall Jackson. Longstreet and Ewell had begun the march north but Hill was left at Fredericksburg in order to screen the movement. There were several days of skirmishing at Franklin's Crossing following 5 June but there was no concerted effort by the Federals to attack either those troops left at Fredericksburg or those on the march. Warner, *Generals in Gray*, 134.

here, he is a good soldier and always ready for duty. I am not very well acquainted with him, not being with the regiment, I don't know much about his habits but think he would drink a little if he had a chance and you know that don't suit me at all. A man can live without it here as well as at home or anywhere else. Lieutenant Vandergriff is sent to Richmond sick.

Molly, we are again near the mountains which look so much like dark clouds rising. I find myself writing yet I had no idea of writing so much, but I must close. Oh kiss the children for me, again write to me when you get your present that I sent by Robert Sandifer. Write me if you please, ma'am. I am your true devoted loving and faithful, never forgetful, ever lonely and lonesome husband taken from your bosom without my consent, left here against my will. When I die you can say he was faithful as a husband. May the good Lord take care of and preserve us all is my prayer. Farewell my dear Molly and babies.

W. R. Stilwell

———

There apparently was a letter dated 15 June written by WRS from near Culpeper. However the daughter of WRS who submitted his letters for judging to the UDC held this letter back. It never got into the archived collection and was subsequently lost.

The following June 20 letter is full of optimism about the current campaign closing the war. Stilwell expects to be in Baltimore or Philadelphia in a few weeks. He doesn't mention Washington; he knows that city is too strongly defended to be taken. There are stragglers and the legitimately sick on this march but the pace is not so brutal as during the previous Antietam campaign and straggling will not affect the outcome of the approaching battle.

Camp at Ashby's Gap in the Blue Ridge Mountains, Northern Virginia, June 20, 1863
My dear and beloved Molly:

This dark dreary rainy day I seat myself to write you and inform you [of] where I am. Ashby's is in Clark County, Virginia in the Blue Ridge Mountains 15 miles southeast of Winchester and about 25 miles from Harper's Ferry. I need not say that we suffered in marching so far I have seen many men lying fainted by the side of the road, some dying from heat, many whose feet are so sore that they could not walk. It was very dusty until day before yesterday, since then it has been wet and cold, Today it is one of those dark drizzly days which always makes one feel bad. I am sitting in the wagon on the gun trunk, the mountains so high on both sides that you can not see the sun till ten o'clock in the morning, nor after four in the evening. We would be marching today but the river is up and we have to wait until it falls. I am [with]in one mile of the Shenandoah river which empties into the Potomac at Harper's Ferry. You have no doubt heard of General Ewell's success at Winchester.[3] He captured six or seven thousand Yanks and all of their stores. He is now in Maryland and Pennsylvania with his army. I think I will be in Maryland if not in Pennsylvania, in a week if I live. We have had some little cavalry fighting for the last two days. I saw 40 yanks go by this morning. My health was never better. I am in good heart. I think we will end the war [with] this campaign. I hope I will be able to write to my dear from Baltimore or Philadelphia in a few weeks. If General Ewell goes on, he will be there soon and we will follow as soon as we can, tomorrow I suppose.

I have got all my clothes yet [as I] get them hauled. I haven't worn my new uniform but one Sunday yet, I am saving it for hard times and I know very well he [hard times] will be along this summer for I met him last year up here in the mountains. We cannot get any news up here from Vicksburg, don't know what is doing there but hope that General Pemberton is still fighting over Vicksburg or whipped them one. Molly I shall not send this letter today, as I don't know exactly when it will go off and I may write

---

[3] The Second Battle of Winchester took place 13-15 June and was a great Confederate success. Union losses were about 4400 compared to Confederate losses of only 269. Boatner, *Civil War Dictionary,* 937.

more. As I can tell more in a few hours perhaps I may have to write it with a pencil. We were five days marching from Culpeper [to] here, sometimes marching until twelve o'clock at night. I would to God that this war would end soon, both nations is ruined forever. I shall write more on another sheet. I may fill it up if I have time. If not, all right.

Molly I will have a good joke on you. In a few days when I get into the U. S., you know that according to the laws of nations when a man is banished to another nation that he can marry again. So I will be free and of course I could find some southern ladies over there, what eh you say, ha, ha, ha. Molly I went to bed last night and the rain run under my pallet until it would have done almost for a floating battery. I had to change my clothes and I crawled up into the second story of a horse stable and done fairly, so will try it again tonight.

My dear you must be sure to write every week though I shall be thankful if I get a letter from you every two weeks. I wrote you a letter from Culpeper the same day that we left which was the 15th. I will write often if I can. At the same time I would say don't be uneasy about me should you not get any in some time. I may be placed so I can't mail letters. Give my love to all our friends and relations, tell them to remember me in prayer and may the good lord preserve us all. Kiss our babies for me. I would give my arm to see them and you. I am yours truly forever till death.

W. R. Stilwell

———

Stilwell is still at Ashby's Gap crossing back and forth over the Shenandoah River.

Camp at Ashby's Gap on the Blue Ridge Mountains near
    Shenandoah River, June 22, 1863
Molly, dear and beloved Molly:
I wrote to you the 20th and did not get to finish it before we had to march again. I sent it off with one blank sheet, something I

never done you before. I would not write again so soon but I have the chance today and may not have it soon again and besides that our mails is so uncertain now and I know if you don't get letters from me when I am marching to invade an other nation amid strangers so many that you will be uneasy about me.

When I wrote to you the 20th we were on the south side of the [Shenandoah] River. We crossed that evening and camped on the north side the next day. Yesterday our cavalry had a fight with the enemy on the south side and we were ordered back and crossed back again.[4] I had to wade the river between nine and ten o'clock at night, the river where I crossed was about 250 yards which was on an average waist deep. I pulled off all my clothes and took it millpond fashion [naked]. It was very swift and the rocks hurt my feet very bad but I got over safe. The Yankees left and we closed to the north side again, making three times to wade the river. I can not tell we may have to cross two or three times yet but I think the next river we cross will be the Potomac into Maryland. General Ewell holds Fredericksburg City, Harper's Ferry and Hagerstown in Maryland and part of his army is in Pennsylvania and [he] captured 15,000 militia over there.[5] We are having stirring times here in the valley of northeastern Virginia. It seems like it has been my luck to be in every active campaign of the war. I have seen as much as any of them. I think we will start for Maryland in a day or two, we are only about 25 miles from the line.

My dear I have not yet any letter from you since the seventh of this month, it seems very hard that I can't get letters from you but I don't blame you with it. I know you write. I think I will get one soon, we had a mail yesterday. I hope I will get one soon. I have got all of my clothes along with me and a plenty of them except socks and I can do a while with what I have got of them. We haven't

---

[4] Lee's movement was accompanied by heavy skirmishing on the fringes of the advance.

[5] The hastily organized Pennsylvania Militia was brushed aside by Ewell's advance but the report of 15,000 captured is doubtful.

drawn any money in four months nor don't know when we will. I have yet enough to do me I reckon as I don't spend any now, only for tobacco, that is very high. Oh dear, you don't know how bad I want to hear from you and all the friends. Do write often and maybe I will get some of them. I must close for this time. I wish Father had the map of Virginia, I could tell him where to find me and that would be about a thousand miles from home, far from those I love. Oh, my wife, my dear wife and children, shall [I] never see thee any more on earth? God grant it. My love to all. I am yours forever more. Kiss em, kiss em, hug em, hug em.

Good bye my dear,

W. R. Stilwell

———

The Army is now in Pennsylvania and is well fed and in good shape. One of Lee's objectives in going into Pennsylvania was to provide food and forage for his army for a time in order to give Virginia a rest. Thus far, he has accomplished this objective.

Rest for two hours away up into Pennsylvania, June 26, 1863

My dear wife:

It is with great pleasure that I pen you a few lines to inform you that I am in good health and spirits although I am very tired and footsore. I am very glad to get to write to you as I know you want to hear from me very bad. I guess you will be surprised to see that I am in Pennsylvania and still going farther. We have stopped at twelve o'clock to rest two hours. I think old Abe is gone up this time. We are getting large quantities of stores of every kind. We passed through Hagerstown this morning, it is in Maryland. The ladies cheered us greatly but they can't fool me, they want to save their property. Beef has come in market again, it is very good. We have not had any battle since the battle at Winchester. I reckon you have heard of that. We took on all Yankee cannon, mules and wagons and commissaries. Molly, I can't write much as we have to leave shortly but I know if I was to only say [that] I am well and sign my name, it would do you a great deal of good. I am writing on a cartridge box and am so nervous being tired that I can't hardly write.

We crossed the Potomac at Williamsport above Harper's Ferry. I think we will go to Harrisburg Pa, that is the capital of this state, but I do not know but one thing sure: we are now making the greatest movement of the war and will make Yankedom howl and I hope to God, make them cry out "Peace, peace." This is the most beautiful country I ever seen, the whole country is covered with cherries. We make them smoke. Apples have not come in yet. Our army is in good condition enjoying plenty to eat and wear and confident of success. Molly, I think this is the last year of the war, God grant it. I am no man for conquest. I had rather be with my wife and children than to be here and subdue the whole Yankee nation. I want to see my Molly and babies. I hope I may see them ever long, oh may that day, that happy day soon come.

No move yet, I will continue my letter longer. Our army is much larger now than it was last year, therefore I hope for success. With the blessing of God we will do valiant things. We should thank him greatly for what he has already done for us. We have had abundance of rain lately and had to wade [through] mud and water. I did not wade the Potomac, I rode over in a wagon, it was not more than hip deep to the troops.

I received a letter from sister Jane [Darnell] dated the 11th but have not received any from you since the seventh. It seems like a long time but I am taking it easy. I leave you in the hands of God. He can take care of you and I believe he will do it. I don't expect to get any letters hardly from you while I am up here. Though I write always anyhow, it will make you feel better to think you have wrote to me. I will write every chance I get, this makes five letters I have wrote since I left Culpeper. I hope you will get some of them though the mails are not regular now. Dear Molly, I must close, I am very tired and must rest some. We have marched 14 miles today by twelve [noon]. Tell Pa, Mother, Uncle William, Aunt P. B., Grandma, Sis [Martha Ann Jane Ragland], Margaret, howdy.

Tell them I am in Pennsylvania and may be in Ohio in a few weeks. We are going that way now. Oh my babies what shall I say of them? God grant that I may have a happy meeting with them and may the happiness which once actuated our fireside again be done. To live and die with thee, for there is none else on earth like the little weekie in the bosom of my family. And now may the grace of our Lord Jesus Christ be with and remain with us all now hence and forever more. Goodbye, my Molly dear, goodbye, fifty thousand dollars reward for one kiss from thee and twenty-five each for the babies. Goodbye now, dear. Yours forever more and more.

W. R. Stilwell

———

Stilwell is continuing to enjoy the riches and beauty of Pennsylvania.

Camp near Chambersburg, Pennsylvania, June, Sunday the 28th, 1863

My dear and beloved Molly:

I wrote you a letter 2 days ago but did not get to send it off, I learn that a mail will leave tomorrow and I thought I would write you a little more and let you know how I am and where I am. My health is good except [for a] cold which I think was caused by wading the rivers and mud and going to sleep wet which I have to do often. We have stopped from 12 o'clock today until morning to rest and let the troops ahead get out of our way. Our present camp is two miles from Chambersburg, Pennsylvania and about fifty miles from Harrisburg the capital of the state, where it is believed is the place next [we go]. We crossed the Potomac at Williamsport and from there to Hagerstown near where the battle of Sharpsburg [Antietam] was fought, from there to Greencastle and on to Chambersburg. The people here are mostly dutch. It hurts them very bad to see the rebel occupying their country. We don't destroy anything, but what we need to eat and wear, such things as vegetables and chickens, honey, has to get eaten. An old dutch woman got after me today while getting some onions from her garden, she gave me fits, but I made her no reply, but yes'em. Remember Fredericksburg and the young ladies; silks torn from their wardrobe, yes'em, yes'em, Our generals don't let us take anything that the people will sell. We caught two or three hens and an old rooster in the presence of the general today. He wanted to know what we was going to do with the old rooster, we told him make soup, it diverted him very much.

We have not had any fights since we come into their country. I don't think we will until we get to the capital. I look for a right smart skirmish there. Chambersburg is a considerable place, some mile and a half or two miles across and is a perfect dutch town, though beautiful, some of the finest buildings I ever seen. The people looked very sour and crestfallen though they hope we will get whipped at the capital. I think not.

Molly, the mail come today and letters up to the 16 but none from you, no letter later than the 7th has been received from you. I hope I will get one soon but if I don't, all right, I don't blame you, I know it is in the mails. I must close. It may be some time before 1 can send another letter but you must take all things easy. Give my love to all. Mr. Lemmonds and Mr. Parker are all right. Kiss em for me. I am ever your affectionate though absent and unhappy and lonely husband. Yours till death and forever more. Pray for me and God take care of you and all my friends.

William R. Stilwell

———

This is the first surviving letter written after Longstreet's great assault on Cemetery Ridge of July 2. There may have been others written in the interim and it's too bad we don't have them in order to better understand the shock of the decisive Battle of Gettysburg. Stilwell doesn't yet know, or will not admit that Lee has been decidedly defeated. But he knows that the regiment is no longer the size of his original company and there is a long recitation of casualties, one of whom is brigade commander Semmes.

Since Semmes didn't survive and no battle report from McLaws survived, the actions and movements of the 53rd Regiment on that fateful day have not been reported by battle historians. Your editor believes that the area fought over by the men of the 53rd was the woods of the Rose Farm, east and south of the famous Peach Orchard. The regiment made several charges down into a ravine and up the other side into the Wheat Field. Somewhere in this ravine, Semmes was mortally wounded. There is no official count of regimental casualties for Gettysburg but in a later letter, Stilwell will present a very graphic account of the severe losses incurred on 2 July 1863.

Camp near Hagerstown, Maryland, July 10, 1863
My dear and beloved Molly:
Thanks be to God that I am still alive and have one more opportunity of addressing you. Many has been deprived of this blessing ever of speaking to their friends through the medium of the pen forever. I know that you must be very uneasy about me, it has been so long since you heard from me. I have wrote several letters to you after we got in Maryland and Pennsylvania but I have no reason to believe that you ever got them as the enemy captured several of our mails going and coming. I have no doubt but they got some of your letters. I have had none from you since the 7th last month. Oh what a long time it seems. It is very hard but I have borne it like a good soldier without murmuring, it is true. I want to hear from you very bad but still I feel more sorrow for you all at home than myself. I have suffered very much; hard marching in mud and rain, my clothes has not been dry until now; in five days and nights, war is like the infidels faith, it will do well until you come to test it and then it makes the heart sick. It has fallen to my lot to try a good portion of it but I still hope that the storm will blow over and all will be well but how long, oh how long, is a word that I often repeat on my pallet at midnight.

You want to know something about the battles. I know we have had a very hard battle and lost a good many killed and wounded. I don't know which got the worst of it as the Yankees had to fall back to prevent General Beauregard from going to Washington and our army had to fall back to support him.[6] You may not understand what Beauregard is doing here [but] neither do I, but the understanding is that him and D. H. Hill is somewhere on the edges with 40,000 or 50,000 thousand men. If that be true you may expect to hear of stirring times more than has been yet. The battle that we had was fought at Gettysburg, Pennsylvania. We took the city, our brigade suffered very much, our regiment lost heavy and more officers than I ever knew. Lieutenant Colonel Hance was killed. Captain Bond from Butts [County] and several more not now remembered [7] Captain Brown was shot through the leg between the knee and ankle. Lieutenant Farrar through the thigh. Sile Walker,[8] Gis Brannon,[9] George Fields,[10] James Fryer,[11] and several more were wounded, all of whom were doing well except James Fryer, he died shortly after he got to the hospital. In Company I from Butts, I don't know many that was killed or wounded except James Weaver killed, Sandy Parker wounded; he was shot through the

---

[6] This rumor is typical of the attitude of invincibility of Lee and his army; i. e., "The loss at Gettysburg was only part of a larger plan to capture Washington."

[7] John Mitchell Dooly Bond, Jr., captain of Company I (Butts County) of the 53rd Regiment, was 26 years old and had married Charity Goddard on 25 December 1859 when she was 16. They had two children. In 1860 he listed his occupation as schoolteacher.

[8] S. L. Walker was 21 years old and unmarried. He was the son of prosperous farmer and slave-owner Charles Walker and his wife Nancy Moseley. In the 1860 census he was listed as living with his parents and noted that he had attended school within the last year. His wound was serious, consequently he was placed in charge of the brigade ambulance train and surrendered at Appomattox. He married Mary Harper in November 1866. In the 1870 census they were living near McDonough with one child and he listed his occupation as retired merchant.

[9] Augustus H. E. Brannan was a 28-year-old Henry County farmer who was a private in Company F. He was married to Mary Livingston on 2 February 1855 and they had several children. He was permanently disabled and was living at home at the end of the war. He attended the 1904 soldier's reunion at Shingleroof Campground.

[10] George Fields was a 31-year-old farmer in Company F. In 1860, he was listed as living with his widowed mother and two sisters. He was listed as AWOL late in the war. No further record has been found.

[11] James Fryer was a 23-year-old private in Company F. In 1860 he was living with his father, John Fryer, a McDonough tailor, his mother and one sister.

hand, not dangerously.[12] John [Parker] was not hurt nor none of the rest of the boys that you know of the friends around there as [I] know of. I forgot to say that General Semmes was wounded through the thigh. I helped to carry him off the field. He said I was a faithful man. A good many of our wounded was captured as our cavalry was mostly gone down toward Washington,[13] they went in [within] three and a half miles of the capitol. In what direction we will go from here is not known but I think we will stay over on this side and have another fight or two. I think General Lee is going to fight the Yankees all this summer on their own land and make the people feel the effects of war. We made them feel it wherever we went. I have lived high on pork, fowls, butter and so, etc. I said I was going to live high if I come over here. Molly, a few more battles and our regiment will all be gone. It isn't much larger now than our company was when it came out. Oh the horror of war, who can tell, if this war lasts much longer there won't be any left. We don't know how the war is going on at Vicksburg nor nowhere else. We don't know anything but what we see as we don't get any papers. I hope they are all getting along well for I do want this war closed this year. I want to be with my family next year by this time if not long before. I have endured enough. I have suffered enough for anyone man, yet there is another that has suffered more. I ought to be, and I trust I am very thankful that I have fared so well but oh my Molly and my Tommy, and my Mother, if it was not for thee, I could give up my life more freely on the battlefield. I lay down night before last very wet and tired. I dreamt that I was at home and on how glad I was but when I woke I found that I was still lying in mud and water, I was greatly disappointed.

Molly, we have not drawn any money in a long time, going on five months but I have got plenty yet. I don't have to spend much

---

[12] James Weaver was second corporal of Company I. In 1860, he was a 28-year-old Butts County tenant farmer living with his son, Alonzo G., age 2.

[13] The regiment's casualties were suffered on the second day of Gettysburg, 2 July. Stuart's cavalry did not return from their ride around Mead's army until the night of the second. What the absence of cavalry had to do with the capture of the wounded is not known to the editor.

now. I have got paper and envelopes yet that I captured from the Yankees at Fredericksburg, and as for tobacco, it is played out [used up] since we crossed the Potomac. I bought four cigars in Hagerstown today to chew; can't get plugs now. I got me a straw hat in Pennsylvania, but it won't last long in service. I have got three pair of socks, I can make them last a good while yet.

Molly, I have wrote a long letter and must now close. I hope I will get a letter from you in a few days. There is nothing to prevent [it] now. I don't think we will stay here but a short time. I will try and write again soon if we don't march. Give my love to all the friends and tell them howdy for me. Write soon to your ever faithful and true Billle, howdy to Pa, Mother, Sister and all. Oh my Molly and my babes, what would I give to kiss thee. This war, this wicked war, God grant that we may meet again. I am as always your absent, lonely and ever faithful husband until death. Goodbye my dear Molly.

W. R. Stilwell

Good by my dear

―――――

Stilwell summarizes the extent of casualties by stating that the brigade has only 550 to 600 effectives remaining and the regiment has 150 men. His company is down to twelve or sixteen guns. "Guns" is a measure of firepower and is representative of the men present and available who carry rifles. It excludes the three officers and first sergeant and all men who have been detailed to support functions, such as Stilwell himself. The loss of firepower from the number of men detailed was significant and was a relatively fixed number that did not decline as overall manpower did. Thus effective firepower was more volatile than total manpower and dwindled severely as the casualty count grew.

Camp Near Hagerstown, Maryland, July 13, 1863

My dear and beloved Molly:

The first letter that I have received from you [since the seventh] was received yesterday dated 28. You may be sure that I was glad to hear from you and to hear that you all was well. We are having hot times over here and are losing lots of our men. I have not been hurt yet. I thank God but don't know how soon I may. The pickets are fighting now and a few hours may bring on a general engagement. Our brigade and regiment is most all killed and wounded. The brigade has not more than five hundred and fifty or six hundred men. Lost over half our regiment [leaving only] one hundred and fifty [men]. My company has twelve or sixteen guns and is commanded by William Norman,[14] the 2nd sergeant. Lieutenant Elliott[15] was shot through the arm and had to have it taken off the other day. Captain Brown and Lieutenant Farrar was wounded at Gettysburg, so you see that we are most all gone. I wrote to you on the 10th in which I stated that General Semmes was wounded. He has since died,[16] so my good old general is gone, never more to wear his sword at the cannons mouth in front of his men. I did him the last favor that I could, that was to help carry him off the field. He is gone but died as a brave man and a Christian. Colonel Bryan of the 16th Ga. Regiment is in command of the brigade now.[17] Molly, we have just heard of the fall of

---

[14] William P. Norman was a sergeant in Company F. In the 1860 census, he was living at home with his father and mother and seven siblings ranging in age from 16 to 1. He was listed as age 19 and recorded as having attended school that year. Home was a modest farm near Locust Grove in Henry County. He was captured at Sailor's Creek on 6 April 1865 and spent a short time as a POW before his release and return to Henry County. He married Sarah Lewis on 31 December 1866. In 1870 he was recorded as a landless farmhand with one child. He died in Henry County in 1895.

[15] Second Lieutenant Baylor S. Elliott was wounded in his right arm, necessitating amputation after a battle at Funkstown, Maryland on 9 July 1863. This was one of the rear guard actions covering the retreat of the Southern army across the Potomac. Funkstown has now been absorbed into Hagerstown. Unknown to WRS at this time, Elliott remained in hospital as the Confederates withdrew and became a prisoner of war on 12 July 1863. He was incarcerated for the remainder of the war at Johnson's Island, a prison on an island in Lake Erie. After the war, he married Fanny Sims in December 1867. In the 1870 census he was listed as a farmer of some substance with one child. He served as tax collector of Henry County in 1869 and 1879. He and his wife were also schoolteachers.

[16] On 10 July 1863 in Martinsburg (West) Virginia where he had been carried by ambulance.

[17] Colonel Goode Bryan was a 52-year-old West Point graduate, class of 1834. He resigned from service in the army the year following graduation. From then until the

Vicksburg.[18] Oh, how sorry I am, that is a great slam on us if it be so and I fear it is. I fear this army will all be destroyed before this campaign is over. We can't fight many more years longer if it don't stop. The men will all be dead. Man's life is as the grass and as the flower of the grass, man that is born of woman is of few days and full of trouble, my God, when will this war close?

Molly, I am glad that you got your pocket and book. In regard to our shoats [young pigs] do what ever Pa thinks best, if he can make meat out of them this fall, do so. Tell him not to bother about me a bit. I will try and make out and as for sending any money, I have got plenty of it, you need never fear about my not having money. I always manage to have it. Molly, as I was sitting writing the mail boy brought me a letter from Brother John all right, very glad to hear from him. He is seeing a good time. I wrote to you in my letter of the 10th of the death of James Fryer killed at Gettysburg, Pennsylvania.

Tell Bob [the slave?] I would like to have some of his cider but can't afford to drink it and as for meat I have eat flour bread until I prefer corn or lightbread. Molly, I like the baby's name very well. I suppose it is Martha Virginia, at least that is the way you wrote it down. I reckon it will be called Martha Molly.

I always speak the truth, I am discouraged, don't believe the war will close in a long time. Everybody is tired of it but they don't look to the right source for help. Give my love to Uncle William, Aunt P. B. and Granma, Pa, Mother and all Sisters. I want to see them all very bad but don't know that I may ever do so. Molly, if I fail, my prayers are for you and the children, my trust is in [the] Lord. If I fall I want to fall at my post though God grant that I may see my family again before I go home. Oh, Molly, I

---

outbreak of war, he was a planter in Alabama and Georgia. Residing in Georgia in 1861, he was elected a member of the Georgia secession convention from Lee County, entered Confederate service as a captain in the 16th Georgia and attained command of the regiment in February 1862. After resigning due to ill health in September 1864, he was semi-retired, living in Augusta GA until his death in 1885.

[18] Vicksburg surrendered on 4 July 1863. The Confederacy was now cut into two halves and the North had full navigation of the Mississippi River.

didn't think that we was ever to be separated this way. Write once a week and may the good Lord take care of us all and save us in his kingdom. I must close. I am as ever your loving husband until death. Kiss the babies for me. Good by my Molly dear

William R Stilwell

———

Stilwell is now back in Virginia. He commiserates about the recent rains and the misery they caused. He does not understand the extreme danger that the rains posed to the whole army. The Potomac was too high to be crossed for several days and you had a defeated army with its back to an uncrossable river. If Union Commander Meade had been more aggressive, the results to Lee's Army would have been disastrous.

Stilwell has no doubt that God is on the side of the Confederacy. Defeat means that God is displeased and is punishing his chosen people for some sin. Thus, Southerners have to discern which actions constitute a sin in the eyes of God. WRS believes that He is displeased with the invasion of "their" country. This belief does not seem to be confined to Stilwell; other Southerners have expressed the same belief but it was far from being universal.

Camp 12 miles between Martinsburg and Winchester,
  Virginia, July 16, 1863
My dear Molly:
Again I engage myself to write you a few lines which will inform you that I am in good health and [unintelligible]. We have stopped for a day or so to rest and clean up our things, where we will go now I know not. I am very much discouraged at the fall of Vicksburg and the threatened fall of Charleston. I fear it will fall too as so many of our men have been sent off from there on our campaign into Maryland, and Pennsylvania has not been very successful, our army is much discouraged, men never suffered worse for the length of time than our army will while we were near the river. It rained most all the time and the mud was knee deep, a great many barefooted and wounded. I am fully convinced that it is

not right for us to invade their country. God has showed his displeasure every time we go over there and has never bless our arms with such success as he has in our own country. Therefore I don't think it is right.

So far as war news is concerned, I refer you to the papers as I have not time now to give details. I am now acting courier for Colonel Bryan, [who is] now in command of our brigade. One of the couriers was wounded and was sent off and may never return and they appointed me to take his place until he comes back, if he ever does. It is a very dangerous position but quite an honorable one. My business is to carry orders and some times I have to take them in the hardest of the battle. I have a horse to ride. I go with the general wherever they go. It is a good place to form acquaintances and friends with the big officers and that is the main thing. I flatter myself that I have made some good friends that will do me all the favors they can. I have no idea how long I will keep the place but as long as they want me to or get a better [man].

I received a letter four or five days ago from you of the 28th and last night I got one of the 21st. I have written several lately. I hope you have got them. Molly, I have bought one pair of socks for one dollar and a half as I am riding finely now for some time. Don't be uneasy about me I always look ahead. I have got money a plenty though I have not drawn any in most five months. I am satisfied with the baby's name. Give my love to all the friends and relatives. Lemmonds and John Parker are well. I wrote you about Sandy wounded. I will write more and better when I have time. Tell all howdy and kiss the baby and may God take care of us all for Christ's sake. I am yours forever more. Goodbye Molly.

William R. Stilwell

————

Stilwell, though willing to fight on, would agree to a compromise settlement to end the war. But does he have any idea as to what could be compromised? Lincoln won't agree to end the war without restoring the Union and Jefferson Davis will accept nothing but independence.

So no compromise is possible and war will go on for almost two more years.

Camp near Winchester, Virginia, July 19, 1863

My dear and beloved Molly:

This beautiful Sabbath morning I take my seat to write you again. Notwithstanding I have written not many days ago, yet I received your letters of the 7th and not having anything that gives me more satisfaction than writing to you, I thought I would write a few lines. Molly, this is one of those beautiful, still and solemn Sabbath mornings and this morning, while walking amongst the cedars I could not help saying "Oh God, how long shall I be separated from worshipping with my family." Oh, if I could just kneel around the family altar with you this morning or could I hear the old church bell toll, it would give me more pleasure than to conquer empires and subdue kingdoms not so. Oh lord, I am hundred of miles from those that I love, from the family altar, from the old church yard without any thing to cheer me except my bible and hymn book but thank God they can furnish me a great deal of consolation and I can kneel though I be thousand of miles from home, yes sweet home and pray to my Father which sayeth in secret and feel that all is well. Oh that God may grant us again to meet and live happy as we have done in days past and gone and may God bless you today is the prayer of yours forever more.

Molly, my health is good as usual although I have fallen away until I am very poor. I think it is caused by hardships and fatigue. I have had a hard time, even my clothes was not dry day or night for most a week but I have got along this far and hope I may be able to do so in future, though what is in [the] future for me God only knows for I don't see any prospect of the war closing in a long time unless we give up and that won't do, but many are of the opinion that we will have to do so. I believe I would consent to a compromise. I want it to stop. If it goes on much longer there won't be anybody left. I hope they will settle if some way this year and stop the flow of brothers blood. I have seen enough to satisfy me forever.

Tell Father that I am obliged to him for his proposal to send me money but I have got plenty and don't need all that I have got. I reckon we will draw some time this year but I am not in a hurry. I have got 25 or thirty dollars in my old clothes. I always keep it on hand. Don't be uneasy about that. I like the baby's name very well but I notice that you called her Sis, stop that. Your letters come very regular now and will from now on I think. I am acting courier now and will be in much danger in a fight, more so than ever but I get to ride, the other courier was wounded. I may quit when he comes back if he ever does, I don't know. My duties are to carry orders. I am your Billie as ever till death.

William R. Stilwell

————

Stilwell is still moving south. His spirits seem to have been revived somewhat by his new duties and the failure of Union forces to take Charleston.

Camp near Culpeper, Virginia, Saturday, July 25, 1863
My dear and affectionate Molly:
I have no doubt but you are very anxious to hear from me. We have been marching for some time past. You will notice that we are making our way back south, we got here on yesterday and will rest today though I don't get much rest myself having to carry round orders every few minutes. I like my position very well but it is a very dangerous one. We have not had much fighting since I last wrote to you as we had however, a little fight the other day in the mountains and the shells came pretty close but nobody was hurt on our side as I heard of. We run them off and come on, the general opinion is that we will go back to Fredericksburg in a few days. We are camped on the road leading there and I think we will go back there. I don't care; I had as live go there as anywhere unless it was home and I see no chance for that in a long time although I believe that God will bring the war to a close whenever it is his will that it should close, and that may be this year or it may be five, but as far

as man can see it looks like it will last a long time. The Yankees failed at Charleston,[19] Beauregard[20] is not Johnston, he fights them whenever they come to him.[21]

My health, dear Molly is very good and while my comrades have fallen by sickness and on the battlefields, yet I am permitted to live and enjoy good health. I try to feel thankful for this great blessing. I am getting along as well as anybody could most in service, I have as many friends and as true ones as any boy in service. Molly, I can't write much this time as I have to see about getting my clothes washed or do it myself and my other duties. Keeps me busy most all the time. I wrote to you few days ago. You may send me one extra pair of drawers when you send my socks. I bought me one pair of socks. Send them [socks] the first chance. I think there will be passing [fighting] before long. Molly, I have passed through the second campaign through Northern Virginia and no one knows what we have suffered but them that has been along. I hope I may never have to pass through another one. I think I will get a letter from you today or tomorrow. Get the children's likenesses taken when you can conveniently. Give my love to all the friends and relatives. Write soon, kiss the boys for me, tell all howdy. As for you, you can kiss this letter and let us worship God for his goodness towards us and pray without ceasing and in everything give thanks unto God. I am as always your ever true, devoted and affectionate husband until death.

William R. Stilwell

---

[19] On 11 July 1863 and again on 18 July, Union forces were repulsed with heavy losses in assaults on Fort Wagner, one of the forts guarding Charleston harbor. *Civil War Day by Day*, 383, 387.

[20] Peirre Gustave Toutant Beauregard was the hero of Fort Sumter. He was one of the full generals in the Confederate army and he successfully defended Charleston from both sea and land attacks. Charleston was never captured until abandoned during Sherman's march through the Carolinas in 1865.

[21] Joseph Eggleston Johnston was another of the full generals in the Confederate army. At this point, WRS is probably reflecting the lack of confidence in him as a result of the loss of Jackson MS and Vicksburg.

We don't read much about couriers in Civil War literature. Such people were usually titled as aides and were lieutenants. Every commander from brigade level up had numerous couriers/aides because that was the only way he had of communicating with his subordinate units. There is nothing that explains how an enlisted private fits into the brigade staff as a courier. As Stilwell describes the duties and cites incidents in later letters, there seems to be little difference in his duties and those of the numerous lieutenants that he works with and whom he calls couriers. So it is quite a position of honor for a private soldier. Stilwell sees it as a great opportunity to make acquaintance with staff officers from whom he can learn and who might provide favors in the future. It fits well with his intense ambition.

This letter is to his Father and Uncle William about obtaining the funds to buy a horse and fittings. Most every mounted Confederate soldier, even the private cavalryman had to furnish his own mount and the $37 monthly pay quoted by WRS is the same pay of a private cavalryman out of which he has to pay for much of the horse's upkeep.

Camp Near Culpeper, Virginia, July 27, 1863
Dear Uncle and Father:
I wrote Molly a short letter on my arrival here in which I stated that I was acting courier in this brigade. I have since been permanently appointed and my object in writing so soon again is to ask for advice and also for some assistance if it can be rendered conveniently. You no doubt understand the duty of a courier; it is that of carrying orders. They remain with the general all the time unless sent off by him on duty. They are allowed feed for their horses, they are obliged to have one. They get 37 dollars a month which is pretty good wages. It is a much easier place than in ranks, they have more privileges, have their things hauled and their rations also and in fact they fare much better than in ranks and then they get more credit and honor. This position I have gained by doing my duty and always standing square. General Semmes, on the bed which would have been his death bed if he had not been removed, said I was a faithful man. This is why I say I have gained this position by

doing my duty. Now I have given you all the information that I can. One reason that I wish the place is that you know I am not stout nor able to carry things in ranks. I have got the appointment but one thing I lack yet, that is a horse. I have one to ride until I get one or for a while at least. I can get a horse, bridle, and saddle for two hundred and fifty dollars. Now the assistance that I wanted is to help me pay that amount. I have about forty dollars; the government owes me for five months service which is fifty-five dollars. I will get thirty seven dollars a month from now on so you see that if I live I can soon replace the money and if I should not [live] the horse will be worth the amount. If my horse gets killed in battle I get paid the full value of him so you see I have no risk to run, only [if] the horse may die. I have given you all the facts in the case. Now I want to know if you can assist me any and if so how much. I don't want either of you to disfurnish yourself, no I had rather go to ranks and bear the burdens than that, but I think I can replace the money in a short time. I want you to consult and determine and let me know as soon as possible if you can oblige me. I shall feel very thankful. If not, I shall not think hard of it in the least. I have not tried to make any arrangements, it may be I could get the money here but the regiment has not been paid off in five months and I prefer getting it from my friends. I believe that Colonel Bryan who commands the brigade would let me have the money. He will be promoted to general soon. It is he that has given me the appointment.

My health is good; we are camped here for how long I don't know. The general opinion seems to be that both armies will go back to Fredericksburg but I think that we will fight before we get there. I have been most covered up in dust by shells during our late battles but thank God I am safe, yet no one, but they that have tried it, can imagine the feelings of a man amidst the bursting shells and flying shot when every valley seems to belch forth the arrows of death. My love to all. I am as ever your affectionate son and nephew always.

W. R. Stilwell

———

Although the new baby at last has a name—Martha Virginia, to be addressed as Virginia, Stilwell continues to take little interest in "it" as he refers to her. The religious revival in the Army of Northern Virginia continues.

Headquarters Bryan Brigade, McLaws Division
Camp near Culpeper, August 1, 1863
My dear Molly:
Again and again have I wrote to you without having received any one from you. I want to get a letter from you very bad. I have not received any letter from you since the 11th of July. I blame the mail and not you. I believe that you have wrote.

We had orders last night to take up the line of march this morning for Fredericksburg, but this morning the order was countermanded, having heard that the enemy was below between us and there. Orders has just come to march. I expect a fight, good bye.

Aug. 2nd—Dear Molly, we lay in line of battle all day or all evening yesterday but no fight occurred. I think that we will march in a few hours perhaps to Fredericksburg. This is Sabbath morning, the sun is just up, our division is now lying in line of battle but I don't think we will fight here though I think we will have to fight soon. I am still acting courier. I have the appointment now. I may fall in the next engagement, God only knows, but if I do I hope I am ready. I feel that I will die in a just cause if I die it will be in defense of my country and the liberty of my people. I very much desire though to live to enjoy the company of my family and to raise my little children. I hope that God may spare me to get home but if I don't, thank God. I have ever been faithful to you and can only leave you and the children in the care of him that is able to take care of you. My desire is that Tommy be educated well and taught that religion is worth more than all else besides. I want him raised that way, as for the other [baby] I love it although I have never seen it; it is yours to do as you think best. I know you will raise it right. You can keep this letter and read it to them perhaps when I fill a soldier's grave though God forbid, nevertheless they will be close to God. You can tell them that it was religion that enabled their Father to endure the toils and hardships and sufferings of a good soldier. Don't let this make you feel bad. I don't do it for that, but that it may do good some day. I feel that whatever is best for us all will be done. I leave the rest of this sheet so that if any move takes place before the mail leaves I can mention it. I have something else to write. [Letter continues in pencil].

No more today. Preaching at dinner and meeting this evening again and to-morrow. If we don't mind we are going to have a basket [?] meeting. Goodbye.

William R. Stilwell
Courier for General Bryan.

———

In the aftermath of Gettysburg, Stilwell describes the army as being in pitiful condition, in need of rations, clothes, and shoes. God has laid a curse on the army.

Stilwell loses his usual even temperament and blasts Molly for her short letters. He gets so mad that part of what he wrote is reported here as unintelligible. Examining the original letter, the editor cannot make any sense of what he is writing in the passage but some awfully hurtful words appear. He regains his composure and moderates his tone with the remainder of the letter but he does mail the whole as a warning to Molly.

Headquarters Brigade, August 6th, 1863, Camp 20 miles above Fredericksburg, Virginia

My dear Molly:

Your kind letter of the 27th July was received day before yes-terday. You may be sure that I was glad to get it for it was the first in a long time and although I never suffer myself to become very un-easy on such occasions, I confess that I was beginning to think some-thing must be wrong. My dear, I am in the enjoyment of good health this morning. You will notice that we are gradually moving down towards our old stand [at] Fredericksburg. We are now about

197

12 miles from Chancellorsville where the last battle was fought. At Fredericksburg, it is very likely that we will have to fight there again as the enemy is moving that way. Oh, the suffering that our troops has to suffer. Just think of the searching rays of sun of August and men marching with their baggage on their back. I have seen men fall by the roadside fainting almost every day. Marching barefooted, their clothes almost torn off them and [on] half rations. God deliver our people from the curse that overhangs them. Our rations are short now and have been for some time. We have to buy or suffer and the men have not been paid off in five months. As for my part I have made out very well thus far. I have about 40 dollars now but I must buy me a horse somehow or other. I can soon make the money back but how to raise it now is the thing. I don't know hardly how I will do it unless Father and Uncle William help me. I have written to them about it. I have a horse to ride now and may have it some time but I had rather have one of my own. Horses are very high now I know, but it is so much better than carrying a musket and knapsack and in fact I am not able to do that. Then I will get 37 dollars a month and can learn more and see more and far better. I would not miss getting me a horse for five hundred dollars. If my horse gets killed, the government pays me for him. If I get killed, General Bryan will sell him and send you the money. He is another clever man and thinks a heap of me, he gave me the appointment of courier over the head of the other one and told me to get me a horse, that he was going to keep me. I tell you, if a man will do his duty and be a man he will always have friends. I always have plenty of friends, I hope I will not be parted from General Bryan like [I was from] Semmes though I feel that he [Semmes] is better off. Just before he died he called for his sword and testament. He placed his sword by his side and locked his hands round his testament and across his breast, thus he died.

Molly, your letters are so short. I do think you and Sis Mag could write more than that [unintelligible]. Your letters are short and sweet like a roasted maget. I know I write more than is necessary but you must forgive me for writing so much to you, but I can't help it for it does me good to write and I imagine that it does you good to read. Mother's poetry was also received. It is the best piece I have seen. I shall write a reply to it and send in this letter though I have not time to do the piece justice. If I had time I could do better. As for more news, I have quit writing on that subject. You did not write to me what papers father and uncle take. I would advise them to take the Savannah Republican as Peter W. Alexander,[22] the noted correspondent of that paper stays at General McLaws' headquarters in our division. By that means they would always get the news direct from our division. I am acquainted with Mr. Alexander, he is a nice man and a good writer. I would be glad if they would take it. I would send them a Richmond paper but they would not get them regular.

Molly, I would give most anything in the world if I could just see in my imagination how Tommy and the baby looks but I cannot. You may think it strange that I can see how Tommy looks but I have been gone so long that I have almost forgot how he once looked. As for the little Jinnie, as I never seen her, of course I never can imagine how she looks. I want you to have ambrotypes taken the first chance you have and send them to me. They would afford me many a pleasant hours pleasure. Yours is most worn out. I have to keep it wrapped up in paper. Molly, somebody stole your little bible out of my coat pocket, it almost makes me cry to think about it. I would not have taken anything for it. I have a larger one with reference to it but it is so large to carry it is unhandy. I am reading *Baxtus Saints*. It is like a good spring in a weary land. Give my love to Granma and Uncle William and Aunt P. B., Pa and Mother, and all Sisters too. Tell Tommy that Pa wants to come and see him bad, [and] to be a good boy and do whatever Ma and Granpa tells him. Teach him to be a good boy and to say his prayers at least twice a day and may God grant that you may be able to raise them right and that if we never all meet on earth again that we may one day form an unbroken family in the kingdom of heaven, to praise

---

[22]This is excellent advice about Peter W. Alexander who was one of the premier reporters of the war. However, it is doubtful that he stayed much at McLaw's headquarters because he ranged all over the South.

him who has been a friend and helper in this life. Pray for me, my dear, I think of thee last thing at night and the first thing in the morning. I hope there is a better day a coming. I am yours as always until death.

Good bye my dear Molly,
W.R. Stilwell

———

A short letter written mainly to acknowledge receipt of the offer for advancing $150 for the horse and to discuss possible means of sending the money.

Headquarters Bryan's Brigade, Camp between Culpeper and
    Fredericksburg, Virginia, August 11, 1863
My dear Molly:
Your letter of the 11th was received today and I hasten to reply to it. I feel very thankful that uncle and father can accommodate me with a hundred and fifty dollars. I would have been very glad if they could have let me had as much as (200) as our regiment have not drawn yet and may not in a month or two but nevertheless, I am very thankful for that much. If you can send it by Lieutenant Farrar do so and if not, wait until further notice. Don't risk it by mail yet, I had rather wait longer, at least for the present. I have no chance to write having wrote to you yesterday. I am well and doing well. I am glad to hear of the meeting, God grant that you may have a great revival that may spread all over our land and country. Give my love to Brother and Henry and tell Uncle Dorman that he was the first preacher that ever put his hand on my head and told me to be a good boy.[23] Give my love to Uncle William' s folks and all the rest—my pen is so bad I can hardly write with it. Molly, send that money by Farrar if you can, if I want you to send it by mail I

---

[23] Brother and Henry are unidentified. In the context of association with Uncle Dorman, they are likely church officials.

will let you know. Don't forget to kiss the baby for me and may we all meet soon is my prayer. I am yours forever more.

William Stilwell

———

Stilwell is in a black mood over the dismal prospects for the Southern cause. Morale of the troops is at rock bottom and rumors of disaffection of the North Carolinians and Georgians are everywhere. The speculators and extortioners have turned God against the Confederates. Stilwell then turns to the question of whether his drawers should be white or colored; such a changeable temperament!

Headquarters Semmes Brigade [Now Bryan's], Camp between Culpeper and Fredericksburg, Virginia, August 13, A .D. 1863

My dear and affectionate Molly:

Your kind letter was received this morning before breakfast. Of course I was very glad to hear from one that I love so dearly. I am in the enjoyment of good health but not of spirits. Oh, Molly, how dark, this indeed is a dark day for the Confederacy, hundreds of our men are deserting and those that remain are discouraged and disheartened and people at home are whipped and want us to give up. To give up is but subjugation, to fight on is but dissolution, to submit is awful, to fight on is death. Oh, what shall we do? To submit, God forbid. To fight on, god deliver. Oh, Molly, when I think of the thousand of mangled forms of human beings crippled [and] torn in pieces, the thousands of widows and fatherless children all over our land, the weeping and moaning and anguish throughout the land, I am compelled to cry out. Oh, God, how long will thou afflict us, how long shall the horrors of war desolate our once happy country. Is the strength of God weakened or is his arm shortened? Nay, but sins of the people have rose like a dark cloud between us and God, yes between us and the mercy seat. We seek the creature and not the creator. Speculators and extortioners seeking gain out of the blood of their brothers and women and children. I tell you dear

201

Molly, unless the great God helps us we are gone and how can we expect him to bless such a people as we are. I once believed in the justice of our cause but we have made it a curse and not a blessing. I believe that the next six months will decide our fate and I fear it will be against us. All that I can say is God forbid.

The men from North Carolina held meeting yesterday, I believe they will go back in the Union.[24] The men from Georgia say that if the army invades Georgia they are going home. I don't believe our army will fight much longer. I know that many will or would say that 'I am whipped.' I would say to them if they would come and see and feel what I have they would feel as I do, as for my part I can do as well as any for my trust is in God but enough of this subject as time will prove my saying. I saw a list of the killed and wounded in the 32nd Georgia Regiment at Charleston yesterday. I reckon Brother is there. It seems strange that you didn't know it the 4th of August for that was the day of your letter.

Molly, you desired to know whether I wanted my drawers white or colored. Colored is preferred if convenient but if not, it don't make any difference. Don't be uneasy about my socks. I have one pair of woolen stockings and a pair of cotton socks yet. I can make them do some time or during the summer. I can do very well yet but thought you had better send them when you could, so you may do so.

Dear Molly, you spoke of my coming home on furlough. There is none gone home now unless sick or wounded. Thank God that has never fallen to my lot yet. You said you wanted to see me. I don't suppose there is a man on this earth that wants to get home any worse than I do, you know my love too well to doubt that, but I have never entertained much hopes of getting home until the war closes. I think through the mercy of God I will get to go then and I don't think it will be long. God speed the day. I am looking for a letter from Father and Uncle and I hope I will get one soon. Molly, you must get them pictures [of the children] taken and send them to me soon.

---

[24] While the North Carolinians were always suspected of Unionist sentiment, I do not think this report was true.

I don't think we will have any more fighting soon, at least in two or three weeks. General Bragg will fall back to Atlanta, I fear.[25] If so, I want Joe Brown to call all of his troops home and if he don't I believe they will go anyhow.

The weather has been extremely hot here for some time. While I write I am sitting upstairs in a fine two story house at the window. Our headquarters have been here for some time passed, it is a beautiful place. Molly, you must not scold me about loosing your little bible. I am so sorry I most cry every time I think of it. I didn't lose it myself but it is gone, it had been with me in and through many affliction and hardships.

John Parker is well, I haven't seen Mr. Lemmond lately, he is off some-where with his wagon. Molly, We are going to have peas for dinner, the first time I have had any in some time. We don't get a bit more than we can eat of late days. We draw some meal lately which I am very glad of. I am very fond of it accordingly. We draw one pound and one quarter a day.

I went last Sabbath to hear the Rev. Dr. Stiles, D. D. from Savannah preach.[26] He is one of the oldest devines in the Presbyterian Church. He made one of his best efforts. You can find his text at Psalm 49, 8th [verse][27]. Oh that such men would stay and preach in the army, they would be worth more than a brigade of wicked men. I must begin to close my long letter. I hope the day will soon come when I will not have to write to you but see you face to face. Give my love to Granma and Uncle William, Aunt P. B., Mother, Sister and all. Oh the babies, kiss em, kiss em, hug 'em for me. Oh, Molly, shall I never see thee again on earth, God grant it

---

[25] Braxton Bragg, another Confederate full general, was in command of the Army of Tennessee and was currently holding a defensive line protecting Chattanooga.

[26] Clay Joseph Stiles, 1814 graduate of Yale Law, practiced law in Savannah until he became a Presbyterian minister in 1825. He organized the first Presbyterian churches in Millegeville and Macon GA and served as pastor in New Haven CO from 1853-59 but re-signed and returned to the South due to rising sectional conflicts. He resided in Savannah until his death in 1875. E. C. Scott, compiler, *Ministerial Directory of the Presbyterian Church US 1861–1941*(Published by order of the General Assembly, 1942) 658.

[27]"For the ransom of his life is costly, and can never suffice."

but if not let us meet in Glory where there is no more partings, sorrow and weeping, all for ever more. I am your true and devoted and loving husband always even to the end. Good by my dear Molly. May God bless us all, amen.

William R. Stilwell

———

Stilwell is still "out of heart" at the South's chance of winning the war. He believes that it is the civilian population that is causing God's disfavor. The army continues its religious revival with WRS, at least, attending two religious services a day.

Headquarters Semmes [now Bryan's] Brigade August 27, 1863, Camp Frederick Hall, Virginia.

My dear Molly:

Yours and Sister's letter was received day before yesterday. I would have wrote sooner but we have been moving and I couldn't. I have not time now to write you a long letter. I am enjoying good health and doing very well although I am out of heart about our independence being gained. I think now that the only way to stop the war is by compromise, and I think the sooner it is done the better for us. I think that Charleston will be taken in a few days. But I am not the one to say when the war should close but don't think it can last long, God grant that it may stop soon, so might it be.

I received a letter from Uncle John the other day with the express receipt for that money which Father, Uncle and some other unknown friend sent me.[28] I have sent to Richmond for it and will be likely to get it shortly. I don't need it yet as Colonel Bryan has not yet got his promotion but is looking for it every day. There is not a prospect of any fighting here soon, in fact it is said that the Yankees is falling back towards Washington and our army is falling back towards Richmond. Our division is not more than 40 miles

---

[28] The editor has no documentary evidence of who is the unknown friend, but guesses that it is Uncle John.

from there, we are in a good camp and will stay here a good while, I think.

Molly, your letter gave me a great satisfaction in regard to the meeting at Pleasant Hill and several other things. I hope that God will bless you all at home and see that they will quit speculating. God has sent his blessings among us; we have meetings most every day. I attend preaching most every day and prayer meeting every night. I was very glad to hear that the children was in so good health but I was very sorry to hear that my Molly had the toothache, for Molly, Billie is not there to sympathize with her. Dear, I shall have to accuse you of being a tory.[29] I think that you would most be glad if the Yankees would whip us if you thought it would bring me home, but I must forgive you when I remember that it is because you want to see your dear boy. You must endure the cross as a good soldier and trust in God to bring your Billie home to you and if he never gets to see you again on earth, it will make our meeting in heaven more sweet. *If we miss that we miss all.*

Tell Sister that I will write to her soon. I have not time now. I will write again as soon as I get that money. I am uneasy about Brother John. I guess he has heard shells bust enough to satisfy him. I don't suppose he wants to hear any more. I hope and pray that he will come out safe. Give my love to Granma and Uncle William and aunt P. B. Tell them I want to see them very bad, give my love to Pa, Mother, and Sister, and Oh, Molly, I would be to God that I could see you yet once more. May God who has kept us thus far keep us to the end and permit us to meet again and that soon. Oh Molly, you can't imagine how my heart yearns for you and the sweet little babies, Kiss them for me. Goodbye my dear Molly. Oh, for one kiss.

W. R. Stilwell

---

[29] To be a tory in the South was to be disloyal to the Confederate cause.

In the tone of this letter, WRS addresses his brother John as an older brother to a younger rather than vice-versa, which is the actual case.

Out comes the startling revelation that Squire Stilwell, father of William and John, is an alcoholic. This explains much about the circumstances of the family and about WRS's personality (as son of an alcoholic). He never mentions this subject again.

Headquarters Semmes Old Brigade Camp, Frederick Hall,
   Virginia September 2, 1863
Dear Brother John:
I have wrote you two letters without receiving any answer and again I propose to address you feeling as I do very much concerned about your welfare. I have thought often of the difference in your experience now and when you wrote me some time ago in which you stated that you had never heard many cannons. I have no doubt but that you have heard enough to satisfy you that there is no pleasure amidst busting shell and flying shot. I hope enough that none of them has hurt you and I hope that God will shield you from harm.

We are prepared here any day to hear of the fall of Charleston. I fear that we will hear it soon. All eyes now turned to Bragg and many fears are expressed that he will do as always, fall back. If we fall back much farther we won't have any place to stand on to fight. Our army is much discouraged at our late reverses and fear that we will not be able to defend ourselves much longer. As for my part I haven't much to say, my hopes and trust is in God, a present help in time of trouble. I hope, dear brother, that you still hold fast to your profession and still do your duty as a Christian. Remember my Brother that if we miss heaven, we miss all and if we gain heaven, it is enough. I am striving more and more every day to live for God and to be a good Christian. I hope you are doing the same, and then if we fall on the field of battle, all will be well with us.

I heard that the 27th [Regiment] was gone to Charleston, if so I hope you will get to see Darnell as he has returned to his regiment. A letter from Uncle John and one from home informs me that all is well except Rany (negro) who is very bad off, her recovery is thought doubtful. Molly informs me that Father does not drink any at all now and that he dresses up, goes to meeting and Uncle John says looks better than he has in fifteen or twenty years. Thank God for that much.

Molly wants the war to close before I get killed and don't care how it goes if I do get killed. I told her she was a tory. Tommy and the baby doing well. Everything is quiet here now, no prospect of active operations soon. I am in hopes there won't be. I have seen and felt enough. I have had good health all summer. Cousin Mary E. Stilwell has not had a letter from you in a long time.[30] She is full of patriotism and so are most all but if they had been where I have and where I fear you had been, they would not cry out more "Blood, more blood." I want you to write soon and give me your general opinion of the war [campaign] for Governor of Georgia and all the news that you possess. That would benefit me. We are about 20 miles from Fredericksburg, 40 from Richmond. I am as ever your affectionate Brother William until death.

W. R. Stilwell

———

"Dear Molly—keep these letters, they may be pearls in time to come—. Thus writes Stilwell and we are grateful that he instructed that these letters be saved and are available for our current-day study, as indeed, they are pearls.

This is a long and lengthy letter on religion in which Stilwell affirms his faith and states that he is a witness in order to encourage all at home to remember their duty to God. Why he singles out the homebodies as opposed to the soldiers he is actually engaged with is not explained. Is this pure faith or is it part of his ambition?

---

[30] Mary E. Stilwell was the 22-year-old daughter of John Stilwell. She had married Samuel Dailey on 16 October 1862. No service record for him has been located. In 1870 he was a railroad conductor living in McDonough with Mary and two children.

Headquarters Semmes Brigade, Monday morning September 7, AD 1863

My dear and affectionate Molly:

This calm peaceful morning I seat myself for the purpose of addressing you a few lines, I am thankful to say that I am enjoying good health of body and mind, in fact my health of either was never better. We are still encamped in the beautiful grove where we have nothing to mar our peace, no prospect of a fight here soon, everything perfectly quiet but I fear that is only the calm that precedes the storm. I fear we will not be allowed to enjoy our repose much longer.

I have been looking for a letter from you for several days but none has come yet. I think I will get one today. I shall not seal this letter until I see. I have no war news here, all eyes are now turned to Charleston and to Bragg's army in Tennessee. I think from what I see that a great battle will be fought near Chattanooga and if we are defeated there, [we will] be in Georgia, but I have confidence in the justness of our cause and the strength of God's arm. If he is for us who can be against us, and if God be on our side who shall be able to withstand his strength and if he is against us, all our efforts will be in vain. He is our only hope and shield, our hiding place, so might it be. God is blessing us in the army, we have a good revival feeling in our brigade and many hopes and prayers are made for great out pouring of the spirit of God. We will continue to hold prayer meeting in our regiment every night. Last night I held meeting in Company G, we had [a] good meeting, some coming to the altar for prayer. I read the 3rd chapter of John and made some remarks from the 14th verse.[31] I have been invited to hold meeting in Company A tonight. I shall try and do so by the assistance of the spirit and grace of God.

Molly, I do not mention this as one item of news but that my friends at home may see that I am trying to live for eternity and for a home beyond this sin smitten and poor world hoping that it may

---

[31]And as Moses lifted up the serpent in the wilderness, so must the Son of man be lifted up.

encourage those at home to remember that we must all appear before the judgment seat of Christ. Oh my dear wife, pray that I may be faithful and discharge all my duty as a Christian. I know it must make your heart rejoice to know that my faith is still unshaken and strong in the Lord and in the presence of his might. What say you my dear wife, does your heart still swell with the love of God? I need not say "Do you love me" I know that but do you love Jesus Christ who has done more for you than I ever can do? You pray with and for our little children and teach them to love God as well as me. Remember dear wife that the responsibility which rests on you is very great. I would to God that I was there to bear part of it, but God has willed it otherwise and let us say thy will be done. Remember that the two little infants which is in your charge must live with God high up in heaven or dwell [with] his frowns for ever. You know my belief in regard to raising children, you know more what the word of God says, train a child in the way it should go. I can not help you, all that I can do is to kneel at the cross of Christ and ask his blessing upon them. I do, every day. Oh, how many prayers have I sent up to the thankful God at the hour of midnight for you and them and for my parents. Oh, God, shall I never see them again in the flesh? Oh, that I could once more unite around the family altar, oh what a sweet spot is that. I know that heaven is as near here as anywhere and heaven is always near the Christian but it seems to me that it would be one of the sweetest placed to die or to fall asleep in Jesus on earth. Oh, the love of God. I love to think about it, to think how I love my little children and God knows I do love them, but then to think what God says if ye being evil know how to give good gifts unto your children, how much more will your heavenly father give good things unto them that ask him. Oh, what love is this, the love of God which passeth all understanding. If ye love me keep my commandments.

Dear Molly, I have devoted most of this letter to the subject of religion. I feel like I could write about and it is more important than any other subject. Keep these letters, they may be pearls in time to come and may God who is able to keep us, preserve us and keep us in his love and save us in his kingdom above. Amen.

Colonel Bryan has not yet got his appointment. He told me the other day that his prospects was better now than they ever had been. I hope he will get it soon. Give my love, respect and prayers to all Uncle William's folks and to Pa and Mother. I leave the other page, if I get a letter this evening I'll write on [more] I shall devote it to Sister Mag [Margaret]. Kiss my boy. I am yours always. Goodbye my dear wife.

W. R. Stilwell

Molly, I love you.

6

CHICKAMAUGA/CHATTANOOGA

This letter is full of excitement. Longstreet is taking two of his divisions to Georgia to support Bragg in his fight with Rosecrans somewhere south of Chattanooga. Stilwell outlines a grand plan of envelopment that never was seriously contemplated but the movement that was put in motion is exciting and innovative. For the first time in the history of warfare, major forces are to be shifted by rail from one front to another over a distance of hundreds of miles.

Headquarters Bryan's Brigade, Camp Hanover Junction, 20
   miles above Richmond, Virginia—Sept. 11th, 1863
Dear and loving Molly:
I wrote you on the 7th and stated that everything was still and quiet, but that evening orders came to cook three days rations and to march the next morning at daylight. We marched to this place and have stopped for the present; that is, our brigade has. The rest of our division is gone on—shall I say where? They are gone to Tennessee somewhere. We will follow in a few days, we are left here for the present but will come on in two or three days. I have no doubt but what I will pass through Atlanta, Georgia in two or three weeks and it may be in less than a week. Oh, how shall I come as close to you as Atlanta and not get to see you but if I do pass through there, I shall cast a look toward you and thank God that I have got so near you as that. If ever I get on Georgia soil again I shall feel like

Columbus when he discovered America. I shall feel like kneeling
down and kissing the earth. Molly, there is one of the greatest
movements now going on that ever has been. I don't know but I
understand it to be about thus.

Ewell is gone by way of Lynchburg and Bristol, Tennessee and
from Bristol he will attack old Burnsides[1] in the rear.[2] His corps is
already gone. Longstreet's Corps will go by way of Richmond,
Augusta, and Atlanta, Georgia and on to some point in Tennessee
and wipeout Burnside and then unite Longstreet and Ewell together
and in conjunction with Bragg will attack Rosecrans and drive them
out of Tennessee.[3] I think it will be one of the greatest movements
ever undertaken and if it can be accomplished will make the
Yankees howl. God grant that it may be done. Oh, God for the sake
of Jesus Christ bless us.

Molly, I shall have to close as we leave for Richmond in a few
hours, we will take the cars there. I think perhaps I may be in
Georgia before this letter reaches you. I am in good health, give my
love to all and kiss the babies. Don't write any more until you hear
from me unless you send it by hand. I must close. Goodbye my
dear Molly. Colonel Bryan has been appointed brigadier general. I
will write again soon, I am your Billie forever.

W. R. Stilwell

———

*Stilwell writes Molly from Atlanta on 19 September, unaware
that the great battle of Chickamauga has been roaring all day and the
great Southern victory will occur on the morrow but Stilwell's brigade
will arrive too late to participate.*

*Stilwell writes some mean and insensitive words to Molly. Despite
all the tenderness he has express to her in many letters, he can be mean*

---

[1] Ambrose Everett Burnside, West Point, class of 1847. He was in command of the
Northern armies at Fredericksburg, which was a disaster. He remained in the army in
lesser positions. At present he commands the Army of the Ohio located in East Tennessee.

[2] This was a false rumor.

[3] William Stark Rosecrans, West Point class of 1842. At present he is a lieutenant
general commanding the Army of the Cumberland facing Bragg around Tullahoma TN.

and strike with the suddenness of a snake. Perhaps this was the typical chauvinism of the Southern white male who was the owner of his universe and all persons within.

Atlanta Georgia, September 19, 1863

My dear Molly:

You may be somewhat astonished to receive a letter from me here though I suppose you will hear of it before you get this. We got here yesterday or last night at twelve o'clock. I tried to get a furlough and go home today but could not, there was so many that runaway and went, that they would not give any. General Bryan tried to get me off but could not. I have not much time to write as all the couriers are gone but me. I am well and doing well. I think we will leave for Dalton or Rome tomorrow. There will be a big fight up there if the Yankees don't run off. I got the ambrotype and drawers and two pairs of socks that you sent me by Lieutenant Farrar. I can see that Tom favors himself a little but not much, the baby looks fat and pretty but you don't favor [each other] or [you]don't look like you did when I left. If it looks like you, you have broke very fast. I fear that you are not cheerful enough, you must not grow old and get ugly before I do come home.

Molly, I seen Uncle John McKibbin today and all of Sloan's Company from Henry [County].[4] Uncle John is going home tomorrow or next day. Molly, I will enclose a letter that I wrote before I left Virginia. I want some of you to come and see me if I get stationed soon, but I will write again soon and let you know where I am. I am very glad to get back to Georgia. Give my love to all the friends. I have not got time to write longer. You need not write to me until I write again. I am yours always till death.

W. R. Stilwell

---

[4] Adam C. Sloan, the father of Thomas Sloan who was the deceased captain of Company F. He was a 55-year-old McDonough blacksmith, merchant and prosperous planter and now commander of Company B, 10th Cavalry Regiment, Georgia State Guards, which was a six month militia unit organized very recently.

———

Stilwell and his unit are settling in for the siege of Chattanooga but he still has to find a horse. He now has a new concern. It becomes very important to him that his Pa comes to visit him.

Headquarters Bryan's Brigade, Camp in front of Chattanooga,
   September 28th, 1863

Dear Molly:

I am writing you a few lines but don't know when I will get to send it off. I would have wrote before now but could not as I had left my knapsack behind. I have been sick ever since I left Atlanta with [a] cold. I am some better now. I have had a very hard time as both the other couriers have been gone but they have come now. If I thought I could get me a horse cheaper by coming home I think I could get a furlough for a few days but I am afraid that they are harder to get there than they are here. If Father or Uncle knows of any horse that I could get by coming home let me know as soon as you can and if not, I want Father to come and see me and bring me some pants. I learn that the bridges that were burned will be built by Tuesday so he can come, if we stay where we are now, [or within] a few miles of us. If he comes tell him to inquire for Longstreet's Corps, McLaws' Division and then for Bryan's Brigade and he will find me here. Molly, I would like for you to come too, but under the circumstances I don't think it best now, there is nowhere for you to stay. If I get sick or wounded, why you can come then.

I have had some very narrow escapes from shells but not hurt yet. You must continue to pray for me. The Yankee still hold the city but it is reported that we have their supplies cut off, but I don't know. We whipped them very bad last Saturday and Sunday.[5] I

---

[5] The Battle of Chickamauga was fought on 19 and 20 September. This was Bragg's and the Army of Tennessee's only clear victory during the entire war, whereby most of Rosecran's Army was sent fleeing back to Chattanooga. It was another bloody affair with casualty rates of about 28 percent on both sides. The battle was unusual in that the number of troops on both sides were roughly equal, Bragg being reinforced by Longstreet's Corps, not all of whom, including WRS, reached the area in time to play a part in the battle.

think they will leave in a short time. Molly, if Father comes to see me, send me a pair of pants and a towel and send me that little testament that I sent home. I had the misfortune to have my bible thrown out of the car. Give my love and respect to all the friends. Write to me soon. Kiss the children for me. I am as every your affectionate husband until death.

William R. Stilwell

Dalton, Ga.

P. S. Direct your letter to McLaws' Division in care of General Bryan

––––––

Butts and Henry Counties each contributed seven companies of regular Confederate infantry. All of these companies (including one each in the 53rd) were assigned to Virginia or to the southeastern coast except for three Butts and one Henry County companies of the 30th Regiment Georgia Volunteer Infantry which were assigned to the Army of Tennessee. Tthis was a great opportunity for a reunion of Butts and Henry County boys from the two regiments. Stilwell also had old friends from Louisiana that he seeks out. These people were now totally isolated from their homes.

Headquarters Bryan's Brigade, Army of Tennessee, Camp
 before Chattanooga, October 2nd, 1863

My dear beloved and loving Molly:

I wrote you a letter a few days ago which I hope you have received. I was very unwell at that time but I am better now. I have not had a letter from you in a long time but have heard from you by several persons who went home from Atlanta. There was 22 of my company that went home but they all went without leave. I couldn't do that, it would not do me any good to go home that way. If I live I think I will get a furlough this winter and if I knew that I could get me a horse by coming home I think I could get home soon. I have still got the money that was sent me but our regiment has not yet been paid off, it is going on eight months since we have been paid off. Molly, I am needing a pair of pants very bad, I want you to send me a pair of pants as soon as you can. I was in hopes that Father or Uncle William could come to see me. They can come within six miles of me on the railroad and if they was to bring anything they could not carry, they could leave it with Major Davis of our brigade who is at the railroad who would take good care of it. I am still in hopes that they will come and see me and bring me something good. Molly, I want you to send me a towel. I wrote in my last letter how for Father to find me but for fear you did get it, I will write it again. Inquire for Longstreet's Corps, McLaw's Division, Bryan's Brigade and there he will find me. If he don't come and can see any one that is coming; if you will send me my things it can be left with Major Davis at the depot and I can get it from there most any day.

Molly, I little thought this fall two years ago when we was together in Chattanooga—so happy together, that today I would be so near there under the circumstances that I am under. I am [with]in two miles of the room where we stayed. I can't help but love the spot, and not only that spot, but all other spots wherever I have seen and enjoyed your company.

But I must tell you, the other day I and James Speer concluded that we would go down our line of battle and hunt up Dick Turner, your cousin.[6] He is Lieutenant Colonel of the 19th Louisiana Regiment. We did not get to see him as his regiment was on picket. He is well. Strolling about, I found Charley Crenshaw, Bob Shurand's son-in-law.[7] I did not know him at first, he has never been home, can't hear from his family. He tells me that old man Shurard

---

[6] Richard W. Turner would become full colonel and commander of the Louisiana 19th Regiment on 25 November 1863. After participating in the Chickamauga and Chattanooga battles, he fought the Atlanta campaign in Hood's Corps. On 28 July 1864, he was in the attack at Ezra Church near Atlanta where Confederate casualties may have been as high as 5000 and included Col. Turner who was badly wounded. He would complete the War in non-combat roles in the Trans Mississippi. How he was related to Molly is unknown. Andrew B. Booth, compiler, *Records of Louisiana Confederate Soldiers* (Spartanburg SC: The Reprint Company, 1984) 11/2: 890.

[7] Old friends from WRS's time of residence in Louisiana.

and the Dr. and one of the others are dead. Jones Lloyd is dead also. It has been so long since he has heard from home that he could not tell me much. He says Miss Malissa is not married yet.

A little further down, I found the 30th Georgia and found Van McKileline lying in the ashes eating parched corn.[8] He is a Lieutenant now and is well and hearty. I found many more of my good friends, all tired of the war and want to get home and all think they have seen the hardest service, but I know what I have seen and history will say so too. The truth is, I have seen so much hard service that I am used to it and feel like I would not be satisfied anywhere else. I assure you dear Molly that I am faring as well us anybody can in service and all of my regiment is astonished to see how some get along and have good friends but the great secret is I do my duty and do it well. I am always at my post though it is sometimes very dangerous. The other day the shells flew thick and fast but I trust in God and fear them that is able to kill both body and soul. I think that we will shell the city in a day or two; perhaps tomorrow; we are planting artillery today. I long to see the Confederate flag wave over Chattanooga. I think I will see [it] before long. We whipped them very bad the other day. Our brigade did not get there in time to get a chance [to fight]. If we can rout old Rosecrans, I think I can capture me a horse. Molly, I don't like to write with a pencil but I haven't got any ink or pen that is any account, if it rubs out you must let me know and I will try and get ink.

Now Molly, because I said I thought I would get a furlough this winter don't you expect too much. Perhaps I ought not to have told you for if I don't get it you will be disappointed. You need not expect much although I intend to try to get one if there is any

---

[8] Most likely, this person is Martin Van Buren McKibben, who was appointed Jr. 2nd Lieutenant of Company B of the 30th Georgia regiment (Butts County) on 16 July 1863, and was assigned to the Army of Tennessee. Van Buren was the youngest son of Thomas McKibben and Elizabeth Ward Duffey, and lived near Fellowship Church. He was currently 23 years old. He was wounded severely at Franklin, Tennessee on 30 November 1864 but survived to experience a long and distinguished Butts County career as lawyer and teacher. He now lies under a most imposing monument in the Fellowship Church cemetery.

chance. Give my love to Grandma, Uncle Em [William] and [Aunt] P.B., and Father, Mother, Sister and all the negroes and friends. A letter from Brother John the other day informed [me] that himself and Darnell was in good health. Oh do kiss the babies all over for me. Oh, how I want to see them but I want to see you more than they. I am yours until death. Goodbye.

William R. Stilwell

P.S. Direct your letters Dalton, Ga. Longstreet's Corps, McLaw's Division, care of General Bryan.

"Ain't I smart." Stilwell buys a Yankee horse for 25 dollars.

Headquarters Bryan's Brigade, Camp near Chattanooga, Oct. 16, 1863

My dear Molly:

I have just received your letters of the 9th. You can imagine how glad I was to get it, it is the first I have got since I left Virginia nearly five weeks [ago]. I have been looking for Father but no word of him. Now if he has not started tell him not to start now. The bridges between here and Atlanta are well washed away and General Bragg will not allow any citizen to come up. He had better wait some two weeks before he comes. I want him to bring me something good to eat and please send me a pair of pants and a shirt. I had a shirt stolen from me a few days ago, also please send me a towel. I am in good health. I have got me a Yankee horse, he was wounded in the fight in the foot. I think I can cure him. He won't cost me but very little. I told the man that I got him from if I cured him I would pay him twenty-five dollars. He is a young horse four years old and, [if] I get him well, will be worth eight hundred or a thousand dollars. Ain't I smart, I think you ought to brag on me, I am smart enough to get me a horse from old Ellic [?].

Molly, General Bragg has just issued an order that no furloughs will be granted for the present. I don't think I will get home before winter, if then, but I will try very hard to come this winter. Molly, if my horse gets well, I shall send some money home soon. I want to send that that I borrowed and perhaps a little more though I shall have to buy a saddle and bridle and they are so high. I don't think I can spare any but that which was borrowed. If he [the horse] gets well. I shall send that.

No sign of a fight here now. General Wheeler captured twelve hundred wagons the other day[9]. Write soon, Oh, do write. No more at present but I remain yours always until death. Goodbye, (kiss).

W. R. Stilwell

P. S. Direct your letters to Chattanooga Tennessee in care of General Bryan, McLaws' Division, Longstreet's Corps.

———

Stilwell pens a poem of tenderness to Molly but Virginia, the newly-named daughter, is still an "it."

Headquarters Bryan's Brigade, October 20, 1863, Camp near
    Chattanooga, Tenn.

My dear Molly:

Your very short letter of the 17th inst. was received on the evening of the 19th making the trip in two days. It reached me in due time and found me in the enjoyment of good health and spirits. I was very sorry that Father could not come to see me and also that I could not get those good things that you had prepared for your ever faithful Billie, but I hope that I may yet get them or some others as good. I have had great misfortune in getting things from home. I think that Father can come before long. I think that he can come in a week or two. Molly, you need not send me my bible. I have got one that was captured at Gettysburg, Pennsylvania. I have

---

[9] Joseph "Fighting Joe" Wheeler, the Confederate boy general, currently 27 years old, was a major general commanding the cavalry of the Army of Tennessee. On 2 October the cavalry under his command captured a large wagon train at Anderson's Cross Roads in Tennessee. The raid continued northward as far as McMinnville TN, only returning to Confederate lines on 9 October. The raid did little permanent damage to the Union forces bottled up in Chattanooga, but it did put the Union soldiers on starvation rations for a while. Boatner, *Civil War Dictionary*, 910-11.

wrote to you to send me a shirt, pair of pants and a towel and any other things that you may have and want to send. That is all that I need at present. I have all my baggage hauled and can take care of my things very well. Molly, my horse is getting well fast. I wish you could see him and the rider too. I imagine if you could see me rein up my fine steed and dash into the battle once, you would say it was not me. I think he will be able to ride by the time we have to march, he is worth all of eight hundred dollars and he will only cost me 200 dollars. I shall have to buy a saddle unless we could have another fight and then I think I could get one. I was sitting in the tent the other day reading a newspaper and T. M. Polk tapped me on the shoulder. I had not thought of him in a long time.[10] You will not know anything about him, but the rest will. He is well. I have been trying to find Cousin John Rea (?) but have not yet found him. If Uncle Washington told what regiment he belongs to I would be glad if you would let me know.[11] I wrote long ago to Aunt P. B. to know what regiment cousin Margaret Glass' two sons belonged to, but have never yet received an answer from her about it.[12] I think it is a mistake about Brother John and Darnell being up here. I think they are still at Charleston, S. C. If they have had come here I should have known it ear [before] this. Molly, the longer I have been in my position, the better I am pleased with it. I would not, as much as I admire office, give it for a lieutenant's position in a company. There is plenty of them that would gladly exchange with me. It is better to be born lucky than rich and with all my bad luck thank God I have some good. I have no doubt it is [He] that has guided me through.

I have received many letters of late. Uncle John's well-written and sympathetic letters are good. He admires my courage very much and says he is proud of me. Bob McDonald is another good

---

[10] T. M. (Marshal) Polk has not been identified. He may have been a descendent of Mary, daughter of Elijah and Elizabeth Stilwell, who married Charles Polk. There was a T. M. Polk present who was a sergeant in the 48th Tennessee Regiment of Cleburne's Division.

[11] Uncle Washington has not been identified.

[12] Margaret Glass and her two sons have not been identified.

friend of mine. Letters from W. N. and R[ichard] M. Everitt have been received.[13] I am going to write to Granma Stilwell this evening.[14] I have never wrote her a letter since I been gone, the reason is I did not know who she could get to read them or write letters but Marshal Polk says aunt Clevet can write.[15] Give my love to Granma, and Uncle William and Aunt P. B. Tell them all howdy for me. Tell Pa to come when he can and to bring me a goose quill for a toothpick. Howdy to Mother and Mag. Kiss the children, God bless their little souls. I want to see them and enclosed you will find a piece of poetry written last night by moonlight. I am as ever.

W R Stilwell

Goodbye, oh for one kiss, oh how sweet.

Evening Moonlight by W. R. S.

1–This world is very lonely now since I'm so far from home, I have not a friend with me to bow before my father's throne.

2–Long and lonely have been the days since I have seen my wife. The moon is dark it hath rays and not much pleasure is my life.

3–I am setting now in the broad moonlight and thinking of the past that awful and that solemn night you held me to your bosom fast.

4–Our little boy was fast asleep, I thought he would not miss and while I stood by his bed to weep upon his cheek I placed a kiss.

5–I am going now where I've often gone to appear before the throne and pray the Father. Oh, how long before I shall see my home, home, sweet home.

6–The Lord has been very good to me. In all the conflicts past he has promised that a friend he'll be and guide me safe to the last.

7–Molly, you have my heart and life and if on the battlefield I die, you are my darling and my wife. My only request is by your side to lie.

---

[13] W. N. has not been identified.

[14] Grandmother Elizabeth Stilwell does not appear in the 1860 census so it is difficult to place her in 1863 when she was 89 and apparently still active as a farmer.

[15] Aunt Clevet may have been Olivia Stilwell Wolfe, a daughter of Elizabeth Stilwell.

William R. Stilwell

Molly, there were several other verses but having to write it by moonlight and with a pencil I can not read them. This morning I have composed many such. Since I have been from home and as I walked past my post at night this will show you that not withstanding my long absence from home and have seen so much murder, I still have the same tender feelings that I once had. Nothing was said in my poetry about Jinney [Virginia] but nothing is known, I know she lives but that is all. I love it because I love you. I will give her a feast some time.

W. R. Stilwell

———

Stilwell is assigned the very unpleasant task of procuring corn in Walker County, Georgia in a very rugged mountainous area that was strong in Union sentiment. He had to take corn from a family whose head was off fighting in the Union Army.

While the Southern Army had Chattanooga invested and were squeezing the Union Army's food supplies, the South's supply wasn't much better. The mountainous area did not supply much sustenance so they were reliant on the rickety Western and Atlantic railroad from Atlanta.

Headquarters Bryan's Brigade, October 27,1863—Camp near Chattanooga, Tennessee

My dear Molly:

No letter has been received from you in some time, the reason is not known. I hope I will get one this evening. I am well and doing well. Some fighting yesterday here and [they] are fighting on the left now about two miles from me. I don't know whether we will have a general engagement or not, everything is ready for a fight as far as I know. I think our division will move camp this evening. So much rain that our camp is almost a pond of water. I don't think we will move for I am in hope we will go nearer the railroad. I would be glad if Pa could come now for fear after this fight is over we may not stay here long and he can come on the railroad now. Buck Lemmond come up a day or two ago.[16] He says anybody can come now that wants to. I think the sooner that he [Pa] comes the better and if we have a fight I would be glad if he could be here.

I just returned last night from a trip of three days up in Walker County, Georgia after corn.[17] I could not find any corn to buy and had to press some.[18] I pressed it from a lady whose husband is gone to the Yankees, It was very hard to do so and she crying and begging but I could not help it, my orders was to get corn and I was obliged to get it. I don't want to go anymore. I had much rather fight Yankees than take corn from women and children. I had a good time otherwise, eating butter and milk and potatoes and other vegetables but it did not last long, but like the hog I had to return to my wallering in the clay and vomit again.

I received a letter from Brother last evening, he is doing well and has good health and thinks many will be the days before Charleston will be tread upon by Yankee invaders. God grant that it may be. Chick Speer is here, got here last night from home.[19] He looks well, better I think than any of the boys, but I fear from what I notice that he will go like the next of the boys.

The bridges that was washed away between Atlanta and Chattanooga have been rebuilt and the cars run through the Chickamauga station. If Pa comes he can leave any thing that he may bring with Mr. Ben Straten at the railroad until he finds me.[20] I can get them most any day from the road. I would be very glad to see him. Molly, them long letters that use to come to me in

---

[16] Could Buck Lemmond have been a nickname for William?

[17] Near the far northwest corner of the state and reputedly a hotbed of Union sentiment.

[18] "Press" was the forcible taking of possessions in return for a promise to pay at market prices.

[19] Chick Speer was probable one of Molly's cousins.

[20] On 2 October, WRS said things could be left at the railroad with Major Davis, the Brigade Quartermaster. Davis resigned shortly after this. Mr. Ben Stratten has not been identified.

Virginia have played out, I don't hardly ever get none at all and when I do they are very short. Come, you must do better than that. Molly, I want this war to close, I want to see you and the children but I have been trying to stop it for a long time and I don't see that the end is any nearer now than when I begin, but I don't think it will last always and if it ever does and I am still alive I shall be very glad. Write soon and often and lengthy.

My love and respects to all the friends. Kiss the children and God grant that we may all live to meet again. I am yours always until death.

William R. Stilwell

Mrs. Mary F. Stilwell Goodbye

Kiss me

———

Stilwell learns to his chagrin that he has been cheated on his horse. It is not a Yankee horse but has been stolen from a Confederate. So he was not so clever after all.

Headquarters Brigade Camp near Chattanooga Tennessee,
November 2, 1863

My dear Molly,

Your letter of the 30th October was received last evening. I was sorry to hear that the baby was sick but hope it is better before now. I am in the enjoyment of good health but am troubled some about other matters. The war seems to have no end and I am tired of living without my family. I don't know what is to become with me and mine. Sometimes it looks like I will go deranged and perhaps it would be best for me. I am tired of the war. I have not had any meat for some time and don't know when I will.

I lost my horse this morning. It turned out that he was not a Yankey horse but belonged to one of our own men. I gave him up this morning. I shall have to buy one as I am obliged to have one and it will pay more to have a horse. I get most out of heart some time but when I remember how much I have been blessed above my fellow soldiers, I don't think I have any right to complain at my lot. I think if I can get a horse by next year I can save some money for you. I am afraid you will need money now but if I buy a horse it is impossible for me to furnish any but I will try and save some by next year. Everything is so high that the soldier can't save much.

I was up on top of Lookout Mountain and took a grand view of everything for many miles around. Our present camp is near the foot of the mountain. Molly, I will try and come home this winter and some time I think if they don't let me go I will go anyhow, but my honor would be injured and I may had as well be dead as to lose my honor. There is but one thing that ever will cause me to desert my post. I need not say what that is for you know.[21]

If you get any chance to send my pants and shirt, do so and let me know when and by whom you sent them. I think I shall write for a furlough soon as Mr. Morris gets his furlough. He is a son of Richard Morris[22] of Henry County; lives six miles from McDonough. Pa will know where he is [lives]. He is one of our couriers and one of my mess and will bring anything for me that Pa will take to his Father's.[23] He has made application for leave of

---

[21] The editor certainly doesn't know.

[22] Richard Morris was a 65-year-old planter with a 55-year-old wife, Naomi, and one daughter living at home. He owned 20 slaves in 1860. None of the family appears in the 1870 census of Henry County.

[23] A. S. (Abraham or Abasalom) Morris had been initially elected Jr. second lieutenant of Company E (Clayton County) of the 10th Regiment which a part of Bryan's Brigade. He is now one of the couriers that could include both enlisted and junior officers. Note that WRS addresses him as "Mr." But they are in the same mess (eating and cooking group). He would be later wounded (date and place not known) and was in a Staunton

absence for ten days. If he gets it I will let you know. I may keep this letter a few days and see if it comes.

My love to all of the folks, tell them all howdy. I want to see them very bad. Write soon. I am yours until death.

William R. Stilwell

Virginia hospital in March 1865. In 1870 he was an unmarried Jonesboro Georgia stable-keeper.

7

EAST TENNESSEE

Stilwell is now an unwitting participant in one of the Confederacy's most disgraceful episodes. General Bragg is purging his command of everyone who might be a replacement for him. Longstreet of course would be a natural and left Virginia with this ambition in mind. In order to separate Longstreet from the army before Chattanooga, he is to be sent to take Knoxville and rid East Tennessee of the Federal occupying forces. So the move suits both men. However, it will prove disastrous for the Southern cause as the inadequate force holding the Yankees in Chattanooga is now even more inadequate. And to make it even worse, Ulysses S. Grant is now commanding the Northern Army.

Camp Sweetwater, Tennessee, November 8th, 9th, 1863
My dear Molly:
You will be surprised to get a letter from this place. Our division left Chattanooga on the fifth and arrived here the 7th. Sweetwater is in the eastern part and lies sixty or 70 miles from Chattanooga and about fifteen miles from Loudon and some five or six to Knoxville. I understand that all of our corps is coming up here. I think that we will unite with some troops from Virginia and then go back to Chattanooga in the rear of the enemy. I only give my opinion and will see if I am right. I fear we will have to march all winter or at least until Christmas. This is a fine country up here,

plenty of pork, beef and vegetables and sure we will live much better here than we have been, though I don't think [we] will stay in a place long. If you should not get many letters from me now for some time you need not be surprised. In the meantime, I will write all I can. I must tell you of some more bad luck. Someone stole my knapsack from the guard as we came up, with one shirt, jacket, bundle of needles and pins, [and] thread. I had just bought two or three quires of paper and the same amount of envelops and stamps, but as good luck would have it, I had given out a pair of drawers and shirt and socks to be washed, and they are not lost. Consequently I have two drawers, two shirts, two pair of socks, two jeans. I miss the paper and envelopes worse than anything else. It could not be helped by me. I was obliged to go with the brigade to another station and that was the reason why I could not take care of it myself. We come on the cars and I never seen my things from the time we left. But so might it be, let it go.

Molly, I had one of the most delightful dreams last night I ever had in my life. I met you and Tommy and kissed each one and had a few pleasant hours in conversation. Oh how happy I was but alas for me I awoke and found it to be only a dream. I would to God it had of been reality. Molly, I fear it will be some time before I can get a furlough now as there is some great move on foot. I shall buy me a horse in a few days. I think it will cost me about three hundred dollars but that will be cheap. I have already bought a saddle. I had to pay thirty dollars. I may write more this evening. Good bye.

W. R. S.

———

Headquarters Bryan's Brigade, Camp Sweetwater Tennessee,
    November 10, 1863
My dear Molly:

Your kind letter of the 4th was received informing me that you had sent my pants by Willis Evans[1]. He has not come yet. I have just sent a letter for you this morning before yours came but the reason I write this morning again is that Mr. Morris, one of our couriers, has a furlough for ten days and I want Father to take a box to his Father's for him to bring to me. He is in my mess and will bring my things for me that you want to send. The young man's name is Abraham Morris, his Father's name is Richard. He says Father knows his Father very well. He lives six miles from McDonough on the Covington Road. Don't send much of anything that will spoil though you must be the judge as to that. I want some butter and fruit, you can send me whatever you think best. I am very glad that you have sent my pants and shirt. Molly, I notice that since I wrote that I thought I would get a furlough this winter that you have been writing every time for me to come home. Now you must stop that as it is only makes me feel bad and I cannot get one now. I will get one as soon as I can. There is no one that wants a furlough worse than I do. I have not tried to write to John and it is so cold that I am trembling now. Tell him that Bob McDonald was joking him about me hanking as I don't hank[2] much but I have a good position. I am yours as ever. Good by.

W. R. Stilwell

Direct to Sweetwater, Tenn.

P.S. No mail went off this morning, my letter has returned. I shall send it by hand to Jonesboro.

W. R. Stilwell

The following letter which has no heading or date was probably written November 15.

---

[1]Willis Evans, son of David Evans, was a private in Company I (Butts County) of the 14th Regiment. He was wounded on 3 May 1863 at Chancellorsville. In November 1864 he would furnish a substitute to take his place in the war.

[2]Unable to determine the meaning of "hank."

Dear Molly:

This is Sabbath evening and I am very lonesome. I thought I could not pass off the lonely hours better than to be writing to you, as it seems like we can never talk to each other [except] only though the medium of writing.

Little did I think when we were married that I must be so soon severed from my dear Molly, but it is the common lot of all to be disappointed and now, instead of being this holy Sabbath evening with my loving family where we could read the word of God together, I am away here in the east engaged in the destruction of my fellow men, but God knows my heart. I do not desire their hurt if they would part in peace. I long to see this war close but I confess that I can not see where it can ever end but I have always thought that God would provide a peace when he thinks best. I still think so, Molly.

If Father comes to see me now, he need not come to Chattanooga, he must come to Sweetwater. If he don't come send my pants and shirt by Mr. Evans or any one that is responsible. I am not suffering for them, but as I have but one pair of pants I like to have a change. I received a letter from Bob McDonald the other day, he says that Brother was at home on sick furlough. You can tell him that I think when he wants a furlough, if they don't give him one, he gets sick and then he is all right. That's smart, if I was as smart, I could get to see my Molly, but never mind, when the war is over I have a loving wife and smart children to greet me. He has none. Oh, how many times I have thought of that memorable day, God speed it. I hope I may live to see it, though I may not. Death is the common lot of all, we all must suffer before the judgment seat of Christ. And oh, that we may all appear there in peace. Molly, let us meet there if we never meet on earth. Forgive me, but it seems like heaven would not be heaven without thee.

Give my love to Uncle William, Granma, and Aunt P.B., Pa, Mother, Sisters and all the friends. I would give the state of Georgia for a kiss [from] you and the children. Oh, God, how long shall I suffer in the flesh? I am yours without spot or blemish until death.

William R. Stilwell

Direct your letter to Loudon, Tenn. All the rest as you did before and send it to Loudon, Tenn.

———

As the Confederates get closer to Knoxville, the fighting intensifies.

Loudon, Tennessee, November 18, 1863

My dear Molly:

I have just arrived here from the front to order our wagons up, we have been pursuing the enemy for several days, fighting some.[3] Thank God, I am not buried as yet though I have been in much danger. I left the division last evening at sundown and had to ride most all night over one of the worse kinds of roads and battlefields, it was very lonesome and cold, it is 33 miles from here to Knoxville. When I left the division they were within ten miles of Knoxville. I expect they are fighting today or will be tomorrow.

I shall start back tonight, it will be tomorrow 12 o'clock before I get there. I have not much time to write but it was the first chance and perhaps the last in some time. I thought I ought to write though I had rather wait until the battle was over but I may not get any chance to write again for some time. I mention this so that you will not be uneasy if you do not get any letter from me soon. I am in good health and spirits and went in front of the brigade all the time, only one man hurt in my company. Ben Walden,[4] son of B. G. had his arm shot off.[5]

---

[3] Most notably, at Campbell Station on 16 November as Longstreet tried to cut Burnside off from Knoxville. Unsuccessful, Longstreet then had to begin the siege of Knoxville.

[4] Ben Walden was a private in Company F. He was wounded in the left arm necessitating amputation on November 16 at Campbell Station TN. He would be discharged 10 July 1864. In 1860 he was a 28-year-old tenant farmer with wife Sara Philips (married

Molly, give my love to all of Uncle William's folks and tell Pa I think he had better not try to come now, I will let him know when I think he can come. I got my pants, shirt and all you sent. You don't know how much good them apples and chestnuts done me. They were so good and then they come from home, from Molly and Tommy. I have not tried on the pants, but I am afraid they are too long, but if they are, C. B. Smith is here and he can fix them.[6] My love to all and write soon. Direct as before. I must close though I would like to write more. Pray for me that God may take care of me and may he guide us all right and permit us to meet on earth again and at last raise us all in heaven. I am yours to the end of time. Good by.

William R. Stilwell.

A kiss for the apples & chestnuts. I am your true husband until death—W. R. Stilwell.

My darling Mary F. Stilwell
Good by Good by.

———

Stilwell's duties as courier are keeping him fully occupied but he finally does obtain a legitimate horse.

Knoxville, Tennessee November 23, A. D. 1863
My dear Molly:
Your kind letter of 10th to hand [arrived] on yesterday. I was very glad to hear from you. So sorry to hear that Tommy was not well. I hope, however that he is well ere this [now]. I am well and doing as well as common. I am camped in two miles of Knoxville. The Yankees still hold the city. We had orders to charge their breast

---

21/9/1854) and two sons. In 1870 he was a relatively prosperous Henry County farmer living with Sara and four children. He would serve a term as county tax collector in 1875.

[5] WRS reversed the initials of Green B. Walden who was a 49-year-old McDonough farmer (in 1860). He had a wife Nancy and six children still at home. None can be found in the 1870 Henry County census.

[6] Smith is a tailor.

works last night at 10 o'clock but the orders was countermanded and we did not make the attempt. I think it will take a hard fight to get the enemy out of the place. I was very glad that we did not attempt to storm their works last night for I thought it very likely that it would be the last works that I would storm. I had commenced writing a letter to you before the order came and I quit but as I am still alive this morning I thought I would write you a few lines.

I have bought me a horse for two hundred and fifty dollars, it is a good Mexican pony. My horse, bridal and saddle cost me two hundred and eighty-two dollars. I owe seventy-five yet. I think I can pay that in a short time and then I can save some money if I have no bad luck but a man never knows what will happen in the army.

I don't think my chance for a furlough is as good now as it would have been if I had stayed at Chattanooga but if ever there is a chance, I will do my best, and I think General Bryan will do all he can for me. There is no chance now as we are in the midst of a campaign. I wrote you that I had got my clothes. You said something about having some cloth to make me a vest, if you have you can do so as the one I have is getting smartly worn but if it is not convenient, never mind, I am not needing it bad.

Nov. 27—Molly, I did not get to finish my letter as the pickets commenced firing. I have been gone ever since from our camp until this morning. I am still in good health. Got a fine supper last night and breakfast this morning at a house over the river where our headquarters was. The pickets are fighting this morning and a big battle is expected everyday. The enemy are strongly entrenched at Knoxville. Molly, there are two things that I need that I can't get here; that is a pocketknife and a handkerchief. Please send me a handkerchief the first chance. There will be no chance for a furlough until this campaign is over and then I will make an effort to get one. Be ye steadfast in the faith till I come. Give your self to prayer, fasting, [and] faith and be ready into any good word and works. My old and highly esteemed friend General Bryan has returned.[7] I have

---

[7] General Bryan's health was poor; perhaps he had been on medical leave.

someone now to tell my trials to, he is truly a good man. Give my love to all, Uncle, folks. I want to see them very bad. Kiss the children. Howdy to all, write soon to your truly loving and affectionate husband until death.

W. R. Stilwell

———

Longstreet's foray into East Tennessee has turned into disaster. On the bitterly cold morning of November 29, Longstreet's Army assaulted a portion of the Knoxville defenses known as Fort Sanders. Though Bryan's brigade was not in the advance of the assault, they were right behind. The assault force was caught in a moat from which they could neither advance nor retreat. The brigade had casualties of 212 men. A comparable count for the 53rd Regiment is not available but an examination of the individual service records indicates a casualty count of at least 65. These levels of casualties are significant for a battle in which absolutely nothing was gained.

This disaster was compounded by Bragg's loss of the Chattanooga lines on November 25 when he retreated in great disorder to Dalton, Georgia. Grant's forces in Chattanooga were now available to drive at Longstreet's rear so he had to put as much distance as possible between his army and Grant's. He moved up the Virginia and East Tennessee railroad to well north of Knoxville into one of the most desolate and isolated areas of the Confederacy.

The East Tennessee and Georgia Railroad bypassed Chattanooga. It ran from Cleveland, Tennessee, to Dalton, Georgia, well east of Chattanooga. Up until this time, even with the Yankees in Chattanooga, this railroad was open from central Georgia to Longstreet's army. Now cut, communications between Georgia and upper East Tennessee had to take a lengthy circular route through Richmond to Lynchburg, Virginia, to Bristol, Tennessee. It was now approximately 1200 rickety railroad miles from Atlanta to Knoxville.

Bryan's Brigade Camp near Radansville, Tennessee, December
12th, 1863

My dearest Molly:

I have no doubt you are very anxious about my welfare. It
seems like a century since I have had a letter from you and I fear it
will be a long time before you can write to me, for your letters will
have to come by way of Richmond, Virginia to Bristol, Tennessee.
I sent off a letter to you yesterday which I hope you will get as it
had been so long and as I suppose you had heard of our charge on the
Yankee fort at Knoxville.[8] I knew you must be very uneasy. I was,
dear Molly, in great danger but God delivered me out of all and
brought me out without being hurt. I wrote you all the particulars.
After our engagement, we learned that Bragg had fallen back from
Chattanooga,[9] that the enemy were marching on our rear in heavy
force and that in a short time would be upon us front and rear, so
there was nothing left us but to retreat as fast as possible. We left at
dark on the night of the 4th and marched all night, one of the
coldest times I ever saw almost, we come here and have stopped.
Whether we will stay or return or go on farther towards Bristol, I
know not. We are about fifty miles from Bristol on the railroad
running from Lynchburg, Bristol, and thence to Knoxville.

Dear Molly, I cannot tell how much I want to see you and the
children although I confess that I have lost many of the sweet
remembrances of home and friends. I confess that I can hardly
realize that I have a sweet wife and two little children. This may
seem very strange to you who [are] at home and [with] those little
blessings of heaven around you, but it is nevertheless a fact. This

---

[8] On the bitterly cold morning of 29 November, Longstreet's army assaulted a
portion of the Knoxville defenses known as Fort Sanders. The fort was a bastioned
earthwork on a hill covered by a ditch 12 feet wide and an average of eight feet deep with
an almost vertical slope rising to the tip of the parapet, 15 feet above the bottom of the
ditch. The Confederate attack was poorly planned and executed and did not allow for
crossing the ditch and scaling the parapet. The assault turned into a disaster with
Confederate losses of 813. Federal losses were insignificant. Boatner, *Civil War Dictionary*,
468.
[9] On 25 November Bragg's Confederate forces suffered the catastrophic and
humiliating loss of Missionary Ridge and were forced to retreat to Dalton GA.

truly is a world of forgetfulness. I often stray off to some sweet place and sit down to think of days that is past and gone, yes, the day when my work was done and come home to meet your smiling face at the door, yes the happiest days of my life. I try to call them to memory but it seems almost like a dream. I know I have a wife, one that I love more than life and that loves me, but those sweet hours have passed and it seems to me like a tale that is told. Don't think dearest Molly, that I have forgotten you for that can never be. God forbid that it should be on earth [and] you in heaven for I hope to meet you there to spend eternity together and may the wonderful and merciful God who has thus far guided me to direct events that we may yet walk together to the old graveyard and pluck the flowers from the same rose bush which once was so lovely. With God all things are possible.

[Remainder of letter missing]

Having been repulsed at Knoxville, Longstreet attempts to maintain some momentum by a raid on three Federal brigades camped at Bean's Station on 15 December. Due to lethargy by some of his subordinates, the attack was unsuccessful, increasing Longstreet's level of frustration and would eventually lead to the arrest and court martial of several officers, including McLaws.

Bean's Station, Tennessee, December 20th, 1863, Sabbath
   morning
My dearest Molly:
Although it may be a long time ere this letter may start for its destination, yet I can't help writing. It does me good to write if I knew you would never get it; for it affords me pleasure to think of you, though I know you can't hear from me, I know that you are thinking of me. I have not had a letter from you since the 1st November, a month and five days. I want to get one very bad but don't expect to in a long time yet. I have been in another fight at this place though not so severe as that at Knoxville. We did not lose

many men. We run the Yankees off from their camp and captured many of their things. Bean's Station is about forty miles from Knoxville where the road running from Cumberland Gap intersects with the road running from Knoxville to Bristol and thence on to Virginia. Our campaign thus far has suffered from the fact of Bragg's path: When he fell back from his position he left our rear exposed and we had to change our base by a side step to the left thus going by Knoxville leaving Burnside's army there and almost starved out.[10] If Bragg had held his position I think we would have captured all of them. We have been living very hard, part of the time on parched corn and some times 1/4 lb. flour per day, but we are getting one lb. now.

Molly, I may fall one day but if I do I intend by the grace of God to fall in the discharge of my duty and with my face towards heaven and, if it must be so, God grant us a happy meeting there. I would to God I could meet you again on earth, but not mine but thy will be done, oh God. Kiss the children and may God bless them. Give my love to all the relations. Oh, my dearest, how long shall I be absent from thee, if it was not for thee, it seems to me I could die willingly in defense of my country, but oh, my dearest Molly, God hastens our meeting.

Write soon to your dearest William

Direct to Bristol, Tennessee

––––––

Stilwell has finally received a furlough. We do not know on what day he left East Tennessee for the 1200-mile journey; his last letter was dated December 20, and thus we don't know how much time he had at home but the usual was to give a man 30 days. Considering that it took him eight days to return, the total time away from camp would have been about 46 days. What is so confusing is that Stilwell dated his next letter 11 January 1864. This is impossible, so the editor, after considerable crosschecking has concluded that the proper date would be

---

[10] General Ambrose Burnside was Union Commander at Knoxville.

11 February and has so noted on the following letter. WRS simply got the months confused.

Another and perhaps unsolvable mystery occurs during the furlough. Stilwell moves Molly and the children out of the residence of William Foster in Butts County and installs them in the residence of Molly's one time guardian, Thomas Speer in McDonough, Henry County. What caused this move? The editor believes that it was the eminent marriage of William Foster to the young maiden, Susanna McKibben There is no record of the marriage, but there is no doubt of the union. Unlike most double tombstones which simply list the names of those that are interred beneath and one simply and correctly assumes that they were husband and wife, the tombstone at Fellowship Church cemetery proclaims: "William J. Foster 2/3/1808–6/27/1875 and Susanna McKibben Wife of William J. Foster 11/21/1838—12/21/ 1927. A clue as to the date of their marriage is the birthdate of their first son, William H. Foster, born on 1 January 1866. William was 56 and Susanna was 26 at the time of their marriage. William Foster's first wife, Mary had died on 12 April 1861, coincident with the beginning of the Civil War.

Susanna was the granddaughter of John and Margaret McKibben, early pioneers of Butts County, and the daughter of Thomas McKibben. Martin Van Buren

McKibben was her brother. In 1867, Penelope Foster, William Foster's sister would marry another of Susanna's brothers, Thomas, a local schoolteacher. Another stone in the cemetery explains some of the circumstances of this marriage: it is a memorial to "Our stepmother Penelope McKibben Born 1811 and Died October 26, 1879."

Stilwell never mentions the union of William Foster and Susanna in his letters. All future letters will be addressed to Molly in McDonough.

Newmarket, Tennessee, January [February] 11, 1864

My dearest Molly:

Arrived at Reidsville [Russellsville (?)] last Tuesday, eight days on the way and all right, safe and sound, found my command where I left it under orders to march on the next morning which accounts for my not writing the day after my arrival. We were two days march [to] here. I [am] now twenty miles from Knoxville, the cars run now in ten or twelve miles of Knoxville to Strawberry Plains.

General Bryan has arrived, everything moving on as usual, no fighting here now of importance. Arrangements [are] making for an advance movement as soon as the weather will permit which will be a month hence, I suppose.

January [February] 12th—Duty prevented the finishing of my letter on yesterday. I feel just like I had got home after a long journey. This feels more like home than it did while there. The weather is pleasant here, everything still, but no doubt, it is the same lull that always proceeds the storm. Short rations, lb. flour, 1/4 pork, nothing else. I had to stay in Atlanta on Tuesday night after I left home and one day at Kingsville, S. C., one at Petersburg, Va. [and] one at Bristol, Tennessee, though I had no breakdowns on the railroad for the first time.[11] My pony is fat as he can be, his back is not well, I am afraid [it] never will be. I think I will have to trade off if it don't get better soon.

I have received two letters from you since I came back, letters that you had written long ago and one from Brother John [Stilwell] and one from Brother Waters that he wrote to Chattanooga. Molly, my pen and ink is so bad that I don't write so that you can hardly read it. I will have to write with pencil and if it runs, let me know it and I will try and get pen and ink. I am in good health and doing finely, I hope you are doing the same. Write soon, give my love to Puss[12] and kiss all the children.[13] One can not help it but think of

---

[11] Kingsville SC is about halfway between Orangeburg and Columbia. It is likely that WRS detrained here to switch to the train to Wilmington NC and thence onto the Weldon line to Petersburg. This is the same route as his unit took on the first trip to Virginia.

[12] Elizabeth (Puss), Speer was a child born of Thomas Speer and Nancy Edwards in 1839. She married first a Sutton and then Allen Washington Turner. He was the richest man in Henry County in prewar days, reporting $122,000 property in 1860. In 1870 he listed his occupation as "trader" but reported only $2000 in property. In 1870 he was 55 and Elizabeth was 31. Living with them were several children from Turner's pervious marriage and a nine-month-old son, Paul, son of Elizabeth.

home, sweet home. My love and respects to Uncle Thomas and Aunt Nancy and all. James is well. Direct thus:

William R. Stilwell

Bryan's Brigade, McLaws Division, Longstreet's Corps (East Tenn.)

I will write more and better in future. You may read this to others but don't show it. Write soon. I am your own dear William.

Goodbye, God bless you. Kiss em for me.

————

William Ross Stilwell is a very complicated man. Perhaps the strangest revelation in all his letters comes in this one. During all the time he was at home on furlough with Molly, he abstained from sexual relations with her. Why? He says that had he yielded to temptation, that afterwards he would never have been able to leave and resume his duties. Perhaps we should take him at this word. His love for Molly is intense, likewise he has developed an intense devotion to his brigade duties and to General Bryan, his commander. He also had the religious temperament to take seriously Biblical injunctions against sex before battle such as Deuteronomy 23, verses 9 and 10, "When you go forth against your enemies and are in camp, then you shall keep yourself from every evil thing. If there is among you any man who is not clean by reason of what chances to him by night—."

Newmarket, February 20th, 1864

My dearest Molly:

I have a few minutes this evening as James [Speer] is going to start home in the morning and I reckon you will be expecting a letter when he comes.

This is Saturday evening and I feel very lonesome, Oh, how anxious I am to hear from you and to hear how you are getting along. I have written to you since I got back but have not had time

---

[13] There were three teen-age children left in the household of Thomas and Nancy Speer.

for an answer yet. Oh, I want a letter so bad to know how you and Tommy and little Jinney, God bless her little soul. I did not know I loved her so well until I came back. I hope you are all doing well.

My health, dear, is very good, never better. I am getting along like always—very well. I had a very cold ride the other night and got my feet frost bit a little I think. Dear, I want you to try and get my hat made and send it and a pair or two of socks by James when he returns I will enclose five dollars as a present. I can't do more now, but hope to do better some time. I have drawn fifty dollars only and I paid that today for my horse. I only owe twenty-five for him now. I want to get all paid up that I can and then the balance is for you.

Everything is still here now, no fighting and no prospect of it soon. I have a good tent and chimney and can keep warm. Oh, but it is not like lying with my arms around you, the dearest of the dear. Molly, did you know that it liked to have killed me to be so distant when I was at home. I knew if I was to let myself do so, I could never have left you until I was drug away, but God give me grace to stand it. God knows my heart, I can never be satisfied unless I die in sight of you for you are my life, my all, and to be absent from you is to be dead to the world. Molly, I could write a book if I had time but I must take my leave. Oh, let us pray much and if we never meet on earth, when we get to heaven we will have a great meeting there. Give my love to cousins, friends, and all Uncle Tommy's folks. [14] Kiss all three of the children for me.[15] I am, dear Molly, your own dear William.

P. S. Direct thus:

W. R. Stilwell, c/o General Bryan, Mr McLaws' Division
Longstreet's Corps, Army East Tennessee
Molly—Goodbye

---

[14] Thomas Speer.
[15] George Alexander Hamilton Speer, age 17; Charles Milton Speer, age 16; and William Absalom, age 13.

Longstreet's army has been told to prepare for a mounted foray into Kentucky. The rationale for mounting the men is that they would be able to move and maneuver through the Spring mud, thus stealing a march on an unmounted enemy. Stilwell seems certain that the plans for this action were firm and perhaps they were at division and brigade level. However, when proposed to Lee and his staff, it was quickly dismissed since the idea would strip the remainder of the army of mounts.

Greeneville, Tennessee February 27th, 1864

My dearest Molly:

I have not as yet received any letter from you since my return. You can imagine how anxious I am to hear from you, this is the third letter I have wrote to you. My reasons for writing so much is our brigade is to be mounted as cavalry and it is thought we will go into Kentucky and perhaps to Ohio, If we do there will be no chance to write. All connections will be cut off, I think it will be three or four weeks before we start though it may be sooner. If we do go and you don't get letters from me you may know what is the matter, you must not be uneasy but trust that all things are for the best. We will not be allowed any baggage except what we can carry on our horses. I am going to cut up my oilcloth and make me a pair of saddlebags to carry one shirt, one pair of drawers, and two pairs of socks. I am afraid I shall have to lose part of my things. Tell James [Speer] not to bring back any clothes with him, if he does he will lose them. He had better come with a horse or [be] prepared to buy one. I wish I was able to get a better horse, the one I have got will not do my business, but I will have to do the best I can until I get in the enemy's country. I will get one there.

I am looking every day for a letter from you and hope I will get one soon, you can continue to write until I can learn more about the arrangement. I will try and write often until we start. I am not certain that we will take the campaign I mention but that seems to be the general opinion. I wrote James a letter that will give him all the information I have and he will have to act from his own judgment. I can only say to him that orders have been received to mount our brigade and perhaps division and corps and is now being done. Transportation [availability] is reduced to almost nothing. Write soon and often for the present, give my love to all inquiring friends. Tell Cousin Puss howdy and kiss all the children. God grant that this war may soon close and let us all meet again, to enjoy the comforts of home and friends as in days past and gone forever, gone. Those were happy days when at setting sun to meet the loving smiles of an affectionate wife. It is delightful to think of those days. Oh, God, will the sun never shine again? I am, Molly, your own dear William.

May the blessings of God rest upon us all, and save us in his kingdom, Amen.

William

———

A religious revival is sweeping through the Confederate Army. Stilwell reports that it is particularly strong in the soldiers isolated in upper East Tennessee. "We have very good meetings day and night."

Greeneville, Tennessee, March 12th, 1864

My dearest Molly:

Your letter of the 27th February was received today, the first I have received since I left home. Oh, with what interest I read each word, it was long, wide and full of good news. Thank God for health, strength, food and rearmament. I was so uneasy or not so uneasy as I was anxious to hear from you. Just think, I left you [on the] 2nd day of January [February] and never heard a word until today. To be absent from [the] one I love, one whose life is my life, is too bad, but not to hear from you in so long, but I trust in God. He has always taken care of me and mine. I think he will to the end. I have written you several letters and would not write now but I feel so glad at getting your letter that I must write and moreover you say, and I have no doubt it is so, that you are so lonesome, I think I may be excused for writing so often.

Dear, I am in the best of health and spirits. I still retain my cheerful manner and look for light out of darkness. I have enjoyed more of the power and joy of religion for several days past than usual. We have very good meetings night and day. We have made considerable improvement in the brigade since Brother Haygood,[16] the missionary to our brigade, has been here. He is a good preacher and a good man. Last Sabbath we had sacrament, we have a good time but when I thought of my dear wife so far away from the sacrament board while I was knelt down by a log away here in East Tennessee. I busted forth in anguish of tears, perhaps some one thought I was a fool but God knows thy grounds and counts thy tears, how best I know in whom I have believed and am persuaded that he is able to keep that which I have committed unto him against that day.

You cannot imagine with what joy thrilled my heart when you wrote me in your letter that Tommy could almost say his prayers himself. That is right my dear, teach him the good and the right way and all will be well. Molly, 1 was called upon last night to lead in prayer. When I began to pray for our wives and little ones at home it seemed to me that I could almost see you bowed before the throne of God at the same time. It was about nine o'clock, perhaps you was. I can almost see you in my imagination as you lay our little ones down to rest and then kneel by their bedside to pray for them and their Father that is so far, far away from them in body, for my mind is there. Thank God [unintelligible] for by faith we meet around one common mercy seat. And Jesus comes down, our souls to greet and mercy crowns the mercy seat.

[Last of letter missing]

---

[16]Atticus Greene Haygood was a young Methodist minister the same age as Stilwell. Educated and already anointed for rapid promotion he would eventually be president of Emory College in Oxford GA and a bishop of the church. The Confederate army's control of chaplains was unsatisfactory to church governance so the church organizations assumed the direct responsibility of providing chaplains. Haygood was one of eight chaplains directly assigned by the Methodist Church to Confederate brigades. Stilwell probably learned much from Haygood. Harold W. Mann, *Atticus Greene Haygood Methodist Bishop and Educator* (Athens: University of Georgia Press, 1965).

———

Perhaps Stilwell is having second thoughts about what did not happen on his furlough. His letters to Molly are taking on a fervor that borders on the erotic. The last part of this letter is missing, which may be a good thing as the expressed level of desire reaches a level which prudence declares has gone far enough-a most remarkable love letter.

Greeneville, East Tennessee, March 23rd, 1864

My dearest Molly:

Although I have received but one letter from you since my return and that has been answered long ago yet I feel like writing and of the abundance of the heart the mouth speaketh, and as you are the light, love and pleasure of my life, I know you will excuse me for writing so often to one whose presence can give happiness and pleasure. I dreamed a most delightful dream last night. I went to sleep after commending you and our sweet little children to God, thinking about, I was thinking how sweetly you were lying in bed perhaps not asleep but resting your weary body and thinking of the one on earth most dear, with one on each side. Oh, how sweet thus I was thinking when I fell asleep. I thought we were together and had walked into a garden of flowers, oh it was so beautiful, we had been walking hand in hand, we came to a pretty bunch of flowers and stopped to look at them, one on either side. I thought you raised your head up to see what I was doing. I looked at you and you smiled. It pleased me to the heart, I sprang over the flowers to catch you around the waist, and just as I caught at you some one called my name and you vanished from my sight and was gone. I awoke, someone was calling me, oh, to think that you would treat me so. If you had just stayed until I could have kissed you once more. I would not take anything for my dream, your spirits must have been hovering around me here. Yet it was so lovely and sweet. I was so much delighted and happy but to think that you would leave me, this without allowing me to embrace you or to kiss your hand, say what made you do me so, you loving creature. I would have been happy all day if you had just given me one kiss. Oh, don't do me so, no more my dearest wife, leave me not thus in anguish and pain but again when we walk among the flowers, let me embrace thee and kiss thy loving brow and be not scared and be not scared of by any one that calls my name. I wish they had been somewhere else and then I could have kissed you and been happy once more. I thank God for dreams for thus making me happy once and hope he will give me another visit soon and if so, I hope no one will interfere with my happiness for I don't have those blessed opportunities often. Still, I am happy today to think that I once more was by thy side amidst flowers and did see thee smile once more, one of those bewitching smiles which only those that love can give. Oh, my dearest, do smile once more upon your unworthy husband, one of those sweet smiles that only you can give. Forgive me my dear if I cause you to shed a tear, if I do I know it will be a tear of love and not of grief. Oh, Molly I have loved as never man could almost. Come tonight and let me kiss you dear.

[Last of letter missing]

––––––

Stilwell and the army have moved up to Bristol, Tennessee on the Virginia State line. They are returning to Virginia to rejoin Lee's army in defense of Richmond, against the army of General Ulysses S. Grant. Several days will be spent in Bristol, apparently waiting for rail transport back to the central Virginia area that they left the previous September.

Bristol, Tennessee, April 3rd, 1864
My dear Molly:
We have been marching for several days of the worst weather I most ever seen in my life. We were four days marching from Greeneville to Bristol, distance fifty-four miles. It snowed most all the time. I am very well and getting along as usual. James [Speer] got here this morning safe and in good health, I was very much surprised at his not bringing me any letter until he told me how and

where he left. I thought I would get my hat when he came back. I hope you will send it by John Stephens as I need it very bad [17] I have not got my socks yet that James brought but will get them today. I am very much obliged to you for them. I would like very much to kiss you for them but you will have to excuse me this time and I promise to do so when I get the chance.

I don't think I will send off this letter for a few days as yet and wait until I have time to hear a little about our move. It is thought that we have come up here for the purpose of going into Kentucky, and I think that by waiting a few days I can get perhaps more information and in the meantime, perhaps a letter from you. I will therefore leave the rest of my letter until a few days passes and I will then complete. Until then I bid you an affectionate ado. Yours ever dear.

W. R. Stilwell

[The following was appended to the April 3rd letter]
Bristol, Tennessee, April 8th, 1864
My dear Molly:
Yours of the 19th and 24th was received today in which you stated that you had wrote me three letters. I have not received them yet. You said that you had wrote one on Sunday before that would give me all the news. I am in hopes I will get it in a few days. You will see that this letter was started on the third. I have not any more news in regard to a move than I had at that time. I was sorry to hear of Mother's sickness but glad she is better. My own health is very good, today is fast day but somehow or other I don't feel the same solemn obligations as in days gone by. I suppose the reason is that fast days come so often with me of late that I can't feel right. I hope it is not for a want of religious interest, nevertheless I have kept the day. C. B. Smith will start home in a day or two and I think I shall send this letter by him. I am glad to hear that you are doing so

---

[17] John Stephens was first sergeant of Company E of the 53rd from Newton County. In 1860, at age 21 he lived in Stockbridge, Henry County with his father, a millwright, mother and four siblings. He was KIA in the Wilderness on 6 May 1864.

well. I am glad you have milk plenty. I know you will drink a glass for me. Oh, this cruel war, this cruel war, how many happy homes have been made desolate and unhappy by it. I hope it will soon end and let loved ones meet again. Oh, how happy I would be if I could hold you to my breast and say, my dear Molly we part no more unless by the hand of a good and great God directs us to part in death.

[Unsigned]

———

Bristol, Tennessee, April 11, 1864
My dear Molly:
I have made several attempts to send off a letter by hand but have failed. Mr. Smith has not got his leave of absence yet. I will therefore write another short letter and send it off by mail. I am very well this morning though very lonesome. Your letter that you spoke about has not come to hand yet. I am afraid I shall not have the pleasure of reading it. We have had an abundance of rain here of late, mud very deep and ground mirery, no movements on foot so far as I know that. I think we shall move before long, somewhere, don't know where to yet.

I am looking for Doss Camel tonight or tomorrow.[18] Oh that peace, happy peace could be once more granted us so that I could once more embrace my dearest wife. Oh, Molly I love you so much and yet I am not allowed to see you nor even kiss thy cheeks, oh, if I would just kiss you again it would do me so much good. I can't see how I ever did leave you when I was at home but God who has guarded us all the time I reckon guarded me in that also. I must bid

---

[18] Johnathan W. Campbell was a private in the 14th Infantry, Company I that was organized in Butts County. He was accidentally shot at Cold Harbor on 3 June 1864, died on 10 June 1864 and is buried in Hollywood Cemetery in Richmond. In 1860, age 18, he was a farm laborer living with his mother and four siblings near Indian Springs in Butts County.

you kiss the little children for me and bid you an affectionate ado I am yours my dear.

William

Good bye my dear Molly. I am your own dear William till death.

8

THE WILDERNESS

Longstreet's Corps is very glad to be back in Virginia. The food is much better and they have mail again. But looking ahead, Stilwell foresees the siege of Richmond and its horrors.

Camp near Gordonsville, Virginia, April 19th, 1864
My dear Molly:
Your letter of April 3rd by John Stephens was received at Lynchburg while on the cars coming from Tennessee. We are now with General Lee's army in Virginia, got here on yesterday and I guess will stay here until the great battle of the war. The Yankees are concentrating a large force here now, so are we. I think we are going to have worse fighting here this spring than we have ever had. I hope to come out safe and get home to those I love. My health is very good, in fact I am doing very well in every respect. I would have wrote to you sooner but for our marching and now I have to write with pencil, you wrote that you would send me a pencil. Who did you send it by? Doss Camel has not come yet, I reckon you sent it by him. Brother Waters sent me two excellent books [delivered] by Mr. Morris. I was very glad to get them. I got a letter from cousin Mag Everitt,[1] one from Pa and Brother John, all on the cars as we come on. I am very glad to get back to Virginia and hope we will

---

[1] Mag Everitt was likely a daughter of Richard M. Everitt. In 1860 his household included a female child, age 14, with initials M. A.

stay here as long as the war lasts. Our people are making great preparations for a siege at Richmond. I don't want to be in the siege, it will be so sickly if we are surrounded and hemmed up in there and then if the Yankees get us in and surround us then I can not write to my dear Molly, but I don't think they will ever get us surrounded. They will have some hard fighting to do first. We get plenty to eat now, the weather is still cold and disagreeable and spring is very backward. I can't write much at this time as the mail will leave in a short time. We can get our mail better now than we could in Tennessee, and will get it sooner. James [Speer] is very well and doing finely. Give my love and respect to all the friends, tell Uncle Thomas [Speer] that he may expect stirring events in this department soon. I must close, the mail is ready. Kiss the children. Oh for one kiss on my dear Molly's cheek. I will write you every week if I can. I am your own dear William.

Good bye my dearest and most lovely and affectionate Molly, your own dear William

Direct thus: William R. Stilwell

c/o General Bryan, McLaws' Division

Richmond, Va.

I love you as ever, may God bless and protect us and ours in this life and save us in the world to come, Amen.

Kiss this spot

———

In the calm that precedes the storm, the big news for Stilwell is the success of the religious revival being experienced in the Army of Northern Virginia.

Camp near Gordonsville, Virginia, April 25th, 1864

My dearest Molly:

I am very well this morning and hope you are enjoying the same good blessing. No letter has been received from you for some time though I am expecting one every day. I wrote to you last Monday morning and I am writing again this morning. We are having beautiful weather now. We had rain last night, the trees and flowers are putting forth and spring with all its beauty and loveliness has come. I need but one thing more to make me happy (thy presence). You know I am a spring bird and love to dwell among the pleasures. You must forgive me for reserving a portion of my love for the beauties of nature and not concentrating it all on yourself. True, you are worthy of all the love I possess, but you must at least permit me to admire the beauties of the flowers; the flowers in spring are not like you. They always remain in my presence but you, whenever you appear to me in my dreams, vanish from me whenever I awake and I see you no more until I again fall asleep. The flowers are not so, when I dream of them in sleep, I awake to find them present with me, nevertheless you are the flower of my heart, the darling of my life, the queen of the flowers. But I must stop or you will think that I am writing a love letter and young people say that [unintelligible] courting a lady after you marry her, however, I never thought so.

I have no war news, no doubt we are having the calm that always precedes the storm, and the silence of the cannon which now prevails will only make its roaring the louder in the future. We have been successful at all points this spring of which you need have heard through the medium of [the] press so I have no war news that would interest you. I have something of more importance to write, news of more profound character.

God has visited us in this part of his vineyard in the outpouring of his holy spirits and many are turning to the Lord. Christians who have back-sled is again returning to the field of Christ, sinners are being converted and the word of God doth run and is glorified among us, thanks be unto God who giveth us the victory through our lord Jesus Christ, now henceforth and for evermore, Amen. Eleven joined the church night before last. I am thankful to say that this good work is not confined to our brigade but as far as I can tell is through this army. I think it is one of the best signs of our success that can be given. Again I say, thank God.

Molly, I sent some money by brother Haygood, missionary of our brigade, to subscribe for the *Christian Advocate* for you, for three months. I want to know if you have ever got it. I will renew it when it is out.

Doss Camel has not yet got here. I am looking for him every day. I hope he will come soon. James Speer is well, all the friends are well here.

Oh, I must tell you, I get just as much coffee and sugar as I can drink. I will send you a grain. I wish you had some. I will make a swap. If you will send me milk, I will send you coffee. I get plenty to eat now. I have not got no money, we have not drawn any yet. I shall have to frank[2] my letters. I hate to do it but can't help it. I could borrow but it ain't here to get. I don't expect there is five hundred dollars in my brigade, no money here.

John Stephens told me about seeing you and the children. He thinks Tommy is a fine boy. If you had of sent my hat by him, I would have got it sooner but I hope I will get it before long, the sun has burned me till you would hardly know me. I have not heard from Mother in some time. I hope she is much better, she was improving slowly when I heard last. Give my love to all the friends. Kiss the babies. Tell Tommy [that] Pa said to be good boy and to do what Ma says. I am dearest Molly, your own dearest. Good by.

William

My dear loving and affectionate wife, oh, God, let this cup pass from me nevertheless, not my will but thine be done.

Your own dear William

Direct—W. R. Stilwell

Care General Bryan, McLaws' Division

Richmond, Va.

May God bless and protect you always and bring us safe through this trial. Amen.

———

When Longstreet's First Corps straggled back into Virginia, the morale of the men and officers was at very low ebb. Longstreet had

---

[2] Recipient pays the postage.

offered to resign but Lee was very satisfied to have his highest ranking subordinate and strong right hand back. Knowing this, Longstreet's spirits improved immediately. Joseph Kershaw had replaced McLaws as division commander, but it is still on a temporary basis, so Stilwell still refers to McLaws Division.

A rare event, a large troop review was scheduled so Lee could work his magic on the men of the 1st Corps. Lee, Longstreet, and their staffs rode the length of the line, so closely they could see each man's face. A chaplain asked Colonel Charles Venable of Lee's staff: "Does it not make the General proud to see how these men love him?" "Not proud," remarked Venable, "It awes him."

Headquarters Gordonsville, Virginia, April 29th, 1864
Dearest Molly:

Your letter of the 20th was received last evening, it was the first since the one you sent by or wrote to send by Doss Camel. I was very glad to hear that you were getting along so well. It does me so much good to hear that you are getting on so well, but Mother, oh, what would I give to see her. I do hope and pray that she may be restored to health again, it is so hard to think that I can't get to see her, nevertheless, my trust is in God who doeth all things well.

We are having a very good meeting, many have joined the church and many more I think will join yet. God has abundantly blessed us. I am well pleased in you having the children baptized. I was marching that day from Charlottesville to this place and was not aware that our children were being consecrated to the service of God. Teach them that we have given them to the Lord and that they must be good. Tell Tommy that Pa says he done pretty and it makes Pa glad. Oh, that God may make us all happy in his soul.

General R. E. Lee reviewed our corps today. There was some ten or twelve thousand men in one field. Oh, if you could have seen it, I would have been so glad and I know that if you had of seen it, I could have seen you and that would have done me more good than a hundred reviews. I am very well, get plenty to eat, plenty of coffee and sugar. We have not drawn any money yet, don't know when we will. I don't need it much, don't you mind about my having money,

I can always make out very well. I have not got my hat yet, I need it very bad, most burned up with the sun, face blistered. I don't think I will ever wear another cap while I live.

Molly, I wrote regular once a week and always do when I can. You said you was not afraid of my forsaking you, unto whom could I go? Thou hast my heart and soul and life, you are my good loving and never failing wife. Love to all and kiss the children for me. Excuse this short letter and believe me to be your own dear William till death. God bless and protect and console and guide you in the way, ever lasting Amen. Good by my dear Molly, yours forever.

William

May 1st.—Dear Molly, As I did not get to send off my letter as I expected, I will write something more, though I haven't a thing of importance to write. I know anything coming from me will interest my dear wife. I have been distributing religious papers this morning for Brother Haygood. I have distributed about four hundred in our brigade and some in others. We have some two thousand papers now on hand. I love to give them out, the boys are so glad to get them and I hope they may do them good. There has twenty or thirty-five joined the church in the last week and the altar is still full of them. Thank God for his goodness and grace. I hope that God may bless the church at home.

There is no expectation of a fight as far as I know soon. Oh, that God may bless us and give us peace that we may get them to worship around our family altar. Oh, Molly, you can't imagine how much good it does me to remember the pleasant hours we have spent on family prayers, and oh, that God would bless you again having that privilege.

Molly, we was one of the happiest couples I think that ever loved most. Oh, how I want to see and kiss you. Oh my dearest Molly, it is so hard to keep us thus separated but let us not complain. God will give us a right and permit us to meet again where we can enjoy ourselves together as in days past and you write as you do. Give my love to Uncle Thomas and Nancy and cousin Puss and all.

Direct your letters thus:

William R. Stilwell, care General Bryan
McLaws Division, Richmond, Virginia.
I am dearest Molly your own dear William, Oh for one kiss, one sweet kiss like you alone can give.
W. R. Stilwell

———

Gordonsville, May 3rd, 1864
My dear Molly:
I have just learned that Mr. Cooper would start home in a few minutes and I thought I would write you a short letter.[3] I am well. It is thought that we will have a battle here soon, though I can't tell. I expect we will have a bad fight. The army on both sides is large and commanded by the best generals that is north or south. May God defend the right and the just cause and may God shield us. I am very uneasy about mother, I hope she is better ere this [by the time this is received]. No letter has been received except from you in a long time. I received one from you the other day and wrote one to you a few days ago. James Speer is well. Give my love to all the friends. I have not received my hat yet. Camel has not come, don't know when he will. I wish he would come back. I must close, not having time to write more. Kiss the children for me. Our meeting still continues, pray for me at sundown, and then we will meet at the throne of God. I am, Molly, your own dear William. Oh to kiss thee my dear wife. I love you as ever. May God bless you and our little children. I am yours until death.
W. R. Stilwell
Goodbye my dearest, loving true and affectionate wife, my all, my life, the one for whom I desire to live and for whom I could die.
Again goodbye, how can I quit? My pencil is not satisfied, it only wants to say my dear Molly and goodbye, but I must bid you an affectionate and loving ado.
William

---

[3] Mr. Cooper has not been identified.

———

Some of the fiercest fighting of the war has occurred since Stilwell last wrote on May 3. Both the battles of the Wilderness and Spotsylvania had occurred during this period. The most notable action for Stilwell's unit occurred on the morning of 6 May, as part of the Wilderness battle. To the west of Chancellorsville, the Federals had broken A. P. Hill's Corps and Lee's entire army was in grave jeopardy. Longstreet and his corps arrived on the scene and immediately counterattacked. By the end of the day, the 1st Corps with two divisions had chewed up five Federal divisions. Bryan's Brigade and the 53rd Regiment were right in the middle.

Losses on both sides were very heavy. Bryan's Brigade suffered 31 men killed and 102 wounded. Fifteen of the dead were in the 53rd Regiment but as Stilwell points out, none was in his company but there were 11 wounded. The Wilderness was the first of the terrible blows that would occur in May and June in Virginia. Grant did not withdraw to lick his wounds as had previous Union commanders.

Longstreet and his men had performed superbly on 6 May. It was Longstreet's ultimate performance, indeed it may have been the best performance of any combat commander during the entire war. Unfortunately, Longstreet was struck down by friendly fire on that evening. He was not killed but was out of service for several months.

Meanwhile, of great relevance to the Georgia troops, Sherman had begun his campaign for Atlanta on 7 May. By 16 May, he is below Resaca, having flanked Joe Johnston out of strong positions at Dalton and Resaca.

Headquarters, Bryan's Brigade, May 16th, 1864

My dearest Molly:

Thanks be unto a merciful God that after twelve or fourteen days marching and fighting, I am still spared to say "My dear Molly." Oh, again I say let us thank God for his goodness and mercy which has been over and around me. I have made many narrow escapes and passed through many dangers. I had one of my friends, a Mr. Curry killed by my side.[4] The other night while asleep, he and I was sleeping together, the ball struck him in the breast, he awoke me struggling, but before I could get a light he was dead, poor fellow, he never knew what hit him.

Oh, God, thy ways are past finding out and thy mercy endureth forever, blessed [be] the name of God. I fear the fighting is not over yet as the enemy [is] still on this side [of] the river. We are now in front of Fredericksburg, the enemy on this side between us and the town. We are ready for them and waiting for them to come, we have whipped them very badly at all points. I hope they will cross the river without any more fighting but if not, I hope that God will give us the victory as heretofore. Oh how thankful we should be for his blessings. I can't think of nothing else hardly. I had eleven men wounded in my company, thank God none killed. Capt. Vandigriff,[5] Israel Sowell, [and] James and Joe Guest are those that you know.[6] Joe Guest[7] lost his right arm, James was wounded in the body.[8] I think both will get well. Poor John Stephens was killed on the field while bringing the flag in and a braver and better soldier never died on that memorable field. Not only me but all who know him mourn his death. I hope our loss is his eternal gain. I talked to

---

[4] Mr. Curry has not been identified. By the use of the title "Mr." and the fact that he was sleeping by Stilwell's side, we can assume that he was a lieutenant courier.

[5] Captain James W. Vandigriff was wounded in the right foot at Wilderness, Virginia. Disabled, he would retire to the invalid corps on 12 January 1865. He married Mary E. Smith on 1 August 1866. In 1870 he was residing in McDonough with his wife and listed his occupation as a retired grocer.

[6] Isaac Lamar Sowell was one of five brothers who served in Company F. He was third sergeant, currently age 28. He was wounded in the right leg at Wilderness, Virginia on 6 May 1863. Disabled by gangrene, he was on detached duty in the Quartermaster's Department in December 1864. In 1870 he was an unmarried farmhand living with other family members in Henry County.

[7] Joseph A. Guest, born in 1843, was fourth sergeant of Company F. As a result of losing his right arm, he would be discharged on 21 August 1864. In the 1860 census, he was reported as a 17-year-old schoolboy, son of William and M. J. Guest, farmers of moderate means who owned no slaves. There were 6 children in the family. Joseph cannot be located in the 1870 census.

[8] James was a younger brother of Joseph Guest. He would recover only to be killed at Cedar Creek VA on 19 October 1864.

him on the subject [of] religion but a few days before his death. I think he was a Christian. Give my respects to his parents and friends and tell them that I share part of their grief. His brother James is still with the company and well.[9] I know you must be very uneasy about me, Molly, and indeed you have reason to be for I have had no chance to write and I know you have heard of the many slaughters and ten days battle. Oh how I wanted to write but [had] no chance. All communications has been cut off, no mail received nor none sent off, and now though I am writing, I can't tell when it will go off. I hope soon for I know you can't rest. Cousin James [Speer] may have wrote but I don't suppose it went off. I have not received any letter from you in a long time. I hope you are well and doing well. I have not heard from Mother, hope she is better.

General Bryan is still safe, thank God. He has paid me quite a compliment and says he will mention my name in his report[10] for my gallantry on Friday's fight in rallying the men in the midst of the fight.[11] All the honor that I ask [for], is to get home after our independence is gained to enjoy the love and affection of my dearest wife and sweet little children, and may God grant that I may, and he alone shall have the honor and glory, for God forbid that I should glory in anything save the cross of our Lord Jesus Christ, Amen. Molly, my mind is not composed and you must excuse this badly written letter but the most important [thing] is to know that I was still safe on the 16th May. As for the morn, let us trust in God and leave the routine in his hands. But now I come to the part of my letter that makes me shed tears to bid you an affectionate ado. Oh God what a trying moment is this to me. Oh, God all things are possible with thee. Take care of me and mine for Christ sake, save us for they mercy's sake. Amen. Send word to all

---

[9] James Stephens was in Company E, Newton County. He was captured on 19 October 1864 at Cedar Creek VA and died in the Elmria NY prison.

[10] General Bryan mentioned couriers Morris and Dobbs but not WRS. About Morris and Dobbs he commented on their forcing to the front the few who were disposed to straggle. (*OR*, 36/1:1063-64.) It was probably awkward to comment on a private having the same duties.

[11] 6 May 1864 Battle of the Wilderness.

the friends. My love to all. I am, dearest Molly, your devoted and ever loving and affectionate and true and never forsaking William.

When you write, direct as before to Richmond, Va., in care of General Bryan, McLaw's Division, Army of Northern Virginia. And now may the love and peace of God and our father and the mercy of our Lord Jesus Christ rest and remain with us now henceforth and forever more. Amen

Good by my dearest Molly.

W. R. Stilwell

Lee has fallen back about halfway from Fredericksburg to Richmond. He must remain between Grant and Richmond and Grant is taking advantage of this, maneuvering on the flanks to make Lee retreat. The 53rd Regiment, as indicated by casualty data, has not had any hard-pressed battles since the Wilderness but have been subjected to skirmishing and hard marches. Stilwell, as brigade courier, is almost constantly in danger in such fluid situations.

Camp near Hanover Junction, May 23, 1864

My dear Molly:

I have written you two letters since the fighting began but I could not give you much satisfaction as the fighting was still going on and even now we are expecting to march. We stopped here last night after having marched all night and day before. Hanover Junction is twenty-seven miles above Richmond. We have fallen back some twenty-five miles as we were not driven back by no means, we had to fall back so as to unite our armies and to get close to our commissaries, having suffered already for want of rations. We have whipped them at every point thus far and I think will in [the] future though I think our people had as well expect a long siege of Richmond. Grant is no doubt going to try Richmond like Vicksburg and you may be assured that I will write when I can but you must not be uneasy if you should not get my letters. I don't expect you have got any letters from [me] in a long time. I have seen very hard times for the last twenty days and passed through many dangers and had many narrow escapes. I had one man killed while sleeping by my side, poor fellow, he was just asleep and never knew what killed him. I had many shots near me but God has spared my life thus far, [for] which let us be thankful.

Molly, I got my hat last night and now have it on. It fits very well and is a nice hat. I am due you a kiss for it and hope to be able to pay it some day. The pencil you sent by John Stephens I never got. I think he must have forgot it, poor man, his remains lie on the farm fields of the Wilderness. He died like a brave man in the discharge of duty and I hope [he] is in heaven.

Molly, you must not expect long letters from me under the circumstances. I got a letter from [you] dated first of May last. I think I will get to see William Darnell, I understand that he is near Richmond. I don't know whether Brother John [Stilwell] is here or not. I will hear in a few days. I must close my letter, we have to move soon. Write soon and between times. You will see that I wrote you this letter on the 23rd and could not send it off. I now finish it. Molly, I know you are very uneasy about me and perhaps in your dreams have seen me lying on some bloody field with the blood running from my veins, but thank God, it is not the case yet. I am still unhurt and in good health. I had to carry some orders to Colonel Simms.[12] One picket [was] at the river bridge when I got there, the enemy discovered me and fired at me across the bridge but missed me. I have made many narrow escapes and I thank God for it all. Molly, I have written to you about the trophy. I have got to send you a silver fork. I also captured two spoons, knife and fork, haversack and coat. I have got the best kind of a Yankee overcoat. It will be so good for next winter, should I live. Molly, I will need a coat before long, I want you to engage enough of jeans to make me one. I will send you the money to pay for it if you can get it. Perhaps you had better get enough for pants and coat if you can do so. I mention it now so you will have time a plenty. You need not be in a hurry, we have not drawn any money and don't know when we

---

[12] Currently permanent commander of the 53rd Regiment.

will. I have written you a long letter, you must write me once a week. I will get them now I hope, and I will write whenever I can and now dear Molly, allow me to bid you an affectionate ado. I am your own dear, affectionate, true, devoted and ever loving own dear William,

Good by my dearest Molly, I am yours always. I don't feel like quitting but must, Good by.

William

———

Lee's Army is now even closer to Richmond. Stilwell realizes a siege is imminent. General Johnston and the Army of Tennessee have temporarily stalemated Sherman on the New Hope Church/Dallas/ Pickett's Mill line.

Richmond, Virginia, May 29, 1864
My dear Molly:
Although this is Sunday I am writing you a letter, my reasons for doing so are I think good as we are either marching or fighting most all the time and this is the first time I have been situated so as to write in a month. You will see that our army is now near Richmond and no doubt here is where the great battle of the war will be fought, and whatever the country or people think, I know not but I can speak for the army. We feel perfectly confident of success. We have whipped them every time we have fought for the last month and with the blessing of God we can do it again. Our army has only fallen back to prevent Grant from flanking us which he could have done by going along the banks of the river as which he done. How long the fighting will last around Richmond I cannot say, but think perhaps most all summer. I think Grant intends besieging Richmond as he did Vicksburg. He may take it but he will have to walk over many a dead and gallant son of the South first. Our cause is just and must prevail. My prayer is that God will defend the right, his will be done, not mine.

I have received your letter of May 1st, the only one in many long and weary days though I did not expect to get many letters under the circumstances but hope I will get some soon now. I am somewhat uneasy about our army under General Johnston at Atlanta, still hope he will give a good account of himself. I have wrote you several letters and hope you have got them. I will enclose a letter that I wrote at Hanover Junction and did not get it off as I don't wish to write much today. Oh, how I long for rest and for the presence of my dearest Molly. I trust in God that if I never get to see my own dear wife that we will meet in heaven where parting and wars are no more and where we can spend an endless eternity together, God grant that it may be so. Oh, that God may bless and protect and shield us from all harm and permit us to meet again with our little ones. Give my love and respect to Uncle Tom[as Speer], Aunt Nancy, Cousin Puss and all the rest. Kiss the children and tell Tommy Pa says howdy and to be a good boy, and now dear Molly, should I fall in defense of my country, I trust I shall rise again and meet you and the children in heaven. Let the two last words I utter be (Molly, Jesus). Molly, I have been true as a husband and would die [and] believe that you had been true as wife. I am your own dearest William.

Good bye

——

Stilwell's brigade has moved back to occupy Malvern Hill, the scene of bloody fighting on 1 July 1862. It has taken the Union Army almost two years to return to where they were when Lee took command of the Army of Northern Virginia and this after trips into Maryland and Pennsylvania. The 53rd Regiment has now been engaged in most of the major engagements during these two years. But by comparison with the 2nd Louisiana, which had been in Virginia a year longer, the 53rd was in good shape, the Louisianans having been annihilated.

Malvern Hill is adjacent to Cold Harbor, where some of the bloodiest fighting of the war has been ongoing over the past few days.

Most of the blood will be from Yankees as Grant ordered another futile frontal charge.

Camp near Malvern Hill, June 14th, 1864
My Dear Molly:

Once more I have the opportunity of writing to you, You will see by reference to the captain of my letter that we are near the memorable spot of Malvern Hill, the first spot where I ever seen an enemy in battle array. Here lies the remains of departed heroes with nothing to cover their bones from the heavens above. Many a loving and affectionate husband, father, or brother's bones lies exposed and trodden under foot, here too lies the skeletons of our enemies, thousands upon thousands, all over the fields and woods side by side enemy lie. When we behold these things we are constrained to say, Oh, God is man that thou art mindful of him or the son of men that there visited him, man in his animal estate is worse than the best of the field but I shall not attempt to describe the scenes of a battlefield after two years has passed since the conflict, and where so many bodies lie moldering in its mother dust. To you it would be an awful sight, but to me it is not. I have seen so much, ah, too much.

I have been quite unwell with dysentery for more than a week but have not quit the field. I feel much better this morning. We have had fighting every day more or less since I last wrote you though we have no heavy engagement. The enemy is moving and several days may pass ere we meet again. It is thought they are going to the south side of James River. That will be southeast of Richmond. I still think as I told you before that I expect fighting here all year, at least all summer. I think the war must have an end this year, one way or other. God grant that it may come and our independence with it. Molly, I received your letter of June 2nd the other day You can imagine my joy when I tell you that it was the first in nearly six weeks and after so long to hear that you and the children was well and doing so well I was constrained to thank God for his goodness and his mercy. Molly, although we have been parted and kept so far from each other, yet God has blessed us abundantly and has kept us safe thus far. Oh, that God may permit us to meet again, let us pray much, remember to pray at sundown and you may be assured I am praying then.

I have seen William Darnell twice lately, he was well and getting along finely. I was very glad to meet with him. He loves to talk on the subject of religion, a very good sign. Out of the abundance of the heart the mouth speaketh. I don't know but from all the information that I can get, I think Brother John [Stilwell] is at Charleston, S. C. I have not had any letter from him since I left East Tennessee.

Molly, I was at the 2nd Louisiana Regiment a few days ago; in the Homer Guards I found eight men, and in the Vernon Guards, three, that is all that is left in the Homer guards. I found Captain Martin, young Dyer Blythe and a Mr. Brown that I knew, they told me a good deal about Homer and all the people though they don't hear from them often. Eli Ragland has lost an arm, Lee Cotton was killed, both the Leakes killed and most all the boys killed or captured. Mr. Maxey is still at home. Mr. Dyer has moved to Kirkpatrick, is still Sheriff. In the Vernon Guards only three remains and only one that I know, that was George Warren's brother Benson that lived with us. He could not tell me anything about Uncle [Robert] Everitt's family. Mr. Warren is dead, so is Nat Knight. Mr. Lloyd has moved off to Texas, he don't know whether he gave up my notes or not but thinks he was broke, both the kids dead. Allen Smith is Clerk of the Court; Whit is dead. Brown who was at home when Robert [Ragland] was sick gives me some information about his death. He says that the people filled the house all the time coming far and near to hear him talk, that he was the happiest man almost ever known. He seemed to welcome death and wanted to be at home, thus giving more light in his death than all his life. Thank God for his grace, oh, that God may grant us grace like him to live like him, to die and like him, to enter heaven to meet him where we will never part again. Amen. Tell the children howdy, tell Tom to be good boy and give Ma and Sister my love to all, and may God for the sake of Christ guide us through life and save us all in his kingdom is the prayer of your loving and affectionate and devoted.

William

Good by-by my dearest Molly. I am your own dear William
Kiss this spot.

9

PETERSBURG

Since he didn't know where his brother John was, Stilwell probably included the following in the letter he wrote to Molly on 14 June. Unbeknownst to WRS, John's regiment, the 32nd Georgia was probably still in Florida, having participated in the victorious battle of Olustee on 20 February 1864—the only major battle fought in Florida.

Richmond, Va. Camp near Malvern Hill, June 14,1864
John S. Stilwell, Dear brother:
If I knew where to direct my letter I would write you a few lines and as I don't know for certain, I will write at least enough to inform you that I am still safe so far, notwithstanding the hard fighting that our army, division and even my Brigade has had to do. Although men have fallen right and left, front and rear around me yet I am still an object of mercy and goodness.

General Grant, after trying Richmond by way of the Wilderness and failed, tried the way of Fredericksburg, failed then by way of the white house, failed, and is now trying the way of Malvern Hill and reports say this morning [he] is under cover of his gunboats in crossing to the south side of the James.[1] The latter I

---

[1] Grant's drive on Richmond in 1864 started with the battle of the Wilderness, then continued with Spotsylvania, North Anna and Cold Harbor. Grant sustained severe casualties in this campaign. Some estimate that he lost half of his beginning army of

think is correct, what success he will have that way is yet to be determined, but I think we have proven to the world that we are able to whip Grant anywhere on open ground. We expect fighting all summer as Grant has staked all on Richmond, he must not fail [and] if he does, down goes another general and the unfortunate Army of the Potomac will again be defeated. Our army is [in] fine spirits although they have had no rest for six weeks. Brother, I don't want to say too much but if you have any more troops in the west like the 20th S. C., you may just keep them.[2] We don't want no such men in this army. They run twice in one day. Their number was eleven hundred and twenty nearly twice as large as my brigade. They want to know how long ere [before] they will get back to Charleston, ha, ha. It's fun to an old soldier in the first army Corps. The 27th Georgia made the most gallant charge of the day a short time since but they were educated at Seven Pines.[3] William Darnell was struck on the arm which paralyzed it for a while but is all right now. I have seen him twice. His health is good. A letter from home informs me all [is] well except Mother, she is improving. Crops look well. Molly is well and doing well, living beautifully. Write soon to your affectionate brother.

W. R. Stilwell

P .S. If you will direct your letters thus they will follow me to victory or to anywhere else.

W. R. Stilwell

Care General Bryan, Kershaw's Division

1st Army Corps, A.N.V.

120,000 men. Finally unwilling to suffer any more frontal assaults on Richmond proper, he was currently transferring his forces across the James River to strike at Richmond's backdoor at Petersburg.

[2] The 20th South Carolina regiment moved from the defense of Charleston to the Army of Northern Virginia in late May 1864. The inexperienced Lawton M. Keitt, a political appointee, commanded them. On June 1st at Cold Harbor, an ordered advance turned to panic in the regiment. Douglas Southall Freeman, *Lee's Lieutenants,* 3 vols. (New York: Charles Scribners Sons, 1944) 3:506.

[3] The Battle of Seven Pines, 31 May through 1 June 1862.

———

Stilwell and his comrades are settling into the static form of trench warfare around Richmond and Petersburg. Mails are erratic and rations are poor although WRS reports that they are still receiving coffee. Purchased foods are even more exorbitant than in the past—eggs are one dollar each.

Petersburg, Virginia, July 1, 1864

My dearest Molly:

Your letter of 16th June was received last evening, although it was so old, yet it afforded me great pleasure to read it. Oh, it had been so long a time without hearing from you. I have wrote to you most every week and I hope you have received them. I received a letter also the same day I got yours from uncle John, his was June 3rd. He said that he had called on Jay Speer to know if there was any thing that he could do for you and that uncle Tom[as Speer] told him that it was his pleasure to attend to that and that he need not give himself any uneasiness on that subject.[4] He also said that if I needed any money, all I had to do was to make it be known to him. I am very thankful to have such friends but I hope I shall not need it. It makes me sad to know that you are so lonesome. Of course it could not be otherwise; a dove without its mate, a love without its lover, yes, a heart without its body. God grant that all may soon be united. You spoke of once getting hold of me that you should never feel like letting me go. I don't think I should make many efforts to extricate myself. Oh, this cruel war. When you spoke of the setting sun and greeting me at the door, you struck the tenderest cord in my heart, to think of those happy days, the joy, love and affectionate happiness we then enjoyed, and now I am not permitted to hear from my dearest, not once a month. Oh, how cruel, how wicked, we can only say that God doeth all things well, trust thou in God and he will yet bless us. I love you. My health is

---

[4] Is Jay a nickname for Thomas Speer?

good except [for a] cold. I have taken a very bad cold a few days since but hope it will subside soon.

You spoke of having vegetables soon for dinner. I hope you may eat them till you get fat and weigh one hundred and seventy-five pounds. I can't get any here, white potatoes is selling at from three to four dollars per quart, onions and eggs one dollar a piece, every thing is out of all reason and still going upward, even apple dumplings is worth one dollar a piece, as for rations, we get plenty, one lb corn meal or flour, 1/3 lb meat, a little rice, peas and coffee.

As for war news, I reckon you have plenty as the war has got down most to you. Here Grant will hold his lines around the city. We still confront him. General Early has scared the Yankees most to death.[5] We still have confidence in Johnston but like you, we think he is very slow. He has been getting Sherman in a trap all spring and summer. I think it's about time the trap would fall, at all events, I want the dead fall thrown ere he gets further south.[6] I trust, dearest, that letters of later date will be received from you soon. I shall write often and long as I can, I have but little else to do. Give my love to all, tell Uncle Thomas to take care of old man Sloan if the Yankees get there.[7] I suppose Uncle H. [blotted out] has gone to the front. Write soon and often. Kiss our dear little children and may God bless and save us all, is the prayer of your own dear William. Be sure and direct thus;

William R. Stilwell,
Care General Bryan, Kershaw's Division
Longstreet's Corps, A.N.V.

———

Action on the defensive lines remains quiet as Stilwell reports no news of warlike actions, etc. Besides he has been off duty with diarrhea

---

[5] General Jubal Early began his Washington raid on 27 June 1864. It is unclear what he would have accomplished by 1 July that would scare the Yankees which, of course he did on 11 July by approaching within a stone's throw of Washington City.

[6] A wish certainly shared by Jefferson Davis and all Georgians.

[7] Adam Sloan, 56-year-old patriarch of the McDonough Sloans was Captain of Company B, Georgia State Guards, a mounted militia unit.

for two weeks. This has allowed much time for him to contemplate religion and write a sermon, "The Ladies of Petersburg." To present day readers, this sermon will seem very curious but contemporary individuals would understand it as a condemnation of the sin of vanity that is causing God to withhold his favors from the Confederacy.

Petersburg, Virginia, July 4th, 1864

My dear Molly:

No doubt you are very uneasy about me. All communication having been cut off two or more weeks and now my only chance is to send this by hand to where it can be mailed.

I have been off duty nearly two weeks with diarrhea very bad, but I shall go to the front this evening, having got nearly well. I do hope and pray that you and the children are well. Still I feel that you are in the hands of God who doeth all things well. Yesterday was Sabbath day. I read a great deal of Barnes, *Notes on the Act of the Apostles*, one of the books brother Martin sent me.[8] I was preaching most all night, you was one of my heroes. I was preaching about the mansion in heaven prepared for the saints' everlasting rest. I was much struck with my idea about that, I remember that all things in this world passed away, health, happiness, friends and riches. Today we might be wealthy and at the heights of fame, but tomorrow we might be beggars, but that inheritance which was undefiled and that fadeth not away in heaven was an everlasting fortune, a never ending home, an eternal mansion. It was very kind in you to come to my appointment, and I hope you was benefited, and I promise to give you a short lecture anytime you will be kind enough to give me a call. It made me so glad to see you and the children paying so good attention. Who knows, but that it may be a vision of the future. God send that it may be. Amen. I believe I am enjoying more of the above and power of Godliness that in all my life before. I bless God for affection and rejoice in all my tribulations. I thank God that I feel that these light affections which

---

[8] Brother Martin is unidentified.

are but for a moment shall work out for me a far more exceeding and eternal wait of glory.

Molly, this is 4th July. I have not got any baked shoat nor turkey nor I haven't got a kiss from my Molly, which would be worth more than all fine dinners. I can tell you what I had for breakfast, it was cornbread, ham and gravy, sugar and coffee. We draw plenty of coffee. I am getting so I can't drink more than three or four cups of coffee for breakfast. I am doing very well so far as money is concerned. I don't need very much of that, there is not much [to buy] today and what little there is, [is] so high that I would not buy it, If I had plenty of money. Onions is worth 50¢ a piece, little apples, from three to four dollars per doz. I don't know when we will get money, I hope you are not needing any. I wish you could see my horse, he is fat and looks fine. 1 could sell him for a thousand or twelve hundred dollars but I don't know where I could get another, so you see if anything was to happen so that I would have to sell him, I would make something. He cost me two hundred and seventy dollars. I think if I can have good luck I can save some money this year, should I live. I hope so at least.

Molly, if you was here it would be heart rending to see the ladies of Petersburg. The enemy have been shelling the city for several days. The woods and all the country is filled with women, from old gray haired mothers down to the infant, driven from their homes without a change of dressing, thousands of them in the wood, without any shelter or protection. Strange to say they most always carry their looking glass in one hand and a frightened child in the other. I have looked at several old ladies to see if they did not have an infant in one hand, the most precious thing on earth, and in the other hand, the dish towel, the next dearest thing, but I have never seen it. But it is remarkable that the ladies never forget the glass. Oh deprived heart, death stares you in the face today, yes, your house with all that you possess will be in ashes, all your fortune shall depart from you. There is all your books of so much value, yes, there is your old bible that your forefathers have bequeathed you, that you value so much. Yes, I price them very high, they are very sacred I know, but let them go. I can't help it but I will take my glass along so that I can hang it on a tree in the woods and look at myself. Oh poor women, I knew that human nature was very bad, I expected that of your girls, but I have seen old mothers carrying the glass. I expect they left their bible, no doubt of it, and I expect many of them [are] members of the church. Forgive me dear for thus speaking of your sex but I think you would have taken Jinnie in one hand and my red testament in the other and several other things I could mention, at all events, I don't think you would have taken the glass nor dish towel, ha, ha. I have seen so much sorrow and suffering that perhaps I don't weep with them that weep, but there are some things very strange, even the pride of the heart. I did not know that a looking glass was so profitable before.

[End of letter—unsigned]

———

Action remains quiet in Stilwell's vicinity but he and his Georgia comrades are very concerned as Johnston and the Army of Tennessee fall back to the Chattahoochee River just north of Atlanta on 5 July. If they cross the river, they will be on the outskirts of Atlanta.

Petersburg, Virginia, July 8th, 1864
My dear Molly:
As I learn that a mail will leave for the south tomorrow, I hasten to write you. In my last I had to inform you that I was sick, I am now in good health, have just left the front on a pleasure ride this evening back to the wagons. I can ride out most any time when we are not busy. I have that advantage of most soldiers, even captains and higher officers do not have the same privilege. I can go anywhere without a pass while all other men in the army have to have them. I was in the city this morning and bought me a pocket-handkerchief, cotton, it cost me eight dollars, such as was sold for fifteen cts before the war. I drew some money the other day but not much. I am going to finish paying for my horse, and the money that I had borrowed. I had to borrow a good deal, at least I had to borrow enough to buy all my tobacco, paper, ink, etc. You know I

borrowed seventy-five dollars from Martin Sowell to go home on when I went home. That after I pay all this, I shall not have much left this time but I think when I drew again I can send some to my dear Molly. When you write again please let me know how much money you have and if you need any and how much you need. If I am permitted to live this year I think I can send you some if it is not much. The government owes me now between one hundred and fifty or two hundred dollars.

The news of General Johnston falling back to Atlanta reached here on yesterday. I have but little or no fears that the Yankees will ever get down to where you are but I think that you will be pestered by our own soldiers, not that I think they will harm you in any way except strolling about and begging for anything that is to eat and stealing your chickens, etc. I had almost as leave have the Yankees around my house as our own men except they will not insult ladies. Everything has remained quiet here since I last wrote, except the Yankees continue to shell the city and some little picket fighting. General Grant says the siege of Richmond is begun, if so we don't know it. It will be like the little man hugging the big woman, he will have to besiege one side awhile and then the other. Tell me not that such an army as ours whose prayers ascend the throne of God day and night can ever be subdued or conquered. Our army is in good spirits and as far as I know, in good condition. Our brigade wants to get to Atlanta, if they must die in defense of their country they had rather fell in defense of their own native state but there is no hopes of our going as far as I know.

James Speer is well, we took a pleasure ride together this morning. Tell Aunt Nancy that James has become quite a ladies man and is making some gallant adventures in this famous city.[9] He enjoys himself only with ladies.

[End of paper—letter unsigned.]

———

---

[9] James Speer's mother.

Sherman breached the Chattahoochee River on 8 July, moving across upstream of Johnston's defenses. This forced Johnston to pull back across the river on July 9. Stilwell foresees the Armageddon descending upon Georgia. But he remains defiant. Should Molly meet the enemy,"Tell them I stand between them and the capital of my country. Tell them that I breathe the air of a true patriot fighting for my God, my country, my religion, my wife and dear children."

Petersburg, Virginia, July 14th, 1864
My dearest Molly:
Time like a never ceasing wave bears all its sons away but still no intelligence is received of your welfare. Just think my dearest, no letter has been received from my own dearest Molly since the 9th of June. I know you have written many kind letters that would have [been] more than welcome. I have written to you often and that consoles me, to hope that you have heard from me. Thanks to a kind providence, I am in the enjoyment of good health and am still getting along as usual.

Much uneasiness is felt in regard to General Johnston's army retreating and leaving our beautiful country to be desolated. Many are uneasy about friends, parents, wives, etc., being left in possession of the enemy. As for my part, of course, I can not but have some uneasiness and anxiety about you but having always trusted you to a merciful and kind providence, God forbid that I should now doubt and fear when danger is near. I therefore think that it is the part of wisdom to ask God still to take care of my dear Molly, and having done this, leave the matter with him who has thus far been our help.

Should you be so unfortunate as to fall in the hands of the enemy, tell them that I stand between them and the capital of my country. Tell them that I breath the air of a true patriot fighting for my God, my country, my religion, my wife, and dear children. Should they insult you it will only cause me to strike the harder blows for all that is near and dear to man. Don't insult them unnecessary. Treat them as enemies but never yield any principle. Should Uncle Thomas [Speer] move, as James wrote him to do, you must advise with him and father about your future orders for it is

275

impossible for me to give any advice at present. I can only say "Believe all things endure, all things hold fast that which is good," and remember my dearest, that what ever befalls I or you, that my only and last days, hours and moments shall be devoted to the love which I bear towards you. I know your heart answers the same. Should all communications be cut off, remember that many noble women have had to endure the same and thanks be to God none more noble or lonely than yourself. Show a determined spirit, endure afflictions as a good soldier, but I do not think that God will thus permit me to be separated from my dear Molly. Still we know not what may be our lot, let us wait and see the power of the Lord.

I will, if I have opportunity, write again in a few days. All goes well here. We have a large army in Maryland.[10] Continue to write until further notice. And now my dearest, may the good Lord guide, preserve, and protect, direct and sustain you in all your trials as is the prayer off your true, devoted, affectionate, love undying husband. I am, dearest Molly, your own dearest William. (Kiss).

My love to all, kiss the sweet little children. Oh, how I love them and pray for them. Your own William. Goodbye. God save you. Molly, you know I love you as few men ever love. I will love you to the end.

Unsigned]

––––––

Stilwell expresses his uneasiness about Molly's presence in McDonough while the Yankees' tighten their noose on nearby Atlanta. He is also worried about the health of his mother, who as his recent letters indicate, is suffering from a long-standing illness. He is in a melancholy mood and ends this letter with a prayer for the safety of his family.

––––––––––––––––––

[10] Jubal Early's force.

Petersburg, Virginia, August 1st, 1864

My dear Molly:

Yours and brothers [letters] was received last evening by James but it was the first in a long time. Of course I was very glad to hear from you and all the rest. Oh, how sorry I am to think that Mother is so low and that I can't get to see her. I am very well and doing well. I am uneasy about the Yankees getting so near you. I hope they will soon come to grief. My division has been at Richmond for the last week, until last evening, we are now camped between there and Petersburg. There was bloody work at Petersburg a few days ago, we whipped them very bad and killed a great many of them.[11] I will send you an account of it with this. You said you did not know what to do about moving to Pa's. I want you to do whatever is for the best, and as I have wrote to Pa to take care of you, I want you to be governed [by this] to some extent, still I think Uncle Thomas will give you good advice. I think you had better remain where you are a while longer. I don't think you are in danger or at least not much danger. I fear that mail matters will be bad if things don't change soon, I don't get any letters from home by mail now, the last one by mail was 16th June. I have wrote you often and hope you have received them. I will continue to write as often as I can. James Speer is well but can't get any letters from home. I have not seen William Darnell lately, he was well the last account. I have been trying to get him transferred to my regiment but can't do it. Molly, my pen is so bad that I can't write I will try and write again in a few days and try and write better.

Oh when will this wicked war close and let us meet again, never to part again on earth? Oh, Molly, let us live near the cross of our Lord and Master and trust in him for life and salvation, Oh, that God may bless and preserve you. Molly, I often steal in the silent grove when supper's over or for an evening prayer that God will take

---

[11] Battle of the Crater, fought 30 July 1864 was initiated by a blast of 8000 pounds of black powder that had been placed in a mine under the Confederate defensive line. It turned into a Federal disaster when the attackers rushed into the blast hole and were trapped. Boatner, *Civil War Dictionary*, 647-49.

care of you and me and the children and that he will do it for the sake of Jesus. Why, you have never wrote to me whether our membership and had been moved to McDonough or not, if it has not been done I want you to have it done as soon as you can and let me know it as soon as you can. I must close for this time. Write often. My love to all, tell Tommy Pa says howdy and to be a good boy till Pa comes home. Oh, Molly, what is the world to me without you. Oh, God, if it be possible let this cup pass from me, nevertheless, not mine but thy will be done. I am, dear Molly, your own dear William. May the God Lord bless us all and save us in his kingdom. I am yours always, Billie.

Good by Dear Wife

(Kiss)

10

CEDAR CREEK

James Speer informs Stilwell of happenings in the brigade while Stilwell is at home on furlough and much is happening. As part of Kershaw's Division, Stilwell's brigade and the 53rd Regiment have been ordered to leave the relative inactivity of the Petersburg lines to reinforce Jubal Early's army in the Shenandoah Valley. Lincoln and Grant have determined to eliminate the Valley as an invasion route to Maryland and Pennsylvania and as a source of bountiful supplies for Lee's army. The Union army in the Valley has been reinforced and General Philip Sheridan has been appointed commander with orders to destroy Jubal Early as a threat and to destroy all food and supplies in the Valley.

Again, we have no advance warning of a home furlough for Stilwell nor do we know of any circumstances that prompted the leave only eight months since his last. Perhaps it was reward for superior service and valor.

Headquarters Bryan's Brigade, New Winchester Virginia,
August 20, 1864
William R. Stilwell:
Dear Sir:
According to my promise I seat myself tonight about (8 o'clock) to drop you a few lines to let you know how we are getting along since you left.

By the caption of this you will see that we are at Winchester, where we arrived on day before yesterday evening.

The only item of news is that General Bryan has resigned and will take his letter to Augusta where he waits the action of the War Department. on his tender of resignation accompanied by Surgeons Certificate of Disability. It is generally thought his resignation will be accepted.

Early had a fight with the enemy at this place on the evening of the 17th. Thrashed them handsomely, taking some 500 prisoners, and 6 pieces of artillery[1].

Should this reach you give my respects to homefolks and everybody else that you see that are worth it, and I remain.

J[ames]. H. Speer

I do not know whether we will go into Pennsylvania or not, but think not.

———

The following note was written to his Uncle John in Griffin on the day that Atlanta fell to Union occupation. He describes an incident that happened the day before on 1 September. Incredibly, Hood's staff, in attempting to clear Atlanta of the wounded, seized an empty passenger train, stuffed it with wounded and started it south on the Macon and Western railroad without informing railroad officials. This train managed to clear Jonesboro just before the Federals cut the railroad there on 31 August. On his way back to Virginia Stilwell was able to hitch a ride on this train as it passed west of McDonough still perilously close to Union forces at Jonesboro. The lack of communication with the railroad resulted in a hideous accident that killed 31 and seriously wounded many more. Stilwell is travelling to Virginia by way of Savannah through Charlotte, North Carolina and Danville, Virginia.

---

[1] Sheridan, while marching northward had left a rear guard at Winchester that had a sharp encounter with the Confederates. The Federal cavalry held well, protecting the main column. The report of men and guns captured is probably greatly exaggerated.

Near Ramsville [Georgia], September 2nd, 1864

Mr. John Stilwell:

Dear uncle, We had a collision between Milner Station and Barnesville.[2] A great many are killed and wounded. The most awful time I ever seen. Thank God I am alive, I jumped off the train, hurt my leg and skinned my face but slightly. I am able to walk. Please send word to Molly that I am safe and gone on to my command as soon as you get this. Oh, God, what an awful time, while I write hundreds of mangled forms lie groaning and howling around me and again I say thank God. I am your affectionate Nephew.

W. R. Stilwell

———

Stilwell's circuitous route requires four days to reach Richmond from Barnesville. We also get a glimpse of the breakdown of law and order in the Confederacy.

Wayside Home Richmond Virginia, September 6, 1864[3]

My dear Molly:

I arrived here this morning after a long and tiresome trip. I am in good health. I got skinned and bruised up smartly by the collision of the cars at Barnesville, Georgia. I never seen such a sight in my life, twenty-six persons were killed and many wounded.[4] I was riding on top of the cars because I could not get inside. I jumped off and got hurt some but I am all right now, and thank God that I got off so light but I have to report another accident that happened to me. I got my carpet sack stole from me and all that

---

[2] About half way between Griffin and Barnesville.

[3] Wayside homes were established all over the South by local residents to assist traveling soldiers.

[4] The official count was 31 persons.

was in it between Columbia, S. C. and Charlotte, N. C.[5] I was asleep and had the carpet sack under me and they jerked out and jumped off the cars while they were running and run off in the woods, so you may tell all that sent sacks by me that they are all gone. I am very sorry but could not help it. I will start up to the Valley in the morning. I can't hear where they are at, [but] somewhere in the valley. I will have to walk a long way. I will send this letter to Griffin in the care of Uncle John [Stilwell] as I don't know how else you can get it. When you write to me direct as before, be sure to send by hand every chance you get. My love to all. Kiss Tommy and Jinnie for me. Write soon. I am your affectionate and loving husband until death. Goodbye.

    W. R. Stilwell

―――――

Confederate authorities reassessed Sheridan's force and Kershaw's division was ordered to return to Lee at Petersburg. But Sheridan attacked at Winchester on 19 September and Early was badly beaten. After six day's march, Kershaw's Confederates were recalled and had to retrace their steps. An ominous note is beginning to appear in Stilwell's letters. He is becoming reckless and a show-off on the battlefield.

Camp [At] Rapidan Station[6], September, 21st, 1864
Mrs. Mary F. Stilwell
Dear Molly:
Since my last we have left the valley and are now enroute for Richmond or some other point south.[7] We will take the cars from this place in a day or two. We had a small fight with some Yankee cavalry the other day at Culpeper as we came on. We come up on

―――――

[5] During the war, a railroad that connected Greensboro NC with Danville VA had been constructed using track taken up from abandoned right-of-way. This allowed a shorter route into Richmond through Charlotte from points to the southwest.

[6] Rapidan Station was located where the Orange and Alexandria railroad crossed the Rapidan River.

[7] This letter is not in the collection.

them very unexpected, we came very near capturing the whole gang but they outrun us. We got about twenty killed, five or six captured, about fifty horses and mules, and three ambulances, and lost none on our side.[8] We have been marching for six days in succession and one half of the brigade is without shoes. James Speer left us five days ago and has not been heard from since. What has become of him, I can't tell. Don't say anything about it for the present. Perhaps he has got on a spree and may come up soon, if not, I will write about it again. The last place he was seen was at a stillhouse and perhaps he is there yet.[9]

Well, dear Molly, I am very well, never had better health in my life and not withstanding General Bryan has resigned and gone home, I still hold my position yet and I think will do so. Colonel Simms of my regiment is in command of the brigade. He has not been appointed a brigadier as yet but I hope will soon. If he does I am all right on the goose sure. I haven't got any war news to write about anything that is going on. I suppose Grant is making a great arrangement to take Richmond and General Lee getting ready to meet him. God defend the right.

I forgot to say that I was complimented very highly for my conduct in the cavalry fight the other day. I was laughing most all the time of the fight and cheering on the boys sometimes from fifty to seventy-five yards in front of the brigade on my horse. I hope you will not scold me dear Molly, for if I fall in this war let me die like a soldier and let my name illustrate the blood of my veins and if I fall, let it be said of me as of the hero John H. Morgan that here lies all that is mortal of the immortal Morgan but I hope for better things.[10]

---

[8] 19 September at Culpeper. This account probably overstates Federal casualties.

[9] James did survive this scrape as family records place him in Henry County after the war. Little is known of him postwar except that he was married, had two sons, then divorced.

[10] John H. Morgan was a Kentuckian who raised a cavalry unit and who later commanded a cavalry brigade that became famous for their raids into Kentucky and north of the Ohio River where Morgan was captured in July 1863. He escaped from the Ohio

Molly, it is most time I was getting a letter from you, none has yet been received. I am very anxious to hear from Mother and all. I don't know where we are going to but will write again soon. The neighbor boys all well, my love to Granma, Aunt Olivet, Pa, Sisters, all. I have just put [on] clean clothes, took a shave and feel very comfortable. This paper it is not ruled and my pen is bad but it didn't cost me anything. Tell Tommy howdy and to save pa some chestnuts and hicks. Kiss, oh, Kiss, God bless the sweet babe and guide its little feet in the ways of truth and may the good and merciful God save and guide us all. I am dear Molly, as ever your own dear William.

[Unsigned]

―――――

In early October, Sheridan advanced up the Valley as far as Staunton, 80 miles from Winchester. (In the Shenandoah Valley, up is down, and down is up because the Shenandoah River runs from south to north. So think upriver and downriver.) The whole Valley from Staunton to Winchester was laid waste and made barren so as to deprive the Confederacy of the rich source of provisions and to make it difficult for a Confederate force to maintain itself in the Valley. As Early moved north again following a Sheridan withdrawal, his supplies had to be moved by wagons from Staunton. The destruction of the beautiful Valley served as a model for Sherman's destruction of Georgia but Sheridan is considered even more ruthless and efficient than Sherman as a destroyer.

Stilwell continues to display a reckless streak on the battlefield.

Strasburg, Valley of Virginia, October 15th, 1864
My dearest Molly:
Mails go and come, I hasten to examine their contents. Yes, I search diligently but no tidings from home, not a letter since I left

―――――

Penitentiary in November 1863 and resumed his command. He was killed in September 1864 near Greeneville TN. Warner, *Generals in Gray*, 220-21.

except the one you wrote two days after I left. Oh, how glad I would be to hear from home but I have given it up and have almost come to the conclusion that I will not get any more and yet I can't tell what is the matter. Others get letters from McDonough and why is it that I don't get mine. Still I believe that my Molly does write me letters.

We had a fight with the Yankees day before yesterday and again I passed amidst danger and death—but unhurt, came out safe.[11] We whipped them pretty badly, our loss very small. I am in the best of health and in my usual good spirits. [I] believe that we will gain our independence and that too when the proper time comes, but Oh, that it would come soon and let the stream of blood which runs so free stop once more and let peace, prosperity, and happiness once more bless our land. Those would be happy days, the meeting of friends, the reuniting of long absent husbands and wives and parents, brothers and sisters. Oh, many have parted never to meet more this side the great bar of God. I have no news from Brother John, none from Darnell, none from home from all my friends and relatives. You can hardly imagine, yes perhaps you can, but none else, how dearly and melancholy the days and nights pass away, shut up north of those mountains where I can not even see the direction of home. This morning, I can not see the sun until eight o'clock for the mountains.

This whole valley is one barren waste, all the barns, mill and public houses have been burned up by Yankees, crops destroyed, dwellings sacked and plundered. The people are generally loyal to the Confederates. The other day after the battle, I seen and talked with two ladies while walking about the garden when the Yankee dead was lying all around them. Think of ladies walking over dead men, laughing as though nothing had happened. They stayed at home all the time of the battle and we fought all around the house. Could you do it, Molly? If you could have seen your own dear Billie as his

---

[11] This was a reconnaissance in force by the Confederates on 13 October that turned into a hot little fight at Hupp's Hill near Strasburg. Confederate casualties were 150 while Union causalities were in excess of 220. Two ranking officers in Kershaw's division, a brigade commander and a regimental commander were struck down. Theodore C. Mahr, *The Battle of Cedar Creek, Showdown in the Valley* (privately published: 1992) 68.

horse went flying over the field carrying orders while the shells and shot was bursting and flying all round him I know you would admire him, if possible, more than ever. You must not scold me Molly for I had rather see Yankees run and fall than any thing else on earth, except you and the children. Of course, I don't want to hurt them if they will let us alone, but if not, I love to see them scatter and skedaddle. I think General Hood will have the Yankees driven out of Georgia soon.[12] Strasburg is (18) eighteen miles from Winchester.

When I last wrote you it was from Hattiesburg, 25 miles from Staunton, so you see we are driving the Yankees before us.[13] I captured a fine pair of white gloves the other day. I would like to send [them to] you as a present, but have no chance. I was too busy to capture much. I am well fixed at present. About my washing. Washing costs now one dollar a garment, say two dollars and fifty cents for washing shirt and drawers and socks. Of course we must have that much washed every week, we can not do it ourselves for we get no soap. Well $2.50 per week would be ten dollars per month. There is four men in my mess and we have hired a negro man for twenty dollars a month, that costs us five dollars a piece a month, and he does all our washing, cooking, makes fires, brings water, etc., [and] any thing else that we want done. He is a good cook, his plate of beefsteak this morning would have done credit to most any cook. He can bake as nice biscuits as any cook woman, so you see that I am well fixed and that at a cheap rate. I have only drawn twenty dollars since I came back but have been trading some little and have managed to pay the fifty dollars that I borrowed to go home on, and have twenty-five dollars left yet.

Give my love to all, tell Tommy [that] Pa sends howdy. Kiss Jennie. Oh, Molly, how bad I want to see you. Molly, if Doss Alexander will bring my clothes, let him do so.[14] I am not needing

---

[12] John Bell Hood replaced Joe Johnston as commander of the Army of Tennessee on 17 July 1864.

[13] This letter is missing.

[14] Second sergeant of Comany F.

them bad but it may be a good chance or the best we will get. Write soon and often. I am, dearest Molly, your loving dear William. Good by, may God bless you. Good by Molly.

[Unsigned]

_____

Stilwell's luck finally runs out.

November 17th, 1864. General Hospital No. 1, Savannah, Georgia

Once more by the goodness and mercy of a kind providence I am in the land that gave me birth. I lost my foot in the battle of Cedar Creek on October l9th, at Strasburg, Valley of Virginia, and was captured the same day. Arrived here in Savannah after being [traveling] on water twenty days. [I] have suffered greatly as my wound is not doing well. I feel sure I owe my life to a Virginia lady, a Mrs. William A. Davis. She came to the place I was kept a prisoner and asked the authorities to allow her to take two or more prisoners that were in the most desperate condition to her home and care for them. As she passed through she stopped by my side and inquired as to how I was getting on. I told her I would surely die unless something could be done for me. She had me placed in her carriage and I was carried to her home. She prepared food that I could eat and nursed me as she would her own son until I was able to travel. She also wrote my wife that I was wounded at [the] battle of Cedar Creek and that I lost my foot and was taken prisoner. She lived at Newtown, Virginia. God bless her.

Finis

[Extract from a letter as condensed by Mrs. R. B. Everett of Covington, Georgia, who was Otelia Stilwell, daughter of W. R. Stilwell.]

_____

Finis. This marks the end of William Ross Stilwell's army career and of his right foot. Tragic as this was, it could have been worse. He could have been one of the 20 percent of Southern military age men who did not survive the conflict at all.

It is distressing that we have only Otelia's summary of at least two letters; Mrs. Davis' letter informing Molly of her husband's grievous wound, and the letter to Molly WRS wrote on his arrival at Savannah. We don't know why Otelia did this in the 1930's when she submitted the letters to the UDC for judging. Nor were the letters included in the collection given to the Georgia Archives and now they are lost. It is likely that Stilwell poured out his heart to Molly in the letter of 17 November 1864 informing her of his arrival "in the land that gave me birth." How I would like to read that letter!

We know something of Stilwell's journey from the battlefield of Cedar Creek to the Confederate hospital in Savannah. He was wounded on 19 October. Between then and reaching a Baltimore hospital on 25 October, he was nursed by Mrs. Davis and transported, mostly by train, to Baltimore. He was transferred to Point Lookout, Maryland on 29 October, formally exchanged, and placed on a ship, probably Southern, standing by to receive badly wounded Confederates. After the ship was filled over several days, it sailed for Savannah, arriving there on 17 November. At this point, Stilwell probably thought he was home. However, On 15 November, Sherman left Atlanta on his March to the Sea, tearing great gaps from the railroads, both the Georgia Railroad from Augusta to Atlanta, and the Central of Georgia from Savannah to Atlanta. It was not possible for Stilwell to get to his home in McDonough during Sherman's march on Savannah, which he captured on 21 December. The next day, Sherman sent his famous message to Lincoln presenting him with a Christmas gift of the City of Savannah.

Shortly thereafter, Sherman would cross into South Carolina and begin his path of destruction through that state. Georgia was now almost clear of Union troops. Immediately, Georgians began to patch up the railroads and inaugurate wagon transportation between the remaining gaps in the rails. Now a reasonably healthy man could have made the journey between Savannah and McDonough and Stilwell was likely reunited with his family shortly after the beginning of 1865. Thus ended nearly three years of warfare for William Ross Stilwell.

Otelia Stilwell was married to R. E. Everitt, the son of Richard M. Everitt, the McDonough saddle maker and brother of Molly's mother. Otelia and R. E. lived in Covington, Georgia in the 1930s

The Battle of Cedar Creek

In far northern Virginia, the Shenandoah Valley points straight for Maryland. Winchester, the principal city of the lower valley, is only 72 miles from Washington and about 99 miles from Baltimore. In contrast, Richmond is 140 miles from the latter. Nineteen miles south of Winchester on the Valley Pike is the old Germanic city of Strasburg. Between the two cities were the towns of Middletown and Newtown. This area was the focus for some of the bitterest and most constant fighting of the war.

In mid-October, 1864, Sheridan forces outnumbered those of Early by more than two to one. Northern forces were about 32,000; Southern forces were less than 14,000. The Union army was camped north of Strasburg centered on Middletown; the Confederates were to the south of Strasburg. On the early morning of 19 October, Early's forces executed one of the most brilliant surprise attacks of the Civil War, or perhaps of any American war. The Confederates found a path that led to the Union forces' rear. John B. Gordon's Division took this path while Kershaw's Division made a frontal attack on the succession of Federal lines. By noon, in combination, they had driven the entire Federal infantry back four miles in considerable disorder. The Southern forces, exhausted, then stopped their attack.

Sheridan was in Washington attending a commander's conference. He returned to the end of the railroad line and then began his famous horseback ride to take personal command of his disorganized men. By late afternoon he had them in a counterattack. Being vastly superior in numbers, they were able to overlap the flanks and get into the rear of the Confederates and put the Southerners into a disorderly withdrawal. At that moment, the vastly superior Northern cavalry hit the Confederate infantry's flanks and retreat turned into a rout. What had begun as a Southern triumph ended in disaster.

Kershaw's Division bore the brunt of the frontal assaults and consequently suffered the most casualties. Bryan's Georgia Brigade counted some 200 killed and wounded. The 53rd Georgia alone suffered 10 killed and 31 wounded, one of whom was William Ross Stilwell. We have no way of knowing just where or when during the advance or retreat that Stilwell was hit in the foot by a shell. We know from his letters that he ended up in a Yankee hospital near the village of Newtown, with his right foot amputated and he was, in his own words, surely dying.

THE ANGEL

Stilwell gives complete credit for his survival to a Virginia lady, Mrs. William A. Davis who was very much a Southern lady even though she had been born in Massachusetts. She appeared magically to have Stilwell placed in her carriage and whisked away to her substantial home and then nursed him as she would her own son, who incidentally, had just joined the Confederate cavalry.

The editor was determined to get information on Mrs. Davis, searching the usual documentary sources such as the census and deed records. In this I had the able assistance of the Handley Library in Winchester. But this type of data was not wholly satisfying in revealing the character of Mrs. Davis. On one of my visits to study Virginia battlefields, I dropped in on Michael C. Kehoe, administrator of the town of Stephens City. Over time, due to directions of the Post Office, the name of Newtown had metamorphosed into Stephens City. Mr. Kehoe knew exactly what I was looking for as he described Mrs. Davis and her family and her home, Sunnysides. Much to his chagrin, Sunnysides, which was located on the northern city limits of Stephens City, had recently been torn down to make way for a modern pharmacy.

Mr. Kehoe suggested that I obtain a copy of a book, *Defend the Valley* by Margaretta Barton Colt (New York: Orion Books, 1994.) This was a history of the Barton family during the Civil War as recorded in their contemporary letters. One of the principal seats of the Barton family was their home Springdale that survives to this day and was located one mile north of Sunnysides. Thus the Barton and Davis families were neighbors; their children were playmates and the adults were friends. The Davis family were minor players in the published letters of the Bartons. *Defend the Valley* is a remarkable record of the Civil War in this area which was fought over on an almost daily basis. As the book had recently gone out of print, I searched to find what must have the last copy for sale in Winchester.

In 1860, William Davis was age 41 and a farmer/physician. Mrs. Davis was age 38. They had two children, Susy, 16, and Charlie, 14. Mr. and Mrs. Davis had indeed been born in the North but as one of the Barton kin expressed in 1862, "Dr. Davis and family are warm Southerners. Mrs. Davis surprises me by the quantity of good she does in every way."

By 1862, Dr. Davis was a highly-placed surgeon serving the Confederacy in Richmond. Mrs. Davis was doing her good works and Susy was the town belle, entrancing the young Confederate officers. Charlie was champing at the bit to get into the war. He joined the Seventh Virginia Cavalry on 4 June 1864, two months before his 18th birthday. He was killed in battle near his home on 6 March 1865. Thus, as Stilwell states that Mrs. Davis nursed him as she would her own son, she later was denied that opportunity as Charlie was killed outright on that day in March only about a month before the war ended.

EPILOGUE

THE REVEREND WILLIAM STILWELL

As soon as the wound on Stilwell's foot had healed, he became active in the North Georgia Conference of the Methodist Episcopal Church (South). He likely was designated as a local preacher which was the equivalent of the exorter status he had attained in Louisiana before the war. Progress in attaining regular ministerial status was slow so he had to maintain his family by other employment. In the 1870 census, he listed his occupation as "merchant" and his residence in Bear Creek of Henry County. His family consisted of Molly and three children: Tommy and two girls born after the war. Virginia had died as a young child. Molly and he added two more girls to the family in the 1870s before her untimely death at the age of 42 in 1883.

Stilwell thereafter married Callie Jane Kennedy and started a second family, fathering seven more children between 1887 and 1901. Callie Jane also suffered an untimely death at age 46 in 1906, just a few months before William Ross Stilwell's death on 7 February 1907. Stilwell and both wives are buried in the McDonough City Cemetery. The deaths of Callie Jane in 1906 and of Stilwell in early 1907 left several young orphans. They were raised by his daughter, Otelia, who had married R. E. Everett, a son of R. M. Everett, the McDonough saddler who probably taught Stilwell the trade of harness making. R. M. had moved to

Covington, Georgia in 1870 and thereafter prospered as a merchant. His son, R. E., followed in his father's footsteps as a prosperous Covington merchant. He and Otelia had no children of their own and assumed the responsibility of raising the orphans.

The minutes of the annual meetings of the North Georgia Conference of the MEC(South) record the slow progress of Stilwell as he worked to establish his ministerial status. In 1872, he was in the list of local preachers ordained as deacons, but he did not attain a full-time position until appointed as supply (temporary replacement) in the La Grange District in 1881. He also obtained such positions, each in a different district throughout North Georgia in 1884-5, 1892, 1893, 1894, 1895, and 1896-1897. It was not until 1898 that he appears in the list of regularly assigned ministers. Between 1898 and 1906 he was minister in six different locations, thus moving about every year. In 1906, his last appointment had been as minister at Jenkinsburg located in Butts County but near the Henry County line. He had finally returned close to home. In 1891 he had been ordained as an elder in the Church. (A summary of Stilwell's appointments in the MEC(S) is published in Harold Lawrence, ed., *Methodist Preachers in Georgia* (Tignal GA: Boyd Publishing, 1984) 531.

At the time of his death in early 1907, he was 68 so he lived a full life. He had sired 13 children; two preceded him in death as had his two wives. He had obviously struggled economically, raising two large families in the impoverished postbellum South. And it was never an easy life for the rural Methodist preacher working a circuit of churches, traveling by horse and buggy, living in poorly furnished parsonages, owning little in the way of possessions.

The state was eventually able to give minimal help to its permanently disabled veterans. In 1879, Stilwell received a one-time grant of $75 given to ex-soldiers with an amputation below-the-knee to allow them to equip themselves with a prosthetic device. In 1889, he began receiving an annual allowance of $50 granted to below the knee amputees. This continued until his death.

Despite the poor conditions suffered by most rural Methodist preachers, as illustrated by Stilwell's struggles to establish himself in his church, there were plenty of men willing to endure the travails in order to benefit from the joy and high standing of their profession. Stilwell had perhaps to struggle more than most in order to overcome his poor education. But from the day that Stilwell accepted the military position of courier until the end of his days, he signaled that honor and reputation were to be the driving forces of his life.

INDEX